Teaching Policy Studies

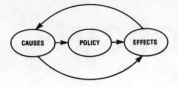

Policy Studies
Organization Series

Teaching Policy Studies

What and How

William D. Coplin
Syracuse University

Lexington Books
D.C. Heath and Company
Lexington, Massachusetts
Toronto

Library of Congress Cataloging in Publication Data

Main entry under title:

Teaching policy studies.

   Includes bibliographical references and index.
   1. Policy sciences—Study and teaching—United States—Addresses, essays, lectures.   2. Policy sciences—Addresses, essays, lectures.   I. Coplin, William D.
HN29.T33   300   77-9186
ISBN 0-669-01829-5

Copyright © 1978 by D.C. Heath and Company

Published simultaneously in Canada

Printed in the United States of America

International Standard Book Number: 0-669-01829-5

Library of Congress Catalog Card Number: 77-9186

To Vicki, Britt, and Richie

Contents

vii

List of Figures

List of Tables

Acknowledgments

I wish to thank Amy L. Herman for providing outstanding assistance on the development of this issue. She was responsible for the organization and the copyediting of the manuscript and for the administrative work required to put the manuscript together. I also wish to thank Stuart Nagel for his confidence in me, his excellent advice, and, on behalf of all of us in the policy studies field, for the work he has done over the last few years in developing the policy studies field. Linda Juachon helped in the final copyediting of the manuscript. Finally, Nancy Dore typed and edited the final manuscript even more quickly than usual.

Introduction

Duncan MacRae, Jr., argues that the field of policy analysis broadly defined should be viewed as an applied discipline—"neither a scientific discipline nor a profession, but a group combining features of both."[1] He shows the similarities and differences between policy analysis as an applied social science, and such disciplines as economics, and such professions as medicine. If the field cannot be easily placed in either the disciplinary or the professional "box," there is a need to explore what this means for teaching in that field.

While MacRae's view raises fundamental questions about the teaching of policy analysis, it is only one of a number of indicators that the study of public policy from a decision-making or problem-solving perspective (as opposed to a theoretical or scholarship-building perspective) is big academic business. The growth in the number of colleges and universities belonging to the National Association of Schools of Public Affairs and Administration[2] (over 174 at last count) and the increase in the number of texts and journals with "policy" in their titles suggests that faculty from various disciplinary and institutional settings are taking a major interest in helping students study public policies.

At the outset, we need to say something about nomenclature. The term "policy studies" is used to avoid quantitative and economic connotation that is sometimes attached to the term "policy analysis."[3] Our conception of policy studies is the same as MacRae's conception of policy analysis[4] and Coleman's[5] conception of "policy research." It includes, according to MacRae, reasoned valuative discourse, a definition of problems, proposals of alternatives, the application of models, methods for testing models, and, finally, a concern for intermediate goals and feasibility.[6] In short, it is the application of the social sciences to societal problems with the emphasis on application.

Notwithstanding the growth of the study of public policy and the clear urgency of the need, the teaching of policy studies as an applied social science could easily be sidetracked by the pressures emanating from entrenched disciplinary and professional school interests. Requiring an ever-changing information base, policy studies could easily become a cover for two types of teaching endeavors: (1) unsystematic discussions of current events, and (2) disciplinary or professional school socialization. Drawing on a variety of concepts, methods, and findings from a broad range of disciplines, policy studies could be viewed as the home of the dilettante and therefore result in institutional sanctions against those who provide applied social science education. Containing a built-in appeal to large bodies of students, policy studies may arouse the jealousies of the disciplines that are in decline and may be used to attract students to courses that are discipline-oriented in content. One should not underestimate the resistance to change operating at most institutions of higher education. Policy studies may be a new bottle for old wines in a period of shrinking faculty resources and growing faculty defensiveness.

The chapters in this book reflect the very nature of the policy studies field. Taken as a group, they can best be described as "eclectic" and "pluralistic." Policy studies as a field requires an open-ended stance toward problem definition, information sources, and methodology. Its only conceptual anchor is the concern for the "causes" and "effects" of public policy. Similarly, no single methodology can suffice. The variety of methods developed in all areas of the social sciences are relevant as long as they are presented as tools to be applied, not intellectual feats to be performed. Given the inherent nature of policy studies, then, discussions of the teaching of it by necessity must be eclectic and pluralistic.

The book is divided into two sections. The first deals with the question of what should be taught while the second explores some ideas of how the content should be taught. These two questions are not answered comprehensively in this volume. The newness of the field and its inherent pluralistic character preclude any attempt at comprehensiveness. However, they do provide an introduction for those teaching or planning to teach in the field.

All of the articles in this symposium are of the "show and tell" variety. They represent the operational ideas of faculty at a variety of institutions of higher education throughout the United States. What they lack in empirical support and rigorous evaluation they more than make up for in creativity and practicality. The ability to combine new ideas with clever applications provides testimony to those who teach in the eclectic and pluralistic field of policy studies.

Notes

1. Duncan MacRae, Jr., "Policy Analysis as an Applied Social Science Discipline," Administration and Society, Vol. 6, No. 4 (February, 1975, pp. 363-88).

2. For more information on the development of public policy teaching at the graduate level see The Policy Studies Directory (Urbana, Ill.: Policy Studies Organization, 1973). Additional information can be obtained from the National Association of Schools of Public Affairs and Administration at Suite 300, 1225 Connecticut Avenue, N.W., Washington, D.C., 20036. Undergraduate programs as described in an unpublished report prepared by David G. Smith of Swarthmore College entitled "Policy Analysis for Undergraduates" (Report to the Committee on Public Policy and Social Organization at the Ford Foundation, 1975 Mimeo).

3. Smith, "Policy Analysis for Undergraduates" (Appendix), discusses the variety of terms and meanings associated with policy analysis.

4. MacRae, "Policy Analysis as an Applied Social Science Discipline."

5. James S. Coleman, *Policy Research* (Morristown, N.J.: General Learning Press, 1972).

6. MacRae, "Policy Analysis. . . ."

Part I
What Should Be Taught?

Part I
What Should Be Taught

A survey of existing articles, syllabi, and textbooks, as well as the work of the National Association of Public Affairs and Administration (NASPPA), reveals that the field of policy studies contains a large variety of substantive content. Quantitative and analytical techniques from statistics and economics are emphasized by some.[1] Conceptual tools such as systems analysis, PPBS, and political feasibility are also included.[2] Finally, institutional information about governmental processes is also included.[3] The report published by NASPPA[4] is relatively comprehensive but not as detailed as some would like.

The difficulty that confronts one in attempting to come to grips with the question of what should be taught is the apparent lack of consensus on concepts, methods, and information. The disagreement that exists in most disciplines is exacerbated by the multidisciplinary nature of policy studies and the vital importance of a good information base for whatever policy area is being studied. Concepts and methods taught under the rubric "policy studies" run the gamut from the most formal data collection and analysis techniques to the least formal uses of logical analysis and the imagination. The information base required for the field of policy studies is not determined by the field but by the context of the policy under study. With such a variety of conceptual, methodological, and informational content, there is the danger that no consensus will emerge and that policy studies may become a battleground for special viewpoints.

However, faculty interested in providing students with applied social science skills cannot afford the luxury of accepting such conflict. It will take all of the strength faculty now have to create an educational environment in which those seeking to socialize students into a particular discipline are thwarted. Hopefully, by beginning a dialogue on the core educational objectives of policy studies faculty, the chapters in this section will contribute to the process of developing a consensus.

General Overviews

The first three chapters in this section take a general look at the content of the policy studies curriculum. The opening chapter, by Ronald John Hy, provides a systematic overview of the entire policy study field. His use of the term "policy analysis" is synonomous with the definition of policy studies articulated in the introduction to this book. While one might quibble with specific aspects of Professor Hy's definition of the field, the chapter represents an honest attempt to interrelate the applied and theoretical dimensions of the policy studies field.

3

The chapter by Fry and Tompkins references, among others, the historical work of the Georges, the conceptual work on bureaucracies of Merton, the psychological perspective of Janis, and the computer simulations work of Davis, Dempster, and Wildavsky, as well as Crecine. The content of policy studies is expressed as a matrix in which the rows are the levels of analysis (that is, individual, groups, organization, system) and the columns, policy processes (that is, policy process, optimal allocation, mutual adjustment, and routines). Regardless of whether or not the authors succeed in their particular formulation, they do introduce many of the concepts now active in the field.

The final chapter providing a general overview of the content of the policy studies field is David G. Smith's chapter on "Policy Analysis and Liberal Arts." Although Smith's article is explicitly focused on the "where" question of policy studies, it says a great deal of the goals of policy studies teaching. Smith's views are as eclectic as the policy studies field itself. He argues persuasively that the policy studies field is both broad and disciplined enough to contain the essential ingredients of what most academicians mean by a liberal-arts education.

Essential Ingredients

The remaining six chapters in this part might be viewed as a wish list. They reveal the authors' views on what they consider to be essential, but sometimes missing, components of a policy studies curriculum. Taken together the six chapters do not cover all items that might be considered essential, but they do treat some of the areas that are important but tricky for the policy studies educator.

Chapter 4, by Jennings and Smith, cites the need to deal with theories of human behavior in the policy studies field. They argue that such theories can be grouped into two categories for purposes of policy analysis. The first are rational choice models and the second are social structural analyses. This chapter is important because it demonstrates how theoretical abstractions can be taught in a way that allows the student to apply them to policy questions.

The next chapter, by Cohen and Rakoff, suggests that an imbalance exists in the teaching of policy studies because the social, economic, and political context in which policies evolve is not adequately explored. Attributing this lack to the "instrumentalism" in the policy literature, the authors call for treatment of the economic, institutional, and cultural-ideological contexts in the policy studies curriculum. They argue that comparative studies is a most effective way to introduce the context of policy. Not rejecting the instrumentalist approach of policy studies, the authors call for even more openness of the curriculum.

One item on everyone's wish list for a policy studies curriculum—particularly given the large role played by political scientists in the development of the field—is treated by John Foster in chapter 6. The chapter discusses the need to alert students to the political role of policy analysis. To try to take the edge off our students' belief in their own infallibility, now that they have policy studies training, it is important to convince them that the origins and the impact of any policy analysis activity are determined in part by the political setting in which that activity occurs.

The last two chapters in the section discuss methods which ought to be taught as part of policy studies. Hambrick and Snyder deal with what everyone agrees is a major educational goal—communications with decision-makers. Unfortunately, most talk about the need for improving the communication skills of policy, but don't do much. Hambrick and Snyder present a clear statement of what the specific communication skills are and what can be done about presenting them.

The final article in this section, by Tom O'Donnell, outlines the entire range of information collection skills that students ought to acquire in any policy studies curriculum. O'Donnell's essay states the obvious, but unfortunately far too few students who complete undergraduate or graduate programs have been introduced to the information collection skills which he specifies.

Notes

1. For example, Edward R. Tufte, *Data Analysis for Politics and Policy* (Englewood Cliffs, N.J.: Prentice-Hall, 1976); and Larry Seidman, "A Course in the Economics of Public Policy Analysis," *Policy Analysis*, Vol. 1, No. 1 (Winter 1975), pp. 197–216.

2. For example, Yehezkel Dror, *Design for Policy Sciences* (New York: Elsevier North-Holland, 1971); and Thomas Dye, *Understanding Public Policy* (Englewood Cliffs, N.J.: Prentice-Hall, 2nd edition, 1975).

3. An example of materials emphasizing information on institutions and their processes is Charles O. Jones, *An Introduction to the Study of Public Policy* (North Scituate, Mass.: Duxbury Publishing Company, 1970).

4. See footnote 2 under Introduction for the address of NASPPA, where copies of the report can be obtained. The full title of the report is *Guidelines and Standards for Professional Master's Degree Programs in Public Affairs/Public Administration*, 1974.

1 An Overview of Policy Analysis Concepts

Ronald John Hy

Introduction

In recent years public policy analysis has become less intuitive and impressionistic and more systematic and empirical. The principal, though not only, reason for this movement toward systematic and empirical analysis is that federal, state, and local governmental officials are being barraged by their respective legislative bodies and taxpayers with demands to provide hard empirical evidence of how well a given policy is performing before they agree to spend additional money on that policy. Due to financial exigencies, legislators and taxpayers are becoming resistive about pouring limited fiscal resources into policies whose impacts are indeterminable.[1] As a consequence, governmental agencies are, with increasing frequency, looking for and hiring persons who can analyze public policy systematically and empirically. As a matter of fact, over the years so many persons have been employed as policy analysis specialists that a new profession is now developing.

To some extent, the rapidly growing number of newly developed administrative units and/or programs solely devoted to preparing policy analysts is a visible sign of this new profession.[2] The emergence of this profession is further underscored by the fact that such units and programs are housed within prestigious research-oriented universities and research institutes and various think-tanks scattered throughout the country. Moreover, many traditional disciplines, particularly the behavioral and social sciences, are beginning to offer undergraduate and graduate degrees with a specialization in public policy analysis.[3] In addition to such programs, a variety of new journals and periodicals devoted either wholly or partially to policy analysis are being published, and a number of other prestigious journals are allocating space regularly to the subject of policy analysis.[4] Thus, the evidence seems to indicate that in a short period of time a new profession has developed, and it is here to stay.

To prepare adequately this new type of professional, universities and institutes must implement new curricula because traditional curricula seldom, if ever, address the needs of prospective policy analysts. This is not to say that many well-established professional schools have not been reshaping their curricula to meet the needs of policy analysts. Many schools are now emphasizing problem-alleviating (commonly called problem-solving) in their curricula, and a growing number of schools also have developed courses which include field

7

experiences, practica, and applied analytical techniques. These developments, to be sure, are broadening traditional curricula.

Despite such efforts, however, traditional curricula frequently fail to meet the needs of prospective policy analysts because many of the newly created or recently modified courses fail to relate effectively to the arena of public decision-making.[5] For instance, traditional curricula tend to stress explanatory rather than prescriptive quantitative and qualitative methodologies. While methodology courses are offered and often required, they emphasize social statistics rather than decision-making (for example, inferential statistics, linear programming, cost-benefit analysis, delphi) and operations research techniques. Moreover, most modifications of traditional curricula normally fail to emphasize enough substantive policy areas (for example, health care, taxation, government and business, law enforcement).

Because of the shortcomings involved with modifying traditional curricula,[6] policy analysis programs need to develop a core curriculum to provide prospective analysts with the background necessary to conduct policy analyses. To meet this objective, the curriculum should incorporate two features. First, it should be problem-oriented, since the primary function of a policy analysis is to supply policymakers with information designed to alleviate problems. Second, the core should be interdisciplinary—not multidisciplinary, as so often is the case—because most problems with which analysts deal are not peculiar to one discipline. (The interdisciplinary nature of policy analysis exacerbates problems encountered when one is trying to develop a core curriculum.)

Yehezkel Dror, an early advocate of a core curriculum for policy analysis, suggests that such a curriculum must be composed of interdisciplinary courses so that analysts will be able to apply nomographic knowledge to ideographic situations. To do this, he recommends a mutiplicity of learning methods. Dror suggests, "These methods in addition to more traditional lectures, readings, exercises, colloquia, and seminars—have to include, as a minimum, gaming, cases and projects, internship, a new type of dissertations, and study tours."[7]

An examination of any established core curriculum indicates that policy analysis does in fact rely on techniques and subject matter from various academic areas. There are three areas, however, from which policy analysis borrows most: physical sciences, management sciences, and behavioral and social sciences.[8] Generally speaking, these three areas provide policy analysts with highly developed prescriptive quantitative and qualitative techniques which when coupled with substantive policy expertise allow persons to dissect and synthesize public sector data for the purpose of proposing viable alternatives in order to alleviate problems.

To be sure, the specific courses that should be included in a core curriculum will differ among policy analysis programs. However, regardless of which courses comprise the core, there are certain policy analysis concepts that should be used to form the nucleus of a core curriculum. Let's take a closer look at these concepts by discussing:

1. The nature of policy analysis
2. The need for a policy analysis framework
3. A proposed policy analysis framework (based on the dynamics of policy analysis)
4. The need for an interdisciplinary policy analysis team.

The Nature of Policy Analysis

A policy analysis is the systematic identification, examination, and evaluation of real and potential impacts of a policy on at least a segment of society. Such an analysis also endeavors to provide objective input to public policymakers by identifying options and clarifying necessary trade-offs associated with proposed changes.[9] More precisely, policy analysis is concerned not only with intentional but also unintentional and unanticipated consequences, whether beneficial or detrimental, which *may* result from policy implementation. Concern with both intended and unintended consequences of a particular policy is central to an analysis becasue the intended effects are seldom, if ever, the only impacts of a policy. In fact, unanticipated aftermaths oftentimes may be even more critical than are intended outcomes.

Besides dealing with intended and unintended consequences, an analysis identifies target and spillover groups affected by policy performance. Target groups are those segments of the population who are intended to be affected by the policy, whereas spillover groups are those other than target groups who are affected by that policy. (These two types of groups, it should be recalled, may be affected either beneficially or detrimentally.) An analysis then dissects intended and unintended policy consequences affecting target and spillover groups by looking at the extent to which a policy's objectives have been or are being realized. To improve objective-realization, an analysis examines alternative policy choices in order to allow analysts to recommend action according to some criteria of regression or progression. But, such an assessment also may recommend that no action be taken. After analyzing all alternatives, an appraisal may, to use a cliché, indicate that the cure is more harmful than the disease.

Need for a Policy Analysis Framework

To conduct a first-rate analysis, investigators need to employ a formalized and systematic framework. This need is apparent to anyone who has ever been required to conduct an analysis. In the first place, reality, unrefined by an analytical model, is too complex to comprehend. Without a blueprint a carpenter is unable to construct a house. The lumber is merely a pile of wood. The blueprint indicates where particular pieces of lumber belong as well as the interdependence of each piece. Like the carpenter's blueprint, a policy analysis framework enables investigators to ascertain where all the pertinent, complex factors belong and how they relate to each other. Likewise a model helps investigators reduce the substantial number of disparate and idiosyncratic factors to a manageable number so that elements which exert influence on policy performance can be discerned.

The primary means for reducing the number of factors needed to make a sound analysis is a framework or model which simplifies reality without omitting integral factors. Stated another way, a model assists investigators by helping them determine first which factors *may* affect policy performance and then ascertain which factors *probably will* have an impact. When a framework is integrated into the assessment process, *more rational* policy analysis can be conducted. (Note the emphasis is on more rational and not on rational.) The function of a model, Gunnar Myrdal once said, is to make an analysis more rational by ascertaining relevant facts and bringing them into their true perspective by clarifying the causal relations between means and aims.[10]

While it would be pretentious to suggest that a single hybrid framework could be applied with equal success to all types of policy analyses, there nevertheless are basic functions essential to all policy appraisals. In the first place, a framework should require investigators to state a policy's objectives clearly and precisely. Failure to specify objectives categorically may lead to overlooking the policy's real achievements, a serious shortcoming when attempting to evaluate policy performance. Without a systematic framework, critically important factors can be easily underrated or even neglected by analysts. (Including all relevant factors is crucial to an assessment because omitted factors may frustrate a policy analysis.)

Secondly, a policy analysis framework should help investigators deal with relational rather than causal relationships, primarily because understanding the latter is a difficult, time-consuming task which is of limited utility to policy analysis. When conducting such an analysis, one need not determine causality. It is sufficient to comprehend that X is so related to Y that X will have an impact on Y. In other words, knowing what causes Y is not so important as understanding the degree to which X will affect Y. In many cases, discerning the cause of Y is not crucial to an analysis. For instance, analysts do not have to determine the causes of crime to analyze the impact of a particular crime policy. They, however, must ascertain whether that policy is meeting its objectives by contributing to a reduction in crime, that is, whether the implementation of a crime policy affects—either beneficially or detrimentally—crime. In this example, trying to find out the causes of crime would be peripheral to the objective of the policy analysis.

Next, a framework should permit investigators to deal with policy dynamics. To be sure, time *does* affect policy performance. Therefore, the element of time must be incorporated into a framework; otherwise, policy will be viewed statically, not dynamically. As the second law of thermodynamics indicates, a static state can be achieved only by cessation of all activity. Since policy does not exist in a static state of suspended animation, a useful framework must allow analysts to examine policy as if it were in a state of quasi-dynamic equilibrium, a condition in which the analyzed policy remains analytically static within a stipulated range of time but in which time is considered an important factor.

Finally, a policy analysis framework should allow analysts to use both qualitative and quantitative decision-making techniques. While scientifically rigorous quantitative analysis is important, there also is a pronounced need for a comparatively simple and completely practical model that strikes a balance between administrative exigencies and available information and strict methodological research requirements. After all, policy analysis frequently relies on information which is not quantitatively precise enough to meet the criteria that purely quantitative models require. More important, however, is the fact that public agencies, especially at the local level, frequently have inadequate and often unreliable data resources on which to make meaningful and significant determinations. Then, too, many factors which are exceedingly crucial to an analysis cannot be quantified. Some critical factors are not prone to quantification because they cannot be assigned cardinal or ordinal values. (Unintended outcomes, in particular, are difficult to quantify.) The aesthetics of a forest, for example, are quantitatively immeasurable. Hence, if one uses only quantitative analysis, prominent factors will be omitted, either intentionally or inadvertently, often causing the assessment to be quite inaccurate.

Any policy analysis framework performing the basic functions just described also possesses inherent, and thus unavoidable, limitations. First and foremost, a model oversimplifies reality through a parsimonious process. It likewise narrows the range of reality to make the complex comprehensible. When reality is oversimplified by any conceptual scheme, the output frequently does not reflect the actual world, thereby making it difficult to determine which factors are integral to the analysis.

An even more important problem facing investigators who utilize a policy analysis framework is the tendency to compartmentalize and thus fragment knowledge which is applicable to an analysis. The danger of fragmentation and compartmentalization is that once the pieces are separated they are difficult to put back together. As Ian Mitroff observed, "We are masters at teaching [ourselves] how to break a system into components (i.e., analysis), but we are poor in teaching [ourselves] how to put the components back together again (i.e., synthesis)."[11] Needless fractionalization makes it next to impossible to put the parts back together because such a cognitive process focuses on components of a policy rather than on the wholeness of that policy.

Keeping these two admonitions in mind, investigators should realize that regardless of the utility and irrespective of the degree of sophistication of any framework, the exact impact of a policy will always be unknown, and there is little one can do about that fact. Thus, a certain amount of conjecture will always be involved in any analysis because paradigms are bound to omit prominent events and effects. The unexpected occurrence of uncontrollable factors, moreover, undoubtedly contributes to this lack of preciseness. (Policy analysis, after all, is based on an interplay between certainty and uncertainty.) At the same time, investigators must realize that oversimplification need not necessarily lead to an unreliable and inaccurate analysis. When an analysis includes the critical factors affecting policy performance, the generalizations generated by the use of a model will be highly informative. In any event, a policy analyst must utilize a framework or be faced with the chaos of reality.

Proposed Policy Analysis Framework

The subsequent model is designed to help investigators simplify a highly complex, somewhat subjective, and quantitatively squishy process in order to assess systematically policy performance in light of its objectives so that corrective action can be taken when necessary. Once the extent to which a policy is achieving stated objectives is determined, analysts can ascertain which aspects of a given policy should be maintained and supported and which should be corrected or abandoned. The framework then is intended to help investigators look carefully at both a policy's accomplishments and failures. (By reviewing strengths and weaknesses of a policy, an analysis can furnish an inventory of data needed for progressive planning.)

Since it is not unusual for such an assessment to be conducted by persons with little knowledge of policy analysis, the proposed framework also is meant to aid neophytes by helping them focus on the essential elements of an analysis and by suggesting pertinent questions to be asked, factors to be examined, and processes to be followed. For instance: Why does a policy exist? What kind of policy is it? What kind of policy is it trying to become? Who is the target group? Which groups are affected by the policy? Does the policy reach the affected groups directly or indirectly?

Although several policy analysis frameworks exist, none can be reduced to a series of mechanical steps. Despite this fact, the procedures in figure 1-1 describe in some sequential fashion the various components of a policy analysis framework.

Identifying Objectives

Since, as stated previously, policy analysis focuses on ascertaining whether a policy is meeting its objectives, such an appraisal must begin with a clear and precise statement of objectives. Defining objectives is by far the most important phase of an analysis because objectives provide parameters for the assessment.

> A. Identify as explicitly and precisely as possible the formal and informal objectives (and sub-objectives) of the policy.
>   1. Determine whether each objective is:
>   a. Procedural
>   b. Substantive
>   2. Develop verifiable, and if possible quantitative, measures for each objective.
> B. Evaluate policy performance in terms of established objectives.
>   1. Ascertain the extent to which objectives are being (or have been) realized.
>   2. Analyze specific performance criteria:
>   a. Effectiveness
>   b. Efficiency
>   c. Effort
>   3. Discover obstacles that prevent objectives from being met.
> C. Propose changes and establish recommendations.
>   1. Revise, modify, and/or rearrange existing objectives in light of rapidly changing conditions and priorities. (Alternatives will be dictated to a large extent by discovered problems and obstacles.)
>   2. Discard unattainable objectives.

Figure 1-1. Policy Analysis Framework

Put differently, specific and clear objectives furnish indispensable criteria for judging a policy's achievements and failures. It is only after objectives, no matter how controversial, have been established that analysts can determine how well a policy is performing.

Ascertaining a policy's objectives is, not unexpectedly, a manifold task because objectives frequently exist in an inchoate form. The first charge, therefore, is to clarify the objectives to be evaluated, with measurement of those objectives to be determined later: before analysts can ascertain a policy's performance, they must have a clear sense of the nature of the activity being evaluated, an intricate endeavor since most policies have multiple objectives—a situation which often creates dissonance among investigators. A case in point is the Model Cities program. According to Harry Havens, the federal policy had variegated aims.[12] It was a:

1. means of concentrating existing resources to demonstrate the impact of such concentrations
2. promise of a massive commitment of new resources to solve urban problems
3. "bricks and mortar" program (an expansion of Urban Renewal)
4. new source of funding for social services
5. way of giving local chief executives more control over OEO-type citizen organizations
6. way to give citizen organizations greater leverage over established local institutions.

Since in theory there is an almost infinite number of formal and informal objectives associated with any policy, investigators need to classify objectives according to some preconceived scheme in order to eliminate or at least reduce troublesome dissonance. Such a categorizing process, which is the initial phase of any systematic analysis, helps investigators identify objectives more clearly and precisely. With the aid of a classfication system, analysts can rationally reduce a substantial number of disparate objectives to manageable and comprehensible groups.

There are various functional classfication schemes that analysts can employ. Generally speaking, policy objectives are handled most easily when they are categorized as either predominantly procedural or predominantly substantive. Procedural objectives are those associated with the administrative implementation of a policy, whereas substantive objectives are those related to the actual accomplishments or failures of a policy. An objective is classified as procedural when it aims to improve internal administrative performance. Substantive objectives, on the other hand, are those intended to attain target goals by concentrating on specific sociophysical targets within the scope of the policy.[13] (Given this distinction, any examination of procedures without a concomitant assessment of substance is meaningless.) Although this dichotomy is not without limitations, it nevertheless is necessary for analytical purposes to group initially—on the basis of prevailing tendency—each objective into one of the two categories, even though an objective may actually fit into both classifications.

At this point, several caveats are worth mentioning. In the first place, the stated objectives may not be the only ones, since every policy has various informal, and in most cases unstated, objectives. Investigators, therefore, must be certain to list all crucial objectives so that they can determine which ones are first-order and which are second- and third-order objectives. Second, there is no commonly accepted way to monitor vaguely stated objectives. How, for instance, can the total effect of a state's welfare policy be ascertained? Finally, objectives seldom, if ever, can be perceived as either static or absolute, inasmuch as environmental fluctuations force constant adjustments in and revisions of a policy. One generally encounters difficulty when trying to determine policy objectives because of the dynamic nature of the environment in which the policy operates. (These limitations, it is felt, can be minimized if one uses the suggested classification scheme.)

Operationalizing Objectives

After categorizing objectives into a manageable number, analysts must operationalize them so that policy performance can be determined. Operationalization is a process whereby specific concrete performances are used to indicate the existence or nonexistence of an objective so that investigators can gauge the degree to which a policy is meeting its objectives. Operationalizing objectives is a formidable task because there usually are a variety of ways to measure each objective. As Herbert Hyman and others have consistently pointed out:

The many difficulties suggested—the breadth of the thing subsumed under a particular objective, the multiple objectives encompassed by many programs, the ambiguity inherent in any or all of the objectives as stated, and the disagreement as to the objectives—are characteristic of many programs and are enough to stagger the imagination of the evaluator.[14]

To reduce the ambiguity to which Hyman refers, analysts must carefully operationalize each objective with performance indicators that meet two methodological rules: (1) indicators used to verify an objective should fit its commonly accepted meaning, and (2) indicators should provide the most accurate verification possible.[15] To insure that these two rules are met, all performance indicators must be both reliable and valid. Frank Scioli and Thomas Cook have concisely and precisely defined each of these two criteria. They state that:

The [criterion], *reliability*, refers to the amount of random error present in the measurement procedure. It is evidenced by the degree of inconsistency of results obtained from repeated applications of a measuring instrument to similar phenomena at different points in time. The greater the inconsistency, the lower the reliability of the measurement, and, therefore, the greater the amount of measurement error present. Closely related to reliability (in a statistical sense) is the question of measurement *validity*. Whereas the above criteria are important to a full assessment of a given measurement procedure, the concept of validity is what might be called the "acid test" for any measurement operation. A measurement procedure may ... be fully objective in providing guidelines for reproduction of the measures, highly consistent in repeated application (i.e., reliable); but if the resultant measures are not validated indicators of the decision-relevant concepts contained in the study, they are suspect—suspect in the sense that they may be irrelevant to the analytical question(s) posed in the study.[16]

Generally speaking, the easiest way to assure that performance indicators meet the criteria of reliability and validity is to use indicators that other analysts have used to operationalize similar objectives, rather than try to develop original indicators. (This statement is not meant to stifle creativity but to control it. There obviously are times when investigators should develop original indicators.)

Another technique that permits investigators to operationalize an objective accurately is to form an index of several indicators. The principal reason for employing such an index is to exhaust, as nearly as possible, all the operational facets of an objective, and no single indicator can do that. By using an index, analysts measure more accurately the procedural or substantive achievements and failures of each objective.

Assume, for instance, that the objective being analyzed is crime prevention. One indicator of crime prevention is a reduction in the number of reported crimes. If the number of reported crimes decreases over time, a person might conclude that the objective of crime prevention is being met. But crime prevention is more accurately measured when one uses an index comprised of several indicators to verify the extent to which crime prevention has occurred. For example, an investigator might use an index composed of the number of unreported crimes, the percentage of households victimized by one or more crimes, the number of persons killed or injured during the commission of a crime, and the dollar property loss from crime as well as the number of reported crimes.[17] If all of these indicators show a reduction over time, analysts will be on much safer methodological ground than they would if only one indicator were used to measure the degree to which crime prevention has been successful.

Whenever possible, indicators comprising an index should be quantified so that investigators can measure precisely how much of an objective is being or has been achieved.[18] But many objectives, though not unimportant, cannot always be operationalized with quantitative indicators. When such a situation occurs, investigators should use indicators whose accuracy can at least be verified; that is, their attainment or nonattainment can be confirmed by more than one person. For instance, if various investigators intersubjectively agree that a given department's morale is low, then it can be considered to be low.

The important point to be made from this seemingly lengthy discussion about objective-operationalization is that only when investigators select reliable and valid indicators will the objective, whether procedural or substantive, be specific, explicit, and precise enough to gauge a policy's performance. In short, regardless of the type of indicators employed, it is essential to note that few productive analyses are conducted without using verifiable indicators.

Evaluating Policy Performance

At this point, investigators should keep in mind that there is a symbiotic relationship between the operationalization of objectives and the selection of performance criteria. Stated differently, the way objectives are operationalized depends upon whether one is measuring the performance criterion of effectiveness, efficiency, or effort, since objectives designed to measure effectiveness are operationalized differently than are those intended to measure either efficiency or effort. Therefore, analysts must decide on which policy performance criteria (or criterion)—effectiveness, efficiency, or effort—they wish to employ when operationalizing objectives.

Effectiveness, which is the most complex of the three criteria, involves verifying (1) the degree to which formal and informal substantive and procedural policy objectives are affecting, either adversely or beneficially, target and spill-over groups; (2) the speed with which objectives are being implemented; and (3) the affected groups' perceptions of how satisfactorily objectives are being met.[19] (The indicators used to construct the crime prevention index are effectiveness measures.)

Efficiency, which is mainly an auditing technique, entails comparing the amount of policy output produced to the amount of effort (workload) required to produce that output—for example, the number of suspects apprehended per man-hour of work.[20] (The heart of the efficiency criterion is cost accounting.) The danger in using only this criterion to measure policy performance is that there is a tendency to assume that whenever a policy is operating efficiently (that is, cheaply), it is meeting the discerned objectives. A policy, however, can be performing efficiently but still not effectively. Because of its possible misuse, the efficiency criterion should never be used by itself, since it frequently leads to an incomplete if not inaccurate performance evaluation.

Effort, often referred to as workload, entails corroborating the amount of work accomplished by an agency—for example, the number of policemen on duty per twenty-four-hour period.[21] It should be noted, however, that although effort is a separate and distinct performance criterion the criteria of effort and efficiency are concomitantly related. More specifically, effort can be measured apart from efficiency, but efficiency can be measured only after the amount of effort has been determined.

Effort, although the easiest of the three criteria to substantiate, is also the most misleading since it verifies only expended effort, not the extent to which objectives are being or have been met. Effort, however, is useful for monitoring changes in the demand for services, inasmuch as it reveals needed changes in current resource allocations. Thus, effort can be used to assess the resources needed to improve policy effectiveness and efficiency. Needless to say, *it is strongly suggested that investigators use all three criteria to assess policy performance because the best evaluation involves ascertaining not only the amount of effort spent, but also the degree to which that effort has been effective and the extent to which it has been used efficiently.*

Once objectives are operationalized and evaluational criteria are selected, investigators must decide which type of analysis should be conducted. Since verifying policy performance is at best an arduous task fraught with difficulties, many foreseen and unforeseen problems can be avoided when one uses two complementary types of analysis—input/output and organization/process.

Input/output analysis relies primarily on aggregate resource distribution data to measure effectiveness, efficiency, and effort. Such analysis is an integral facet of performance evaluation because all data, even qualitative data, can be assigned at least nominal properties. This circumstance, coupled with the profusion of new high-powered statistical techniques, means that powerful parametric and linear statistics can be used to analyze all types of data, statistics such as discriminant analysis, cluster analysis, regression analysis, and multiple classification analysis, to name a few. Besides these statistics, there are a heterogeneous number of nonparametric statistics which provide alternative methods for analyzing data that do not meet the assumptions of parametric statistics.[22]

In spite of all of its advantages, input/output analysis alone usually leads to somewhat incomplete policy evaluation, primarily because it ignores the effect of structures and processes on policy performance. When investigators arbitrarily decide to use only input/output analysis which allows them to perform powerful and precise statistical computations, numerous relevant factors may be excluded. As a result, input/output analysis can be enhanced considerably (and omissions minimized) by combining it with *organization/process analysis*.

Such analysis uses verifiable, though in some instances nonquantifiable, data to help analysts examine the direct and indirect linkages between target and spillover groups affected by a policy and agencies responsible for implementing that policy. Put differently, organization/process analysis reflects the extent to which administrative organizations and procedures influence policy performance. Such an analysis is accomplished principally by reviewing the linkages among budgeting processes, target and spillover groups, clientele and interest groups, and any other group that might be interested in objective-realization.

Once the performance criteria and method of analysis are determined, analysts must decide on the type and amount of information needed to verify the extent of objective-realization. The next step, then, is to find out where data are located as well as what techniques can be used to gather such information. Reasonably accurate and relatively complete and comparable data which measure effectiveness, efficiency, and effort can be gathered from various sources. (Whenever possible, data should be collected both before and after policy implementation.)

Some essential *data sources* are as follows:[23]

For Input/Output Analysis:
1. Existing records and statistics—routinely collected agency information
2. Interviews and surveys—target and spillover group satisfaction
3. Field observations—professional ratings
4. Experiences of other governmental and quasi-governmental agencies—procedural and evaluative comparable data (for example, personnel records).

For Organization/Process Analysis:
1. Organizational structure—flow of authority and responsibility
2. Investment return—cost benefit outcomes
3. Productivity—ratio of input to output

4. Resource capability
   a. Technical—actual and potential state of technology
   b. Financial—capital structure and availability of credit and equity
   c. Physical—condition of equipment and utilization capacity
   d. Human—skilled personnel and personnel policies
5. Social responsibility—types and extent of activities.

Some *data-gathering techniques* include the following:[24]

1. Observation (analyzing records, recording events, obtaining physical evidence)
2. Surveys and interviews
3. Tests
4. Subjective ratings by professionals
5. Direct measurements, such as clinical examinations.

When gathering information, analysts are encouraged to rely on routinely collected data since such a procedure can save time and money. However, diligence must be exerted because until recently record-keeping and data collection traditionally have been given low priority in most governmental and quasi-governmental agencies; thus the data frequently are invalid, unreliable, and incomparable. Data, even when reliable and valid, are not always comparable because various agencies tend to collect them differently, a situation which reduces the usefulness of the information when conducting the performance evaluation phase of a policy analysis. Despite these shortcomings, existing records and documents usually provide the best available information required to conduct a performance evaluation, especially over time.

In summary, the purpose of the policy evaluation phase of policy analysis is to provide specific information about the consequences of a given policy, not to determine and isolate cause-and-effect relationships. When appropriately used, the evaluation furnishes useful information concerning the extent to which structures and processes affect objective-realization. The assessment also provides investigators with some knowledge of the intended and unintended consequences affecting not only target but also spillover groups. Performance evaluation, furthermore, allows analysts to compare the intended outcomes with actual results by raising questions such as: Are the actual consequences more desirable than the expected results? Whose objectives are being met? What strategies should be pursued to reach objectives? Are major opportunities to achieve objectives being overlooked?

Translated into its simplest terms, performance evaluation is a twofold process. One first evaluates performance via input/output analysis and then modifies that assessment with data obtained by means of organization/process analysis. Thus performance evaluation is an iterative procedure which involves examining the continuing interplay between formal and informal objectives and the structures and procedures designed to meet those objectives.

Proposing Alternatives and Recommendations

The final phase of a policy analysis involves developing *viable* revisions and modifications to ameliorate objective-realization and/or discarding unrealistic or unattainable objectives. To determine which policy elements should be altered and which should be discarded, investigators must become familiar with the underlying priorities of each affected group, inasmuch as analysts will be forced to choose from among bewildering sets of conflicting priorities.

When making such perplexing decisions, analysts must consider both the target and spillover groups' explicit and implicit preferences. For instance, group A may prefer to change objective X, whereas group B may be disposed to option P. The reason group A favors a change in objective X is that it incorporates more of group A's values than does option P. The same reasoning holds for group B and its preference for option P. Given the fact that target and spillover groups generally have competing sets of priorities, it is evident that investigators seldom satisfy all groups when trying to propose alternatives and recommendations to ameliorate objective-realization. Only by considering each group's priority scheme can analysts determine the alternatives that are likely to be accepted and/or rejected by policymakers.

When suggesting corrective action, investigators also must take into account the number of years a policy has been in effect. Analysts should remember that few policies are planned rationally; most are the product of incremental non-rational (not to be confused with irrational) responses to demands from vested interest groups with sufficient power to see to it that a particular policy is proposed and implemented. Thus, an implemented policy always has a vested clientele who will be reluctant to support major revisions or modifications. Drastic alternations, therefore, rarely are viable because many policies, especially well-established ones, are "enmeshed in networks of alliances with other policies; are governed by rules, regulations, and laws; and have survived many threats to their continued existence."[25] Consequently, large-scale policy alterations will seldom be received favorably unless a relatively new policy is being analyzed, since its vested interest groups probably have not been solidified.

Despite these admonitions, analysts nevertheless must develop a list of optional suggestions to ameliorate objective-realization. Since there is an almost infinite number of conceivable alternatives from which to choose, one should by necessity restrict the number of viable recommendations to no more than five or six.[26] (Inventorying inviable alternatives is a waste of time and effort, unless one is brainstorming for new, innovative ideas.)

Inasmuch as it would be a mistake to assume that a policy is meeting all its objectives, the best strategy is to propose at least one alternative from each of the following categories of action:

1. Extend the scope of the present policy
2. Make only minor changes in the present policy
3. Develop major revision in the present policy.

Besides developing their own notions as to which aspects of a policy need to be changed or discarded, investigators should review some of the following sources for possible ideas:

1. Specific governmental proposals
2. Legislative statements and laws
3. Positions and expressions of public and private sector groups and individuals
4. Personnel statements of various agencies.

A Policy Analysis Team

Before this review is concluded, a brief word about putting together a team of investigators is in order. By now it should be apparent that it is difficult, if not impossible, for one person to execute a policy analysis. As a result, a team of investigators customarily is employed.

Generally speaking, an analysis is conducted by a team of researchers selected either from the agency which primarily is responsible for implementing the examined policy (inhouse study) or from a coterie of outside experts who usually are associated with research-oriented universities, research institutes, or consulting firms (contract study). Regardless of which type of study is conducted, there are, according to Vary Coates, some major advantages and disadvantages connected with both inhouse and contract studies. Figure 1-2 highlights the pro and con arguments as they are cited by Coates.[27]

Which type of study is best? The answer is unclear since it depends largely upon particular circumstances—for example, whether accountability is more important than autonomy. For many public agencies, however, the question is inappropriate because they do not have sufficient funds for letting contract studies. Consequently, such agencies have come to rely on inhouse studies which, evidence suggests, are most informative when the appraisal is performed by an interdisciplinary team comprised of organizational subordinates and superordinates, all of whom rely on a variety of analytical techniques to scrutinize a policy.[28] (The analysts, regardless of which tier they represent, must understand

	Inhouse Study	Contract Study
Advantages	has greater credibility for agency management	provides less institutional bias and greater objectivity
	shows greater likelihood of producing institutional change in the agency	has greater external credibility
		permits more disciplines to be used than are present in most agency offices
	protects individual evaluators from constituency pressure by their bureaucratic anonymity	allows the regular work of the staff to proceed without interference
	provides available data to the agency	
	develops and maintains inhouse expertise	uses highly technical and specialized skills
	permits flexibility, scheduled assessment activity in terms of time, resources, and work load	
Disadvantages	lacks a multidisciplinary staff in most offices	has severe difficulties of coordination and management when agency and contractor are geographically separated
	lacks external credibility	
	permits the possibility of institutional bias	tends to tell agencies what the agencies want to hear (as the contractor perceives it)
	makes it easy for analysts displeased by the findings or implications to suppress information	may have its reports ignored or suppressed by agency management

Figure 1–2. Advantages and Disadvantages of Inhouse and Contract Studies

each other's orientation and not let differences interfere with their ability to cooperate.)

The advantages emanating from the utilization of a two-tiered policy analysis team are apparent. In the first place, one group often considers somewhat different factors than does the other group. Information generated by these two distinctive, yet similar, groups frequently furnishes an integrated and seemingly composite picture of policy objectives and performances. Secondly, and not surprisingly, corrective recommendations resulting from the analysis are more likely to be supported when both viewpoints are represented and considered in the assessment.

Despite the frequent necessity for conducting an inhouse study, one should keep in mind that, whenever possible, a policy analysis team should consist of a hybrid combination of inhouse and contract investigators. The inhouse group can play a major role in defining and formulating a policy's objectives, while contract analysts, in cooperation with the inhouse group, can analyze the data to see the degree to which objectives are being or have been reached and to recommend any changes deemed necessary. At that time, the inhouse group would have responsibility for implementing the suggested changes.

Conclusion

The concepts just discussed should, as previously mentioned, serve as the nucleus of a core curriculum for policy analysis. For instance, courses showing prospective analysts how to determine policy objectives and how to measure policy performance should be made an integral part of a core curriculum. Courses introducing students to various quantitative and qualitative techniques also should be offered. Techniques which allow persons to integrate both input/output and organization/process data and utilize iterative procedures showing the dynamic interplay between the two would be particularly useful.

More specifically, core courses which address the following topics would be especially serviceable to prospective policy analysts:

1. Research design
2. Mathematical and statistical programming
3. Descriptive and inferential statistics
4. Policy formulation, implementation, and evaluation
5. Political economics
6. Resource management and development
7. Public sector–private sector relationships
8. Policy and program management
9. Public values.

When developing a core curriculum, one should keep in mind the symbiotic relationship between core courses and substantive policy areas. After all, students eventually will have to combine such interdisciplinary knowledge with knowledge of a substantive policy area to analyze some public sector problems, usually in workshops, practica, and/or internships. Thus, a core should provide students with a sufficient enough background to examine policy effectively and efficiently.

At this point one admonition is appropriate. Core curriculum developers should recognize that a core cannot be inaugurated irrespective of public sector needs. In the broadest sense, the types of courses included in the core will be determined by the public sector. (After all, most curriculum developments are the result of external pressures placed on a school.) Therefore, the core curriculum has to coincide with the needs of the public sector if the core is to be useful to analysts.

Regardless of the types of core courses that are instituted, there is no question that developing a sound, serviceable policy analysis core is a formidable task, but one that cannot be ignored. The effort is an essential step in developing an effective policy analysis program for the decade ahead.

Notes

1. Don C. Gibbons et al., *Criminal Justice Planning: An Introduction* (Englewood Cliffs, N.J.: Prentice-Hall, 1977), p. 166.
2. Henry Winthrop, "Policy and Planning Programs as Goals of Scientific Work: Interdisciplinary Training For Social Planning as a Case Study in Applied Social Science," *The American Journal of Economics and Sociology*, 34 (July 1975), 228-29; Stuart Nagel and Marian Neef, "What Is and What Should Be in University Policy Studies?" *Public Administration Review*, 37 (July/August 1977), 384.
3. Ernest A. Engelbert, "University Education for Public Policy Analysis," *Public Administration Review*, 37 (May/June 1977), 228.
4. Winthrop, pp. 230-32; Engelbert, pp. 228-29; Nagel and Neef, 284-86.
5. Engelbert, p. 234.
6. For a more developed view, see Yehezkel Dror, *Design for Policy Sciences* (New York: American Elsevier, 1971), Chapters 1-4.
7. Dror, p. 105.
8. Dror, pp. 28-29.
9. Vary T. Coates, *Technology and Public Policy: The Process of Technology Assessment in the Federal Government*, Prepared for the National Science Foundation by the Program of Policy Studies in Science and Technology, George Washington University, July 1972.
10. Gunnar Myrdal, *Value in Social Theory* (London: Routledge and Kegan Paul, 1958), p. 35.
11. Ian I. Mitroff, "Who Looks at the Whole System," in Henry S. Brinkers (ed.), *Decision-Making: Creativity, Judgements, and Systems* (Columbus: Ohio University Press, 1972), p. 230.
12. Harry S. Havens, "MBO and Program Evaluation, or Whatever Happened to PPBS?" *Public Administration Review*, 36 (January/February 1976), 41.
13. The difference between goals and objectives should be kept in mind. A goal is a desired future condition which does not have to be achieved within a given period of time. An objective, which is more concrete and specific than is a goal, is a desired accomplishment that should be reached in a particular period of time. For a more comprehensive discussion of the differences between goals and objectives, see Chester A. Newland, "Policy/Program Objectives and Federal Management: The Search for Government Effectiveness," *Public Administration Review*, 36 (January/February 1976), 24.

25

14. Herbert H. Hyman et al., *Applications of Methods of Evaluation: Four Studies of the Encampment for Citizenship* (Berkeley: University of California Press, 1962), p. 3.

15. Ronn J. Hy, *Using the Computer in the Social Sciences: A Nontechnical Approach* (New York: Elsevier North-Holland, 1977), p. 79.

16. T.J. Cook and F.P. Scioli, "Impact Analysis in Public Policy Research," in Kenneth M. Dolbeare (ed.), *Public Policy Evaluation* (Beverly Hills, Cal.: Sage Publications, 1975), p. 101.

17. The Urban Institute, *Measuring the Effectiveness of Basic Municipal Services: Initial Report* (Washington, D.C.: The Urban Institute, 1974), pp. 40–41.

18. For a simple yet sound discussion of the quantification and measurement of variables, see Kenneth R. Hover, *The Elements of Social Scientific Thinking* (New York: St. Martin's Press, 1976), pp. 85–93.

19. The following has been extrapolated from The Urban Institute, *Measuring the Effectiveness of Basic Municipal Services*, p. 3.

20. Ibid.

21. Ibid.

22. Some of the most useful nonparametric statistics are the Sign test, the Mann-Whitney test, the Kruskal-Wallis test, and Wald-Wolfowitz test, and the Spearman Rank Order test.

23. Jack L. Franklin and Jean H. Thrasher, *An Introduction to Program Evaluation* (New York: John Wiley & Sons, 1976), p. 72.

24. Ibid., pp. 72–73.

25. Ibid., p. 116.

26. J. Klein, *The Study of Groups* (London: Routledge and Kegan Paul, 1956), p. 42.

27. Coates, p. 4.

28. Anthony P. Raia, *Managing by Objectives* (Glenview, Ill.: Scott, Foresman, 1974), p. 121.

2

Some Notes on Public Policy Processes

Brian R. Fry and
Mark E. Tompkins

Recent years have witnessed a substantial increase of interest in the field of policy studies, both in the governmental sector and in academia. Despite this interest, no clear consensus has been formed as to what constitutes appropriate training in the field. With the exception of some agreement on the requirement for rational-comprehensive analytic skills, the content of curricula in policy studies exhibits substantial diversity. Our intent is to propose a framework for policy studies encompassing several processes and levels of analysis in search of a more satisfactory definition of the domain of policy studies.

Several forces have produced a potentially expanding market for policy analysis in the public sector. Most visibly, the growth in the size and range of functions performed by government, particularly over the last decade, has produced a growing demand for accountability regarding the results of governmental programs and more careful consideration of new programmatic ventures. An important component of this growth has been an increase in intergovernmental transfers from the federal government to both state and local governments. These transfers often carry planning and evaluation requirements and have done much to stimulate activity by state and local governments in those areas.

Another factor has been the reassertion of legislative/executive prerogatives as elected officials, sometimes in tandem, sometimes separately, have sought to exert tighter controls over the bureaucracy. This has led to both additional efforts within agencies to justify programs and to the development of staff capacities independent of the agencies for the purpose of program planning, monitoring, and evaluation.

Yet another factor has been a change in the role concept of the public administrator. Emerging from the protective Wilsonian cocoon of neutral competence, the administrator has either assumed, or has been charged with, the role of policy advocacy based upon professional standards or, more recently, clientele expectations. In this role, the administrator incurs responsibility not only for managerial efficiency, but also for policy effectiveness.

This, of course, is only a partial inventory of forces leading to an emphasis on policy analysis in the public sector. Whatever the reasons, the manifestations are all about us. Perhaps the most obvious of these have been the much heralded, and perhaps oversold, reforms of the budgetary process. The lexicon of budgetary reform has become part of the everyday language of the administrator. Consider, for instance, the familiarity of such terms as performance budgeting, cost-benefit analysis, cost-effectiveness analysis, systems analysis, management by objectives, and, the latest rage, zero-based budgeting. The establishment of the Congressional Budget Office and the continuing efforts of the General Accounting Office in regard to "comprehensive audits" have enhanced congressional policy analysis capabilities. Parallel developments are evident at the state level and, to a lesser extent, the local level.

Much of the activity described above represents a desire to make public decision-making more rational and has generated a demand for persons schooled in rational analytic techniques of resource allocation. For example, as reported in the *Political Science Utilization Directory*, 50 percent of the governmental practitioners responding to a questionnaire listed enhanced training in decision-making techniques, quantitative analysis, economics, and analytical capabilities as requirements for more effective education in political science.[1]

The academic response has been fairly substantial and, to a large degree, apparently conditioned by the nature of the market demand. Though reliable, and interpretable, information is difficult to come by, available resources allow some reasonable inferences about the extent and nature of academic efforts in the field of public policy.

The 1976 *Policy Studies Directory* lists more than seventy-five institutions offering degree programs relevant to training in public policy.[2] A survey by the National Association of Schools of Public Affairs and Administration indicates that nine institutions offered masters' degrees specifically in public policy in 1975.[3]

Although the content of programs in public policy exhibits considerable diversity, a common thread running through most of the programs is the emphasis on rational-analytic techniques. In the nine institutions designated by the NASPAA survey, course requirements were listed in thirteen academic areas. Courses in policy analysis, economics, and quantitative analysis were required by half or more of the programs. No other single academic area was required by more than two schools. Much the same pattern emerges from Dunn's analysis of seven masters' level policy programs with the exception that political science joins quantitative methods, economics, and statistics as course requirements in half or more of the programs.[4] Dunn offers some further elaboration of the content of core curriculum requirements and faculty backgrounds. Core courses were drawn from fifteen academic fields. However, courses dealing with rational-analytic techniques constituted at least half of the required curriculum in six of the seven programs examined. The same emphasis, though to a lesser extent, is evident in the composition of the faculty in these programs. Faculty with academic backgrounds in computer science, quantitative analysis, economics, mathematics, statistics, and operations research constituted one-third of the total faculty in these programs. That figure rises to 40 percent when Stanford, where the program is located in a School of Management, is excluded.

Is this an undue emphasis? Perhaps not. However, the combination of apparent agreement on rational-analytic techniques of resource allocation, coupled with an apparent lack of agreement on what else might constitute appropriate training in public policy processes, raises questions about the adequacy of extant perceptions regarding education in public policy. In our view, the study of policy processes extends over a wider range of questions than those examined by what we have called the rational-analytics approach. Further, a curriculum in public policy should encompass that broader perspective. As Trow has argued, "It is clear that good policy analysis must pay much more attention to the political contexts and organizational structures in and through which public policies are effected."[5] In the discussion that follows, we shall elaborate one possible map of public policy processes by drawing distinctions among processes of decision-making and among levels of analysis for the purposes of describing pertinent models of analysis and prescribing arenas in which the policy analyst should be prepared to function.

The first dimension of the map is policy processes. In this regard, we propose that policy may be viewed as the resultant of optimal allocation, mutual adjustment, and routines processes. These processes are not necessarily distinct in practice, but an examination of policy through the conceptual framework implied by the various processes will serve to highlight different types of phenomena. Moreover, each process requires different analytical tools and skills on the part of the actors involved.

Optimal allocation processes have formed an important, albeit illusive, goal in the study and determination of public policy. However imperfect such analysis may be it has been an important benchmark against which action is measured, both within government and in its constituencies. Ideally, optimal allocation demands the operational statement of objectives, an exhaustive consideration of alternatives, and the selection of the most efficient alternative (or optimal combination of alternatives given multiple and conflicting objectives). The process is purposive in nature. Requisite skills are basically analytical (drawing heavily from the fields of mathematics and economics) with a "single best solution" bias. The ultimate objective is policy which is optimal with regard to overall system goals.

The second process involves the examination of multiple goals and conflict and reconciliation processes, and embodies such concepts as negotiation, bargained outcomes, coalition formation, and compromise. The tensions implicit in the interaction over the varied sets of objectives and their resolution (or quasi-resolution) constitute an important set of phenomena for explaining and understanding public policy. This process is also purposive in nature. However, the outcomes desired are more likely to represent areas of agreement or compromise than single best solutions. Negotiation skills are paramount, and analytical techniques are restricted to the assessment of partial and partisan interests.

The final process is routinized activity in the formulation and implementation of public policy. Routines are typically employed for the purposes of simplifying the decision environment and avoiding conflict in the policy process. The result is standardized procedures and criteria for dealing with policy questions or the accumulation of actions and/or decisions which eventuate in policy. A critical distinction between routinized activity and the other policy processes described is that the process is not necessarily purposive in nature—that is, policy may represent an accidental accretion of events rather than a series of conscious choices. Where skills are required, they are likely to be in the area of organizational design and the formulation of decision premises. Desired outcomes tend to be "satisficing" rather than optimal, and the perspective is likely to be partial in scope.

Levels of analysis are the second dimension of the proposed policy map. Aside from the obvious differences in scope, differences also exist among levels in the degree and form of penetration by other actors, the complexity of relationships among the actors, and the complexity of the problems themselves. Four levels of analysis have elicited varying degrees of interest in the study of public policy: the analysis of individual behavior, the analysis of small groups, organizational analysis, and systemic analysis. Each of the levels noted seems to be at least conceptually separable and of potential analytic importance.

In developing a map of these processes' domains, each process can be crossed with levels of analysis yielding the twelve-cell matrix shown below. For each cell, we have attempted to identify some relevant models utilized in academic inquiry. In this effort, it quickly becomes apparent that some cells have been more extensively explored than others. The most common shortcoming is that the relevant model has not yet been sufficiently related to questions of public policy. The map thus represents an agenda for future development as well as a survey of the existing literature. The models listed obviously do not constitute a complete inventory. Rather, the map is intended to be suggestive and is offered as a guide for the development of more comprehensive programs in public policy. Our discussion will proceed through the map by considering each process through successively higher levels of analysis. This approach highlights the variety of analytic models employed as the scope of the goals is enlarged. In addition, we can begin to isolate important skills and relevant understandings implied by the cells of the map.

Considering optimal allocation processes at the individual level (Cell I), analysis structures goal inventories, provides a method for arraying alternative methods to accomplish selected goals, and formulates criteria for selecting the best mix of alternatives given the individual's understanding of the environment. The dominant paradigm in this form of analysis is rational (that is, goal-directed) behavior within the framework of utility theory. However, employment of the utility function, even where it is derived through revealed preferences (and where it is elaborated to account for uncertainty), poses substantial problems. The analytic is perhaps best thought of as a useful theoretical heuristic, with potential predictive power.

Table 2-1
The Map of the Policy Processes

Levels of Analysis	Policy Processes	Optimal Allocation	Mutual Adjustment	Routines
	Individual	I	V	IX
	Small Group	II	VI	X
	Organization	III	VII	XI
	System	IV	VIII	XII

As other individuals are introduced into the analysis (Cell II), a new set of constraints is introduced. For the "rational" actor, the possible requirement for strategic behavior and the threat of nonachievement of goals are raised as a product of interaction with other actors possessing potentially conflicting goals. In this case, the major work on the interesting portion of the phenomenon (where interests conflict) is found in the field of "game" theory. Though no dominant "solution concept" has emerged (that is, one which specifies a most desired allocation under a generalizable set of conditions), the paradigm does provide models for strategic behavior (for example, minimax and maximin along with assorted "threat" strategies in particular situations). Thomas Schelling's work suggests that these models may be useful in the study of public policy.[6]

As the focus is enlarged to organizations (Cell III), the problem becomes one of rational allocation of resources pursuant to subsystem goals. Analysis is limited to subsystem goals because of environmental uncertainty and the probable limited perspectives of organizational actors. Analytic approaches abound in this context, derived from the theory of the firm and microeconomics. In the public realm, cost-effectiveness analysis, operations research, and some forms of cost-benefit analysis rely on this analytic literature. PPBS (and the associated family of planning and budgeting procedures) are also associated with the attempt at optimal allocation at the organization level.

At the systemic level (Cell IV), the search for optimality must be broadened, since broader goals (system goals) are involved. Here analysis must deal with questions of allocation among governmental organizations as well as between public and private sector activity. The field of macroeconomics and the welfare economics literature provide us with the core analytic research in this context. Among others, operational activities focus on the tools of monetary and fiscal policy.

Substantially different reconciliation and selection processes are subsumed under the heading of mutual adjustment. At the individual level (Cell V), the phenomenon involved is divergencies among internal beliefs and values. The crucial processes at this level revolve around the resolution, toleration, and revaluation of these conflicting elements of the individual psyche. Festinger's work on dissonance processes is perhaps the most familiar to students of public policy; other frameworks (for example, attribution theory) are also relevant.[7] Contemporary learning theory, with its interest in individual information processing, examines these processes, to the extent that they take place with reference to divergent beliefs and values.[8] A literature is emerging in education on "values clarification," focusing on the skills needed to cope with the complexity of individual belief and value systems and to employ them constructively in behavior.[9]

In small groups (Cell VI), divergent individual goals pose a new set of issues—namely interaction among partisan interests in search of mutually satisfactory allocations. These are examined in the extensive literature on bargaining among individuals and on informal group processes and social comparison theory. Some skills associated with personnel management are appropriate in this context. Thompson provides a catalogue of techniques for conflict management within and among organizational groups.[10]

At the organizational level (Cell VII), the conception of divergent goals is central to Cyert and March's formulation of the "quasi-resolution of conflict" in the presence of organizational slack.[11] Crozier's examination of the competition among groups for organizational spaces of uncertainty taps the phenomenon as well.[12] On another theme, work on union-management relations in organizations is relevant, with the present analysis setting out the task of generalizing this work to other organizational contexts involving conflicting goals. Both the literature and actual practice offer an extensive menu of negotiating skills. Alexander George has developed a set of prescriptions for organizational mutual adjustment under the rubric of "multiple advocacy."[13]

Consideration of the problem of conflicting goals at the system level (Cell VIII) leads to the substantial body of work on "pluralist" systems. In addition, investigations of interorganizational relations provide material of interest in this cell of the matrix. Whether we take Neustadt's relatively benign view that the power of the president is the power to "persuade," or Lindblom's more acerbic listing of "methods, stratagems, and tricks . . . (including) throwing one's weight around, forming alliances and coalitions, taking a partisan position, scheming for advantage, as well as horsetrading, back-scratching, log-rolling, jockeying, threatening, deceiving, lying, bluffing, but not excluding persuasion and courteous negotiation . . ."[14] there is a sizable body of skills associated with this context.

When we consider routinized behavior, we find overlapping, as well as relatively untapped, bodies of work that bear on questions of public policy. The analysis of purposive choice, alone, involves a substantial bias in much of the work in policy studies and ignores situations in which policy may result from the mere accretion of events and decisions.

At the individual level (Cell IX), there is a wide variety of literature that examines routines affecting individual activity. Merton, for instance, argues that the bureaucratic organization produces a personality type which stresses rigid adherence to rules, often resulting in the displacement of goals through the substitution of instrumental values (rules) for terminal values (objectives) in the organization.[15] Another set of studies examines the personality structures and "operational codes" of important figures in search of regularities in behavior that affect policy. Work in this area by George and George, Barber, Kearns,[16] and others can be directly related to policy outcomes. Steinbrunner[17] attempts to integrate what he calls cognitive theory and a cybernetic paradigm to understand better how individuals deal, on a routine basis, with an overly complex environment. His work, in turn, springs out of information processing studies in individual learning theory which suggest important regularities in the processing of environmental inputs by individuals.[18]

In small groups (Cell X), a variety of routines can be identified. A large body of work exists on the power of commitment in small groups (for example, Janis's "groupthink"[19]). Other work examines aspects of the small group decision process. Among those of interest in the present context are deference to group leaders, group norms, and dominant positions within the group.

In organizations (Cell XI), the work of Cyert and March,[20] along with that of March and Simon,[21] clearly employs organizational routines as central features of their analysis. The formers' model of organizational learning and the latters' work directly on organizational routines examine the phenomenon at issue in this cell. Other lines of inquiry, such as Downs's examination of routinized search procedures in organizations[22] and Dubin's concept of the institutionalization of conflict in union-management relationships, deal with facets of routinized behavior at the organizational level.[23] The primary skills practitioners employ here involve organizational design, focusing, as Simon has suggested, on the structuring of decision premises (tell them what to do), organizational incentives (encourage them to defer to organizational routines), and attention cues (see that they recognize the appropriate routine to apply under a given condition).[24]

As the system level demonstrates (Cell XII), some early work on "homeostatic" political systems posits a form of routinized activity. Although the level of analysis is not always readily discernible, studies on the budgetary process suggest the existence and importance of system level routines, such as incrementalism, that may determine policy. Examples include Davis, Dempster, and Wildavsky[25] as well as Crecine's work on municipal budgeting.[26] In addition, such process norms as "contained specialization," "mutual deference," "integration," and "bipartisanship" illustrate routines applied at the system level.[27] Wildavsky offers prescriptions for budgetary routines based on known limitations on cognitive and analytic capability.[28]

In reviewing the foregoing discussion, it can be seen that a much wider set of phenomena is identified by this map than we typically find in the partial maps which characterize much of the current study of public policy process. We would argue that an examination and elaboration of the work identified, and more importantly, the phenomena involved, will establish the relevance of this broader set of work for the study of public policy. If this is correct, these models must be more directly related to questions of public policy, and transmittable skills within the various policy processes should be identified and incorporated into curriculum in the field.

Notes

1. Stuart Nagel and Marian Neef (eds.), *The Political Science Utilization Directory* (Urbana, Ill.: Policy Studies Organization, 1975), p. 13.

2. Stuart Nagel and Marian Neef (eds.), *The Policy Studies Directory* (Urbana: Policy Studies Organization, 1976), p. 10.

3. A. Lee Fritschler and A.J. Mackelprang (eds.), *Graduate Programs in Public Affairs and Public Administration* (Washington, D.C.: National Association of Schools of Public Affairs and Administration, 1976).

4. William L. Dunn, "A Comparison of Eight Schools of Public Policy," *Policy Studies Journal*, IV, I (Autumn 1975), pp. 68–73.

5. Martin Trow, "Public Policy Schools Attuned to Modern Complexities," *Policy Studies Journal*, I, 4 (Summer 1973), p. 251.

6. See, for example, Thomas C. Schelling, *The Strategy of Conflict* (New York: Oxford University Press, 1963).

7. The central statement of the former is in Leon Festinger, *A Theory of Cognitive Dissonance* (Evanston, Ill.: Row, Peterson, 1957); the latter is set out in Daryl J. Bem, "Self-Perception Theory," in *Advances in Experimental Social Psychology*, Vol. 6, Leon Berkowitz, ed. (New York: Academic Press, 1972), pp. 1–62.

8. Contemporary work in this field is only suggestive; however, see Donald A. Norman, *Memory and Attention: An Introduction to Human Information Processing*, Second Edition (New York: John Wiley and Sons, 1976), chapters 2, 3, 4, 8, and 10 for an overview of current research. John D. Steinbrunner, *The Cybernetic Theory of Decision* (Princeton, N.J.: Princeton University Press, 1974), chapter 3 ("The Cybernetic Paradigm") involves, in part, an attempt to employ this body of research in the fashion suggested.

9. See Sidney B. Simon, Leland W. Howe, and Howard Kirschenbaum, *Values Clarification* (New York: Hart Publishing Co., Inc., 1972).

10. James P. Thompson, "Organizational Management of Conflict," *Administrative Science Quarterly*, V, 1 (March 1960), pp. 389–409.

11. Richard M. Cyert and James G. March, *A Behavioral Theory of the Firm* (Englewood Cliffs, N.J.: Prentice-Hall, Inc., 1963).

12. Michael Crozier, *The Bureaucratic Phenomenon* (Chicago: The University of Chicago Press, 1964).

13. Alexander George, "The Case for Multiple Advocacy in Making Foreign Policy," *The American Political Science Review*, Vol. LXVI, #3 (September 1972), pp. 751–85.

14. Richard Neustadt, *Presidential Power* (New York: John Wiley and Sons, 1964), and Charles Lindblom, "Bargaining: The Hidden Hand in Government" (Santa Monica: The Rand Corporation, 1955), p. 2.

15. Robert K. Merton, "Bureaucratic Structure and Personality" in *A Sociological Reader on Complex Organizations*, Second Edition, Amitai Etzioni, ed. (New York: Holt, Rinehart and Winston, 1969).

16. Alexander L. and Juliette L. George, *Woodrow Wilson and Colonel House* (New York: Dover Publications, Inc., 1956); James D. Barber, *Presidential Character, Predicting Performance in the White House* (Englewood Cliffs, N.J.: Prentice-Hall, Inc., 1972); and Doris Kearns, *Lyndon Johnson and the American Dream* (New York: Harper and Row, 1976). Unpublished work by Hosti, Rosenau, and Anderson has come to our attention on the issue of "operational codes"; this research agenda is clearly continuing.

17. Steinbrunner, *The Cybernetic Theory. . . .*

18. See Norman, *Memory and Attention. . . .*

19. Irving L. Janis, *Victims of Groupthink* (Boston: Houghton Mifflin Co., 1972).

20. Cyert and March, *A Behavioral Theory. . . .*

21. James G. March and Herbert A. Simon, *Organizations* (New York: John Wiley and Sons, Inc., 1958).

22. Anthony Downs, *Inside Bureaucracy* (Boston: Little, Brown and Co., 1967), pp. 167–74.

23. Robert Dubin, "Society and Union-Management Relationships," in *Complex Organizations: A Sociological Reader*, First Edition (New York: Holt, Rinehart and Winston, 1961), pp. 285–301.

24. Herbert Simon, *Administrative Behavior*, Second Edition (New York: The Free Press, 1957).

25. Otto Davis, M.A. Dempster, and Aaron Wildavsky, "A Theory of the Budgetary Process," *The American Political Science Review*, LX, #3 (September 1966), pp. 529–47.

26. John P. Crecine, *Governmental Problem Solving: A Computer Simulation of Municipal Budgeting* (Chicago: Rand McNally, 1969).

27. See Ira Sharkansky, *The Routines of Politics* (New York: Van Nostrand Reinhold Company, 1970) and Richard Fenno, Jr., *The Power of the Purse* (Boston: Little, Brown and Company, 1966).

28. Aaron Wildavsky, "Toward a Radical Incrementalism," in *Congress: The First Branch*, James A. Robinson, ed. (Washington, D.C.: American Enterprise Institute, 1966), pp. 115–66.

3 Policy Analysis and Liberal Arts

David G. Smith

The "where" of policy analysis directs attention to the fact that the subject is taught within universities and colleges as well as in separate "institutes" and that it is taught to individuals who may never become policy analysts. This observation leads to a second: that policy analysis, like other enterprises, can be evaluated both for its product and for its by-product or "externalities." The latter is the primary, though not exclusive, focus of this discussion of policy analysis and the liberal arts: the value of policy analysis for the student and for the academic curriculum, rather than the value of analysis for policy.

The argument that follows rests upon two main propositions. One is that the future of policy analysis as an intellectual or practical enterprise as well as the career tracks in that field are uncertain—sufficiently so to counsel against overinvestment in a narrowly professional version of policy analysis curriculum, especially at an undergraduate level. A second is that policy analysis and the liberal arts can make important contributions to each other. A corollary to this second proposition is that policy analysis can relate the social sciences, the humanities, and the sciences more effectively, serving as a "third culture" relating the other two,[1] to the considerable benefit of individuals who will "mature" professionally some fifteen to twenty years hence.

Almost any statement about the future careers of contemporary students or the best training for such careers is likely to be proven wrong within a short period. Even more dubious would be predictions about professional careers and the demand for future professionals: for example, lawyers, engineers, *or* policy analysts. Thus, an important although essentially negative point, is that policy analysis curriculum ought to be planned with an awareness of great uncertainty about the career prospects of today's students. As concerns policy analysis, that uncertainty is doubly compounded. The field is young and developing, many denying that it is a "discipline" and doubtful about its future. Furthermore, the professional future of policy analysis depends on how government decides to use it; and decisions about major parameters of policy, such as program-budgeting or technology assessment, as well as public administrators' acceptance of the policy analyst could greatly alter the future. A hedge against these uncertainties would be emphasis upon the traditional liberal arts as opposed to a highly structured

This chapter is taken from a study prepared for the Ford Foundation and released for limited distribution in January 1975. Another version, "Policy Analysis for Undergraduates," appeared in *Policy Studies Journal*, Vol. V (1976), pp. 234–44.

professional version of policy analysis curriculum, especially for undergraduate or joint-degree students.

Moreover, policy analysis as it has developed to the present has been, in the view of some, excessively oriented toward a microeconomic, cost-effectiveness model of evaluation. Some increasingly salient current issues suggest that this model may be of less importance for the future. One such issue is, broadly, technology and society: whether as energy, the ecology, or the biomedical revolution. The second is "rights" or "entitlements," expressed as a demand for equality, for enhanced social services and quality of life, career mobility, and so forth.

In the main, the existing models of policy analysis—the microeconomic or the problem-solving—look to a utilitarian economic or a technical means-ends calculus of rationality. One or the other is essential as a calculus, to pursue analysis through to a conclusion. At the same time, the first is deficient in its capacity to confront questions of technology, the latter in dealing with equity, and both in treating with "rights" and quality of life. At a minimum, these considerations argue against a narrow definition of policy analysis, especially for the undergraduate. More broadly, they argue for a curriculum that includes some of the traditional liberal arts, especially sciences and the humanities.

To consider policy itself, the technical and the humanistic need to be more effectively "factored in" both in the design of solutions and in the evaluation of consequences. Thus, aesthetic or humanistic values—say, in the planning of geriatric facilities, a concert hall, or a parkway—can easily be "designed out" unless the humanist participates in the process. Long-term effects of economic solutions, for instance in energy or nutrition, may also be ignored without the longer and deeper perspectives of the scientist or engineer included as part of the initial calculations.

Representatives of the two cultures—sciences and the humanities—should be involved in designing policy. Just as important, they should reflect upon policy, stand outside the process and provide needed perspective—of historical origins, of long-term physical consequences, of the unobserved human price of a policy. Those who choose policies need to know about the origins of the Cold War; about the consequences of strip-mining; the culture of Appalachia; or about "growing old."[2]

To turn from policy itself to curriculum and instruction, the effects of such a joint endeavor upon the student of sciences or the humanities can also be salutary. For the scientist, who often tends toward absolutism and naive optimism in social prescription, acquaintance with policy analysis may teach prudence. For the humanist, both outraged by and impotent to change policy constructively, such an involvement could provide some leverage in the making of policy. As a further point, both are enabled to contribute constructively to the design of policy.[3]

Policy analysis considered not as a professional program but as a broader, more catholic intellectual enterprise also offers attractive prospects for improving the traditional liberal-arts curriculum in the social sciences. These benefits are important for both faculty and students, providing another reason for not confining policy analysis within narrow professional bounds.

For an instance, economics can be both austere and frustrating for students, unrelieved intellectual fare and disappointing to activists who want to "do something" about their convictions. Meanwhile, teachers of economics complain that professional economics attracts those with a highly cerebral interest in economics, who pursue theory exclusively, and that it "turns off" those concerned with bettering society. Policy analysis could provide one alternative between econometrics and the Union of Radical Political Economists.

Political science, on the other hand, acquaints the student with the complexities of institutions and the constraints that limit policy but with little else. The political scientist can point out the difficulties of implementation and identify democratic values that should inform and constrain policy, but lacking an analytic calculus, cannot recommend a specific policy. This failing of political science is often remarked upon with impatience or with condescension by economists, by policymakers, and by students. The point, though, is not to decry political science, but rather to insist that its contribution to public affairs could be enhanced by associating it with policy analysis. Also, for the student, carrying thought forward to a policy recommendation is more intellectually responsible and emotionally satisfying than the impotent celebration of complexity.

The sociologist, in contrast to either the political scientist or the economist, tends to look especially at "social problems" and to state policy in terms of a contrast between social "needs" and an undesired reality. Thus, he looks neither to the costs of policy nor to the practical means for implementation. Often the results are both unreality of prescription and "diffuse revolutionary frustration."[4] Yet the importance of sociology to policy analysis is enormous, for instance, in programs providing services or developing human resources. Policy analysis could contribute to the student of sociology, in turn, an awareness of the "trade-offs" of a policy and the practicalities of implementing it.

A further point is that policy analysis *can be* interdisciplinary in more than the usual, formal sense of including courses from different fields. Thus, when well done, it brings to bear the analytical tools of economics, the institutional lore of political science or law, the behavioral knowledge of sociology, and the technical component of physical sciences upon a specific problem, at the same time requiring the various professionals to modify their own disciplinary predilections. In general, such an activity is good for either student or instructor. But further, it is just this kind of interdisciplinary enterprise that makes one discipline the corrective for others.

Thus, to summarize briefly, policy analysis and the liberal arts can be valuable complements to each other. On the one hand, policy analysis can increase the mind-stretching and the liberalizing, liberating effects of existing liberal arts curricula. And, on the other, the liberal arts, including the sciences and humanities with the social sciences, provide tools to extend and improve the perspective of the policy analyst and strengthen the autonomous criticism of policy.

Finally, to return to an earlier time, policy analysis can be, in a modest way, a third culture more effectively relating the two other cultures of science (or technology) and the humanities to the evaluation of policy. Apart from the benefit for the scientist or the humanist, this particular contribution of policy analysis would seem to be especially valuable for the future professional—doctor, lawyer, scientist, or engineer—equipping and motivating these future influentials to think critically and with awareness about their professional lives.[5] For the reasons adumbrated above, a combination of policy analysis and the liberal arts might well promote this objective better than either the liberal arts or policy analysis alone.

Applications

A combination of policy analysis and liberal arts may have merit, in theory, both for the student, for faculty, and for the future maker of policy. Nevertheless, for a particular institution the attractiveness of this prospect depends upon how it can be adapted to local circumstance and need. Described below are several different ways of combining liberal arts and policy analysis, with reflections upon their diverse merits.

For most universities or colleges, the likeliest approach is an interdisciplinary enterprise with a "center" and a director similar to earlier efforts in planning, international relations, or American studies. The University of North Carolina at Chapel Hill has begun such a program. On a smaller scale, so has Swarthmore College. Williams College has had for years an outstandingly successful joint undergraduate major in economics and political science with some elements of policy analysis. Programs of this type cost little, expenses being mainly for limited curriculum development, some minor perquisites and fringes, staffing an administrative post, and funding a key faculty appointment or two. Such programs may also be the only way to reach majors within established departments. On the other hand, these programs are likely to be hard to "institutionalize" and dependent upon the accidents of leave policy, the personality of directors, and the philosophies of incumbent provosts or deans.

A second possibility—particularly for technical institutes—is to use policy analysis as a way of combining liberal arts and the sciences or engineering. This alternative is an exciting one because it approaches directly the relating of the "three cultures." A second, less obvious benefit is that of applying policy analysis to foreign as well as domestic policy: for instance in fields such as nutrition, ocean science, defense procurement, and energy. Merely to mention such fields is to make a strong case on grounds of relevance. The methodological perspectives these subjects would bring into conjunction are also worthy of note. Finally, approaching policy analysis by way of science and technology may make it more accessible to and more interesting for minority students, typically attracted to programs such as engineering, with readily accepted credentials.

Several schools have already ventured toward this combination of policy analysis, the sciences, and the humanities. MIT, where students and faculty have a thoughtful concern with technology and with the public sector, has developed an array of policy-related courses in technology and courses and seminars relating technology and humanistic concerns. Carnegie-Mellon University has a strong policy component for its undergraduate programs in social relations and pioneering courses in "applied humanities," associating humanists through problem-oriented curriculum in the design of policy solutions. Several institutions with strong programs in the liberal arts and an "engineering sciences" emphasis are interested in policy analysis as a way to bring engineering closer to the main body of the undergraduate curriculum—for instance, Swarthmore College, Claremont Colleges, and the California Institute of Technology.

This much said, it is also true that prospects for introducing policy analysis at most engineering or technical schools will be poor. Career orientation of the students is one reason. Departmental structure is another: traditional and often separatist departments within both engineering and science. The incentives of the faculty also create a problem: in science, oriented toward research; in engineering, toward lucrative consulting.

Schools of public administration can also use policy analysis as a means to revise their curriculum and make it more consistent with liberal education. A policy analysis version of public administration could be an advantage to the student, for the public administration curriculum, and for the public service as well. For the student, the advantage is training that includes more quantitative skills and traditional social sciences, thus equipping him better for graduate training and future citizen roles and leaving him, probably, no worse off for government service. Such a program would enable a school of public administration to compact its curriculum, increase interdisciplinary offerings, and encourage more sophisticated research. It offers a fresh option for schools embarrassed with faltering or stagnant public administration programs. And if such a revised program could attract more capable faculty and students, government would ultimately benefit.

Realistically, though, this alternative also faces substantial difficulties. Most schools of public administration appear to be weighted down by their past—of faculty appointments, alumni relations, and established government clientele.

Many schools are parts of departments of political science, making effective interdisciplinary efforts difficult. Nevertheless, a few schools, for instance the School of Public and Environmental Affairs at Indiana University and the School of Public Administration at the University of Southern California, have the capabilities for and an active interest in this alternative.

Conclusion

Policy analysis and the liberal arts could be a happy combination in several ways. As the liberal arts ought to inform policy analysis, so the latter could add practical consequences to the former. In times of uncertainty both about the discipline of policy analysis and about career tracks, this joining would be a sensible hedge against risk. And, more positively, there is a creative "third culture" role, increasingly important given the technical constraints and human dimensions of contemporary policy issues.

Yet this proposed joining of liberal arts and policy analysis curricula is also risky. Policy analysis is itself a synthetic discipline and, made part of yet another synthesis, might be lost in the collage—a matter of grave concern for those with ambitions for policy analysis as a discipline in its own right. Also, such a program could well go the way of most interdisciplinary efforts: suffering over time for lack of student interest, faculty or administrative commitment, and from the centrifugal pulls of the primary disciplines.

Considering the prospects of benefit together with the difficulties and the risks entailed suggests that this policy analysis–liberal arts venture is not for everyone. To state a tentative and diffident conclusion, perhaps what is most needed is a period of unambitious experiment by institutions possessing the requisite capabilities, the will for quality control, and strong, local incentives to move ahead in a difficult, interdisciplinary enterprise.

Notes

1. C.P. Snow, *The Two Cultures and a Second Look* (New York: Cambridge University Press, 1963).

2. The daily newspapers and TV commentary provide plenty of evidence of the "visibility" and urgency of such issues and of their growing importance relative to more utilitarian concerns, such as cost-effectiveness.

3. William W. Cooper, Dean of the School of Urban and Public Affairs, Carnegie-Mellon University, has argued that one trouble with the humanists' critiques—and to a lesser extent that of scientists—is that they are "meaningless," that they lack the "means" for implementation. Perhaps this lack of means, that is, to alternate policies, may account in part for the occasional extremism in

critique of public policy by scientist and humanist alike as well as their Luddite tactics when confronted with the contemporary "technostructure."

4. Martin Rein, "Social Policy Analysis as the Interpretation of Beliefs," *Journal of the American Institute of Planners*, Vol. 37 (1970), p. 297.

5. For the significance of this point, I am especially indebted to Dean Cooper, S.U.P.A., and to Joel L. Fleishman, Institute of Policy Sciences and Public Affairs, Duke University. Among the professions to be considered should also be included future public administrators. Thus, many administrators report that they missed most in later professional life not the "nuts and bolts," but courses that enabled them to cope better with the "ideas and issues." Roy Crawley, Executive Secretary for the National Academy of Public Administration, reports designing some years ago a conference for mid-career public officials that included the following elements: (1) political theory and political systems; (2) economics and public policy; (3) management sciences and human relations; (4) introduction to foreign affairs; (5) science, technology, and E.D.P. The list is interesting because the curriculum was designed to meet expressed needs of officials. Also, it comes reasonably close to a mixture of policy analysis and a traditional liberal-arts curriculum in the social sciences.

4 Human Behavior and Policy Studies

Edward T. Jennings, Jr. and
Michael P. Smith

Public policies are based on theories of human behavior, either explicitly or implicitly. This is one of the most important insights that can be taught in public policy courses. To teach this lesson effectively, students must be exposed to different theories of human behavior and required to apply these alternative perspectives to public policy analysis.

When people make statements about the desirability of a particular policy, they are making implicit judgments about the desirability of the ends or consequences of that policy and such intermediate consequences and side-effects as it may have. They also are making empirical (cause-effect) statements about the expected consequences of a particular action or set of actions set in motion by the policy. Such empirical statements are based on underlying assessments of why people behave as they do. At a minimum, students of public policy must learn that there are alternative theories of human behavior, that different theories may lead to different policy recommendations, but that different theories may also complement each other.

Our undergraduate classroom experience has taught us that posing puzzles about human behavior is a good way to capture students' interest, stimulate their curiosity, and tap their latent talent for solving problems. This approach to teaching has been especially useful in our courses on urban public policy. Urban policies for health care, social welfare, education, crime, unemployment, housing, and transportation rest upon underlying assumptions about human behavior. For the most part, these "policies" are a complex web of incentives designed to induce human beings to behave or cease behaving in certain specified ways—for example, to provide and use health-care services, to go to "magnet" schools, to shift from renting an apartment to home ownership.

For this reason, the effectiveness of these policies rests squarely on the validity of their underlying assumptions about human behavior. In our classes,

This essay is a direct outgrowth of our work on the Learning Analysis in Political and Social Science project of the American Political Science Association. An expanded version of our thoughts, which contains suggestions for classroom applications and student exercises, can be found in Michael P. Smith and Edward T. Jennings, Jr., *Distribution, Utilization, and Innovation in Health Care* (Washington, D.C.: American Political Science Association, 1977). The critical comments and advice of task force and steering committee members of that project helped shape our thoughts on these matters. We are, of course, solely responsible for any errors of fact or interpretation in this essay.

we have found that providing students with vividly concrete illustrations of this insight gives them a sense of discovery (the Aha! experience) and goes a long way toward sustaining their interest in solving the puzzles posed by underlying policy dilemmas.

Consider, for a moment, the following two brief scenarios that have proven to be especially useful classroom "attention grabbers."

Scenario 1: An urban subway system is built with very few stops in order to maximize speed. This policy rests on the assumptions that man is a utility maximizer and time is a highly cherished good. Once constructed, the subway attracts too few riders to sustain its costs. What could have gone wrong? Student discussion brings out that the subway designers have sacrificed convenience for speed. Does this invalidate the theory that man is a utility maximizer? Continued discussion reveals two points of view. Implicit adherents of the general utilitarian theory argue that a useful refinement of utilitarian assumptions would be to substitute convenience for time as a valued good. Others argue that policy-makers would have been better off if they had considered that our culture values "self-sufficiency," and that this value contradicts the interdependence required of users of mass transit. The instructor points out that proponents of this latter viewpoint are actually rejecting a general theory of human behavior in favor of a culturally specific one.

Scenario 2: Urban policymakers assume that the flight of upper-middle-class whites to suburbia can be reversed by increasing the stock of luxury housing in central cities. This assumption is based on a utilitarian theory of housing choice which holds that, viewing their home as an investment, people move to improve the quality of their housing. After twenty years of constructing luxury housing with public subsidies, the net return of the upper middle class to the cities is far less than expected, suburbanization continues, and much low-income housing has been destroyed in the process. What went wrong? Students are again informed that this policy starts from a classical economic model of man as a rational maximizer of economic utility. They are further informed that this general theory of behavior overlooks alternative conceptualizations that root human behavior in particular cultures and social structures. Discussion elicits a "social conformist" theoretical position, which predicts that in a frontier-oriented culture such as ours, where open space is an important value, dense urban housing programs are doomed to failure. While pondering this conclusion, drawn from their own analysis, students are informed that a social structural theory of human behavior might also have predicted failure. This approach would have focused upon certain structural features of our society (for example, the highway-auto industrial complex, institutional racism in lending and home-building) responsible for continuing suburbanization. Students are then asked to suggest alternative cultural and structural factors that might impinge upon federal housing policy. They respond intelligently and creatively. They join with the instructor in a quest for coherent, theoretically well-rooted policy choices.

When it is pointed out that scenarios 1 and 2 were actually drawn up on the basis of the BART subway system in San Francisco and upon one of the urban redevelopment strategies of urban renewal, student interest is further solidified. Abstract theory has been linked to actual practice. Theories of human behavior have been tied to their concrete consequences in the real world. Once the relevance of theory has been demonstrated, the stage is set for using more theoretically explicit and refined models of human behavior to shed new light on policy analysis.

Although the social sciences may not be dominated by paradigms (in the Kuhnian [1970] sense that one theoretical approach defines the important questions and implies the methods of inquiry for a particular field of knowledge), it is clear that there are distinct, well-developed theoretical approaches to the explanation of human behavior. Each approach tends to define certain questions as important and others as unimportant, to specify the key units of analysis, and to set parameters on the research enterprise (for example, see Allison, 1971 and Alford, 1975). In this sense, each approach might be considered a latent paradigm in search of adherents.

Elsewhere, we have developed a teaching module that distinguishes between and uses rational actor and social structural paradigms to explain alternative policy outcomes (Smith and Jennings, 1977). These terms denote relatively distinct theories of human behavior. The paradigms tend to ask different questions, focus on different units of analysis, and specify different factors as important predictors of behavior. The application of these paradigms to particular policy questions can lead to contradictory conclusions about the consequences of particular actions and policy incentives. Yet, because the paradigms frequently operate at different *levels* of analysis, they also can be used to complement each other in the shaping of policy proposals.

In the following pages we consider the principal concepts and concerns of the rational actor and social structural paradigms and their application to public policy studies. We then demonstrate their utility by applying them concretely to a particular health policy problem. We conclude with a commentary on the importance of explicating alternative theories of human behavior as a teaching strategy in policy studies.

Rational Choice Models

Rational choice models of behavior are based on the assumption that people are rational actors.[1] The rational actor, as defined by rational choice models, is one who examines alternative courses of action, assesses the consequences of each in terms of estimated costs and benefits, calculates the net benefit associated with each alternative, and selects that alternative which provides the greatest net benefit.

Such models of behavior are known by a variety of terms in the social sciences: rational actor, rational choice, decision theoretic, and utility maximizing. Rational actor explanations for behavior are based on the assumption that people value some things and, within the limits of available resources, will try to increase their possession or attainment of whatever it is that they value. The rational actor is a utility maximizer; he seeks a maximum return on his resources. Utility is the value assigned to things which the actor values. Resources include any valued object which may be exchanged for other valued objects: skill, knowledge, training, labor, capital, friendship, money, status, and power are some examples.

We should take care to note that the rational actor can consider more than one value in making a decision. The rational actor need not pursue one goal at the expense of all others. To do so would frequently result in outcomes that the actor would regard as undesirable. Instead, the actor can take into account the impact of a decision on various values and the relative weight that he places on those values.

In addition, it should be clear that the values pursued by rational actors need not be simple economic self-interest. Other values that people might seek to realize would include such things as social justice, friendship, self-esteem, or a stable social and economic order. Rational choice models are therefore compatible with the belief that people may act in humanitarian ways.

The rational choice approach assumes that an individual will place different values on different states of affairs. Generally, however, we are unable to measure the quantity of value that people derive from different states of affairs. Not only are we unable to quantify value directly, we frequently cannot quantify it indirectly by reference to the quantities of the objects from which people derive utility. Many of the things which people value cannot be measured in standard units.

Although we may lack the ability to measure standard units of value, or of the things that people value, people do place relative values on things. People prefer some states of affairs to other states of affairs; they generally prefer to have more rather than less of a valued object. For this reason, rational choice theories employ the concept of preference orderings. A preference ordering is a ranking from most to least desirable of alternative objects, outcomes, or states of affairs. The theory of rational choice assumes that people will have preference orderings—that they value some things more than others.

The rational actor selects from among various courses of action that which has the most favorable expected consequences. Consequences may also be called outcomes or states of affairs. Consequences include both the costs and benefits of action. A cost is anything which represents a loss of value to the actor.

Costs include actual losses as well as "opportunity costs." Opportunity cost is the value that could be derived from some other use of the resource. The benefits of the decision include anything which provides value to the actor. Although a number of people have tried to classify the kinds of benefits that people derive from their actions, we will content ourselves for now with the notion that benefits can be of many types.

The rational actor considers a variety of alternatives before making a decision. The alternatives are different courses of action. As we have mentioned, each alternative has consequences, and the consequences consist of effects which carry costs and benefits. The actor calculates the costs and benefits associated with each alternative and selects that alternative which has the highest expected net benefit (or difference between expected benefits and expected costs) as his course of action.

Some rational choice models assume that decision-makers assess all possible alternatives and possess perfect information on the consequences of each alternative. Others accept the consideration of all possible alternatives as a condition of rational action, but accept limits on information, asserting that actors consider available information and make subjective estimates of the probable consequences of alternative courses of action. Still others assert that actors cannot possibly know what all the possible alternatives might be. Instead, they consider known alternatives, or the alternatives which they can conceive, and work with the best available information to derive subjective probability estimates of the outcomes associated with each alternative. The latter is a somewhat weaker interpretation of rational behavior, placing fewer conditions on the behavior which will be considered rational.

These alternative models of rational behavior rest on different assumptions about the availability and cost of information. If we assume that information is costly, as it generally is, then we can assume that decision-makers will not seek all possible information. Instead, they will seek information within the limits imposed by time, money, and technical constraints. Within these constraints, search will cease once the decision-maker reaches a subjective judgment that he possesses sufficient information to reach a decision.

If we assume value maximization as the criterion of rationality, the actor is faced with a dilemma. The search for alternatives and better information may yield new alternatives and information which will produce a more beneficial outcome. On the other hand, the search may cost more than any additional benefits that it produces. The actor's dilemma is that maximization models provide no basis for deciding when sufficient search has taken place, since we cannot know, and frequently cannot estimate, whether the benefits of additional search will outweigh its costs.

To avoid this dilemma, many theorists suggest that actors will engage in "satisficing" behavior. They will review alternatives and assess expected costs and benefits, but they will limit this analysis to the most likely alternative courses of action and the most important values that might be affected by the action. In effect, they attempt to find a solution which they regard as satisfactory, given their value structure.

Rationality, as an *explanatory* model of behavior, does emphasize making a choice among alternative courses of action, after estimating the costs and benefits associated with the estimated sequences of each alternative. Whether the behavior is maximizing or satisficing, rationality dictates the selection, from among alternatives considered, of that course of action which provides the greatest net benefit.

Rational actor models of human behavior are based on a series of important assumptions about behavior. The rational choice analyst assumes that people do make decisions before they act—decisions based on a conscious consideration of alternative courses of action and conscious calculation of the cost benefit ratio associated with each alternative. This implies: (1) that behavior is goal directed; (2) that behavior is not, in general, impulsive or instinctual; (3) that behavior is guided by information; (4) that people search for information before arriving at decisions; (5) that individuals can estimate, at least subjectively, the costs and benefits of alternatives; (6) that people have preferences (that is, that they attach greater subjective value to one state of affairs than to other states of affairs); and (7) that people seek to obtain as much as possible for their investment.

Social Structural Analysis

Social structural theorists start from the basic assumption that people interact with each other in the context of norms and expectations, rewards and punishments, and objective opportunities and constraints.[2] These "structures" collectively shape the attitudes, interests, and ultimate behavior of differently situated individuals and groups in the overall social system. A social structure is a regularized pattern of interaction and communication. Through interaction, individuals learn social roles and groups develop social norms. These norms and roles channel behavior by shaping inducements, expectations, and life chances. Among the most significant forces shaping behavior, according to structural analysts, are occupational role, social class and status position, and the prevailing economic and political structure within any given social system.

Social structural analysts focus upon the material and psychological rewards and punishments attached to various roles and statuses that people occupy in society. Social structures mold people's environments. They are the sources of roles, norms, and sanctions. In its most general sense, a social role may be thought of as a set of expectations regarding behavior deemed appropriate to an individual occupying a given position or status within a social system.

According to structural analysts, the way in which people act is conditioned by informally socialized expectations that people hold concerning the behavior suitable to their own position and to the roles of other members of their social system. Collectively, the constraints established by these expectations comprise social *norms*. Norms guide behavior by serving as "standard operating procedures." Within a stable social system, members share the same norms and expectations. Behavior that conforms to the norms and expectations of others is rewarded; punishments are attached to deviant behavior. The rewards and punishments attached to particular role-related behaviors are called *sanctions*.

There may be conflict as well as consensus among participants in any social system about how given roles in that system should be performed. For example, people occupying different roles in that system may have different expectations about a particular role, especially if that second role influences their own role. Since this is frequently the case, conflict, as well as consensus, about roles can be expected as a normal by-product of social structure (see Smith, 1974).

Social structures provide opportunities and constraints that affect people's expectations and their aspirations. They affect how poeple think, how they view the world, and how they react to it. A person's identity is closely tied to his position within the social structure. If either his position or the structure changes, the person's values, beliefs, aspirations, and even his social identity are also likely to change (see Tallman, 1977: ch. 3).

Complex social systems such as America's are highly stratified, professionalized, and characterized by ethnic and subcultural diversity. In such systems, some people's interactions are quite restricted to a limited number of social circles. Particular *substructures* of interaction and communication such as the workplace, the residential neighborhood, the professional circle, or the ethnic enclave socialize many Americans into particular subcultural views of the world and their place in it.

In homogeneous substructures that have limited contact with others, the behavior of members is conditioned by roles, norms, and sanctions which are relatively clear and generally accepted. Such substructures provide a relatively stable value system for their participants. Because of this stability, role perceptions, values, and identities change very little over time. In contrast, other substructures are very open to outside influence. Their members are more diverse in backgrounds and attitudes. Conflicting expectations enter into the everyday life of members. These diverse cues can create role stress. Contradictory role expectations can create psychological cross-pressures which, in turn, become driving forces of social conflict and change. Furthermore, open social structures can be expected to undergo continuous change as new interactions by "insiders" (for example, professionals) with outside structures (for example, government, clientele groups) create new expectations, new aspirations, and eventually new social roles and personal identities.

In social structural analysis, people are viewed as products of their environment. They act in ways determined by the constraints, opportunities, and learning experiences provided by that environment.

Varieties of Social Structural Analysis

Social structural analysis encompasses a variety of approaches to understanding human behavior. Some of these approaches emphasize stability in human relationships; others stress sources of change in role expectations, norms, values, and goals which lead to changes in human behavior; still others focus on dominance and conflict as the key dimensions of social life.

We might, for example, distinguish the functionalist, segmental, and class-conflict approaches to analysis. Each involves social structural analysis, but they lead to different expectations and conclusions. The different perspectives, although all variants of the paradigm of social structure, can lead to different diagnoses of problems and different policy proposals.

The functionalist approach perceives society as basically homogeneous. Its members are viewed as sharing a common sense of identity and similar values, role definitions, and interests. Deviations from this stable value system are seen as temporary dislocations that can be absorbed without fundamentally disrupting the social structure. In this view, members are socialized and ritually inducted into the core norms, expectations, roles, and values that govern the conduct of members of the society. Once socialized, new members become part of a highly stable social order. The behavior of the society is a by-product of members acting out their roles on the basis of the society's norms, expectations, and values.

Supplementary to this view is the model of social structure that may be termed the segmental or pluralist perspective. This model views any social system as a collection of "segments" or subsystems, each of which is a shared interest grouping. In this view, each segment is seen as capable of engendering unique role expectations, norms, values, and goals. Societies that contain such diverse interest groupings are seen as subject to internal competition and social innovation and change.

In the pluralist perspective, behavior is a by-product of several factors. Interactions among segments clarify competing interests. Particularized role expectations motivate the segments. Generalized norms and role expectations channel conflict among the substructures. Competing subsystems and groups seek support from other subsystems which either have no direct stake in the conflict or which have an ambiguous stake in the outcome. The resources and skills each segment can bring to bear in the competition to define the society's mission and allocate its rewards determine the outcome of the competition.

A third approach, the class-conflict perspective, views the overall social structure as dominated by elites that have bent the conomic and social relationships of American society to serve their own interests. By dominating the American political economy, elites also are seen as responsible for distributing rewards and punishments that result in unequal opportunities to obtain the benefits society provides its members. From this perspective, change in public policy occurs as a result of either elite initiative or mobilized class conflict. The sources and use of power provide the key to understanding social life.

Comparing Paradigms

As the preceding discussion of the two paradigms suggests, each tends to emphasize somewhat different aspects of social reality and each is generally used to address questions somewhat different in nature. Despite the differences between the two, they are not necessarily contradictory and they are frequently used to investigate comparable questions. Many analysts intertwine the two paradigms in their explanations of public policy.

To assert that people derive their values, interests, and resources from their position in the social structure is not to deny that they act rationally. To assert that people are rational actors is not to deny that they are shaped and influenced by the social structure. We will take some time now to explore the relationship between social structural and rational choice analysis.

One way to view the relationship between the two paradigms is to assert that they deal with different dimensions of behavior. What we mean by this is that one approach tends to emphasize factors which are rather immediate and specific to behavior being analyzed, while the other tends to emphasize the general context within which behavior occurs. In this way, the two types of analysis tend to supplement each other. The rational choice analyst asks what values, costs, and benefits produce a particular action or pattern of behavior. The social structural analyst asks how social structures and processes shape and determine the values, costs, and benefits considered by decision-makers.

Thus, whereas rational choice explanations emphasize the values people hold and their estimates of the costs and benefits of alternative actions, social structural analysis frequently attempts to explain the sources of differences in cost-benefit estimates. The structural analyst does this by assessing the extent to which social structure distributes values, information, beliefs, and opportunities among the population. He also focuses on the way in which social structure affects the costs of particular actions to differently situated individuals, groups, and classes and the resources available to them.

Some would argue that there is a basic incompatibility between rational choice and social structural analysis. The one emphasizes choice as the key determinant of behavior; the other stresses social determinants of behavior.

Thus, one might conclude that the two approaches imply quite different explanations for behavior. In the one case, one freely chooses to do something; in the other, one's behavior is determined by one's position in the social structure. As our preceding argument should suggest, however, this is not necessarily the case.

Complementary Uses of Paradigms

Social structural analysis is often quite compatible with rational actor models of behavior. For instance, both the functionalist and segmental perspectives on social structure are compatible with the view that social structural forces vitally influence the ends that people pursue, but still leave room for rational calculation and choice of means to attain given ends. Social structure constrains choice. The roles and expectations that people have, the role conflict and stress that they experience, and the consensual and conflicting norms and values they hold combine to provide the individual with a basic value structure. This value structure may be stable, as the functionalists contend, or fluid, as the segmentalists suggest. In either case, the value structure provides a set of ends that individuals pursue. In this pursuit, the rational calculation of the best means to achieve given ends is possible.

Even Marxist class-conflict theory, which holds that Americans have been socialized into a rampant individualism which makes them incapable of perceiving their interests as social beings (false consciousness), may be compatible with rational actor explanations of human behavior. From the Marxist perspective, the very rationality and calculability by which individual Americans pursue their *individual* interest is taken as evidence that their socialization experiences have rendered them incapable of developing social consciousness. People act rationally in pursuit of inappropriate ends.

Another way that we can compare the paradigms is to ask how they would handle change in a particular variable. If we postulate change in an independent variable which is important under one mode of analysis, do the alternative approaches predict similar consequences? For example, information is a crucial component of rational choice anlaysis. It is crucial because it determines the array of alternatives, consequences, costs, and benefits which the decision-maker considers. What likely consequences do the paradigms predict for behavior, in general terms, if new information is acquired?

In the rational actor model, access to new information is likely to alter behavior because it will alter estimates of the consequences of alternative courses of action. The segmental or pluralist view of social structure would also suggest important changes in behavior as a consequence of the dissemination of new information. The creation of new segments is associated with changes of interaction and communication in the social structure. It is also associated with the generation of new information and ideas. Information also provides part of the basis for bargaining and conflict among segments. Thus, information ultimately affects patterns of behavior and outcomes. Under some functionalist interpretations, however, new information is likely to be filtered selectively through prevailing belief systems and patterns of action. As a consequence, new information is likely to have minimal impact on behavior.

Competing Uses of Paradigms

As this last example illustrates, rational choice and social structural explanations of behavior can be competing research paradigms. In many cases, this is true because of the concepts and explanation patterns utilized. Certain forms of social structural theory, for example, minimize the importance of calculation in human behavior, asserting instead that behavior is something which is inculcated in the individual through his position in the class structure and patterns of social interaction. People learn to act in certain ways without consciously calculating why they behave one way instead of another. Instead, emulation and cue-taking provide the basis for action.

Rational choice analysts tend to assume that different actors will reach similar conclusions when confronted with the same body of information. They may differ in their preferences and, consequently, adopt different courses of action, but their conclusions regarding consequences, alternatives, costs, and benefits will be similar. Social structural analysts are less likely to share this belief. They would argue that all information must be interpreted and given meaning. Because people situated differently in the social structure have different life experiences, they are likely to interpret the same body of data quite differently. As a result, even when they share goals and information, their behavior is likely to differ because their interpretations of the data will lead to different estimates of the consequences of alternative courses of action.

In addition, some social structural analysts would argue that social structures and processes inhibit the ability of many people to engage in rational calculation. For example, the class-conflict perspective normally tends to focus upon the ways in which class structure and political economy create structural barriers that systematically disadvantage the lower social classes, thereby impeding their ability to calculate instrumentally their political interests.

An Application

A recent issue of the *Public Interest* contains an excellent example of rational actor analysis applied to a public policy problem. In "Blood Policy Revisited: A New Look at the Gift Relationship," Harvey Sapolsky and Stan Finkelstein discuss various problems associated with blood supply systems. We will summarize part of their argument because it provides a very clear and straightforward application of rational actor assumptions to a public policy problem. We will then suggest how a different view of health-care behavior, one based on the social structural paradigm, leads to different conclusions about how the problem can be solved.

In "Blood Policy Revisted," Sapolsky and Finkelstein discuss various aspects of the collection and supply of blood. Two problems which they address are how to insure an adequate supply of boood and how to maintain efficiency in blood banking systems. Transfusion-related hepatitis is the third item on their agenda, and it is their analysis of this problem to which we now turn.

According to Sapolsky and Finkelstein, transfusion hepatitis is an important medical problem, leading to an estimated 1,000 to 3,700 deaths and 90,000 to 120,000 hospitalizations in the United States each year. They expect the transfusion-related hepatitis problem eventually to be solved through technological improvements, including: (1) improvements in screening tests, (2) decontamination techniques, and (3) the use of artificial blood. In the meantime, they argue, something should be done to reduce avoidable suffering.

Although increased volunteerism and regionalization of blood supply systems have been advocated by structural reformers as solutions to this problem, Sapolsky and Finkelstein feel that there is little hope that these approaches will work. Volunteerism will not work because most donations are already unpaid and there is a great deal of variability in the infection risk associated with volunteer blood donations. There is little reason to suspect that regionalization might help because it is directed primarily at supply problems rather than problems of quality.

Market reformers have urged the application of a strict liability standard for transfusion-related hepatitis. In most jurisdictions, blood supply agencies are currently legally exempt from liability for infection caused by blood that they supply. Removing this exemption would submit the agencies to the financial burden of hepatitis infection, thus providing an incentive for them to reduce the infection rate of the blood that they supply.

After arguing that such a policy change is not politically feasible, Sapolsky and Finkelstein go on to suggest that the same goals could be achieved by informing the public about the variable risk of hepatitis infection in different hospitals. This would allow the public to compare the risk of hospitalization in different facilities. They argue that:

The fear of lost patronage would force hospitals to seek their blood supply from the safest possible source. Blood collection agencies, in turn, would then have more reason than they now demonstrate to be concerned about the hepatitis risk of the donors they solicit.[3]

This argument clearly rests on rational actor assumptions about the behavior of people requiring hospitalization. It is assumed that prospective patients consider alternative hospitals, that they compare the costs and benefits associated with each alternative, and that they select the alternative which provides the greatest net benefit. It also assumes that hepatitis rates would contribute sufficiently to this equation to make a difference in the relative standing prospective patients assign institutions with respect to their net benefits, thus causing the patients to alter their utilization patterns.

Social structural analysts would suggest a very different theory of patient behavior. They would begin with the assumption that such behavior is the product of structured relationships involving patients, doctors, and hospitals. Stressing, as they do, social relationships and patterned interactions, they would next ask how people get into hospitals and what opportunities and constraints shape their behavior in seeking health care.

To begin with, the structure of the medical-care system includes a "gate-keeper." The basic hospital-patient relationship is mediated by the patient's doctor and by the normally superior-subordinate doctor-patient relationship. Entry of the patient into the medical-care system generally is controlled by the doctor. Admission to the hospital is regulated as much, if not more, by the doctor, as by the hospital.

The role relationship between patient and doctor is characterized by dominance and submission. The doctor is dominant because of a presumed competence in medical matters. The patient is submissive, allowing the doctor to make most, if not all, of the important decisions affecting the treatment of illness. Since patients rely on the judgment of the doctor in so many things, they are likely to rely on his or her judgment in hospital selection.

Since most doctors are associated with only one or a few hospitals, most patients are not likely to have much of a choice about where they would like a blood transfusion or operation performed. Instead, their choices are severely limited by the doctor's own special relationship with medical institutions in the community.

Despite this criticism, one might argue that doctors themselves, loath to have their patients die, would consider transfusion-related hepatitis risk rates in deciding where to conduct their practice. Thus hospitals might improve their records out of fear that they would lose professional staff.

This line of reasoning seems to assume, however, that doctors conduct themselves as if there were a hospital market, choosing, on a day-to-day basis, the sites of their operations. Instead, there is a structured relationship between doctors and the hospitals where they operate. Physician choice in these matters is constrained by institutional practices and professional interactions.

Doctors do not freely choose their hospital affiliations. Instead, they must be accepted for practice by the hospital. Once this happens, a structured and stable relationship is established. Doctors do not move freely from one hospital to another on a day-to-day, or even a week-to-week, basis. Once affiliated with a hospital, we might presume that doctors, like others in other work settings, develop supportive relationships and adapt to the norms, mores, and behavioral patterns of the institution. Breaking off these relationships is likely to be personally stressful. One doubts that this shift would be undertaken simply because the hospital has a somewhat higher hepatitis risk rate than some other institution in town.

Furthermore, doctors, like most people, tend to develop loyalties to the institutions with which they are affiliated. These loyalties are a product of interpersonal interactions in the institution and the rewards provided for their service to the institution. Such loyalties are as likely to lead to rationalizations for risk rates as they are to lead to attempts to pressure the institution to alter its practices. Following these lines of argument, social structural analysts would conclude that disseminating information about hepatitis risk rates will have little impact on those rates.

Thus, we have shown that policy analysis based on alternative paradigms leads to quite different conclusions about a policy proposal intended to resolve a significant health-care problem. In our experience, in-depth, concrete examples such as this can provide students of public policy with both a stimulating puzzle to resolve and a deeper appreciation of the theories of human motivation and behavior that underlie public policy.

Implications

We have argued that policies, policy proposals, and policy analyses ultimately are linked to theories of human behavior. Policies are adopted to influence behavior. Policy analysts attempt to demonstrate that influence. As we have shown in the preceding application, alternative theoretical traditions frequently lead to quite different estimates of the effectiveness of policies. Because this is so, we believe it is essential to ground "policy studies" firmly in the study of alternative theories of human behavior.

Quite obviously, a wide range of theories of human motivation and behavior cannot be dealt with in all of our policy courses. At the same time, we cannot be indifferent to such theories. A partial answer to this problem is to ensure that students of policy studies take ample theoretical coursework in such disciplines as psychology, sociology, and economics. But this foundation must be followed up with explicit concern for theories of human behavior in substantive public policy courses. This sould be done, first of all, to demonstrate the applicability of different disciplinary traditions to public policy problems. This reflects the interdisciplinary nature of policy studies. It should be done, secondly, to confront students with the most significant issues in policy analysis—issues involving the appropriateness, validity, and usefulness of alternative analytical traditions.

A broad theoretical orientation can provide students with a variety of basic analytical models that can be applied to different policy problems in different contexts. Instead of providing students with a received body of conventional information and assumptions, a thorough exposure to alternative theories of motivation and behavior will enable students to act creatively by developing their own policy analyses. Their analyses can then be subjected to the tests of logic and evidence that determine their utility or truth value.

We have presented here the outlines of two paradigms and applied them to a concrete issue in health-care policy. One, rational choice, stresses individual values and the conscious calculation of the benefits of alternative choices; the other, social structure, emphasizes the importance of structural relationships and the constraints and opportunities imposed by social structures. These conceptual frameworks do not capture all of the key distinctions that can be drawn among analytical traditions in the social sciences. The distinctions considered, however, do capture important differences that have separated a great deal of social science theory and research.

Accordingly, students who are exposed to the concepts and central arguments of these paradigms will have a firm basis for critical reading and analysis of many of the public policy studies to which they will be exposed. They will be able to explore the underlying theoretical bases of many policy proposals and assess the conditions under which a proposal is likely to achieve its intended goals. Furthermore, a firm grasp of these and alternative theoretical paradigms will provide them with an essential handle for explaining unanticipated policy consequences. As they enter the field of applied social science they will be equipped to approach their work with greater realism, perspective, and humility.

Notes

1. For general discussions of rational actor models and their uses, see Braybrooke and Lindblom (1963), Simon (1965), Allison (1971), Thompson (1976), and Shepsle (1973).

2. For general discussions of social structural analysis, see Parsons (1970), Merton (1968), and Tallman (1977).

3. Sapolsky and Finkelstein (1977).

References

Alford, Robert. 1975. *Health Care Politics: Ideological and Interest Group Barriers to Reform*. Chicago: University of Chicago Press.

Allison, Graham, 1971. *Essence of Decision: Explaining the Cuban Missile Crisis*. Boston: Little, Brown and Company.

Braybrooks, David and Lindblom, Charles E. 1963. *A Strategy Decision: Policy Evaluation as a Social Process*. New York: The Free Press.

Kuhn, Thomas S. 1970. *The Structure of Scientific Revolutions*. 2d ed. International Encyclopedia of Unified Science, vol. 2, no. 2. Chicago: University of Chicago Press.

Merton, Robert. 1968. *Social Theory and Social Structure*. New York: The Free Press.

Parsons, Talcott. 1970. *Social Structure and Personality*. New York: The Free Press.

Shepsle, Kenneth A. 1973. Theories of collective choice. In Cornelius Cotter, et al., eds., *Political Science Annual*, no. 5. Indianapolis: Bobbs-Merrill.

Simon, Herbert. 1965. *Administrative Behavior: A Study of Decision-Making Processes in Administrative Organizations*. Second Edition. New York: The Free Press.

Smith, Michael P. 1974. Elite theory and policy analysis. *Journal of Politics*, 36(November, 1974):1006–1032.

Smith, Michael P. and Jennings, Edward T., Jr. 1977. *Distribution, Utilization, and Innovation in Health Care*. Learning Analysis for Political and Social Sciences. Washington, D.C.: American Political Science Association.

Tallman, Irving. 1976. *Passion, Action, and Politics*. San Francisco: W.H. Freeman.

Thompson, Victor A. 1976. *Bureaucracy and the Modern World*. Morristown, N.J.: General Learning Press.

Sapolsky, Harvey M. and Finkelstein, Stan N. 1977. Blood policy revisited: a new look at the gift relationship. *The Public Interest*. no. 46 (Winter, 1977): 15–27.

Teaching the Contexts of Public Policy: The Need for a Comparative Perspective

Larry J. Cohen and
Robert M. Rakoff

The past decade has witnessed a veritable explosion of interest in the qualitative and quantitative evaluation of public policy. Not surprisingly, American educational institutions have responded quickly to this development, with many now offering graduate level training in policy analysis. Admittedly, there are many important differences in emphasis and design across these programs. However, our review of a large cross-section of them[1] does reveal what we feel is one basic deficiency shared by most of them. For reasons that will be explored below, each tends to focus narrowly, and largely unreflectively, on the policy process manifested within a particular economic, cultural, and institutional environment, typically that of the late twentieth-century United States. Consequently, students are limited in the extent to which they can seriously consider alternative viewpoints on the policy process in which they are, themselves, immersed. Indeed, without some basis for comparison, students cannot fully appreciate the strengths and limitations of their particular policy process.

The purpose of this discussion is not so much to extensively criticize existing program curricula as to offer some means of overcoming this basic deficiency. For this reason, we will not dwell on the nature of the problem, except to note its pervasiveness and some of the more important reasons why it may be difficult to overcome. Instead, the main part of our discussion will concentrate on outlining a basic framework for what we will call a "contextual orientation toward public policy analysis." In brief, we contend that a complete understanding of any policy process necessarily depends not only on an awareness of the basic ordering of the society in which it is located, but also on an awareness of competing responses to basic questions about the possible ordering of societies generally.

Our point about the nature of existing policy analysis curricula is well illustrated by the types of courses typically required in these programs. Nearly every "core" includes a general introduction to the policy process, an overview of organization theory, and an examination of evaluation methodologies. Many programs further insist on some training in quantitative analysis, and a small but increasing number now require either basic economics or public sector economics. The policy process course would seem an ideal opportunity to address the basic issues mentioned above, but catalogue descriptions suggest that this is rarely done. Instead, students apparently learn about the nature and determinants of national and local policy formulation and implementation in the United States. Similarly, the economics courses seem to restrict their focus to a narrow range of conventional economic issues. Admittedly, organization theory courses do offer at least one aspect of the contextual orientation we propose, but the dominant theme of these programs is clearly fixed on a particular and narrow view of policy analysis.

There are several compelling reasons for the predominance of this instrumental orientation in existing policy programs. One institutional reason involves a rational response to the changing market for the employment of M.A. and Ph.D. recipients. As academic positions for policy students have become increasingly scarce, the major potential employers of policy analysis program graduates have become government agencies and allied private research firms, organizations whose interests and needs demand candidates with substantive expertise in particular policy areas and attendant evaluation skills. Instrumentally designed programs may well enhance the employment prospects of students in this market. In any event, there is certainly little incentive, and perhaps even some disincentive, for students to pursue a course of study beyond or critical of the instrumental expectations of their potential employers.

Another important institutional underpinning for the instrumental orientation lies in the relationship between policy researchers in private agencies and universities, and government agencies which fund the policy evaluation studies. Typically, the government agency seeks assessment of the success or effectiveness of the agency in meeting the statutory goals of a particular program, as those goals have been defined and interpreted by legislators and executive policymakers. The instrumental approach is tailored to such research because it typically takes these goals as given, rarely seeking to investigate or critically analyze them. Here again, then, the institutional needs of policymakers and the educational orientation of university policy programs are mutually supportive.

Finally, these institutional characteristics are reflected in and reinforced by the narrow theoretical nature of "mainstream" policy literature. In describing the general field as an "applied social science," Duncan MacRae, Jr., correctly observes that policy research is "aimed at the world of action,"[2] although this "world" is usually defined rather narrowly. That is, one finds in this literature a desire to locate the immediate governmental sources of policy decisions and outputs, and their consequent impacts on intended beneficiaries. Little effort is made to place the resultant findings within the broader context of the economic, institutional, or cultural environment within which policymakers operate. Furthermore, the point of view adopted in this work is almost always that of the policymaker. Neither the structural sources of this viewpoint nor alternatives to the policymakers' perspective receive much attention.[3] As a result, this literature has contributed little to the development of a genuine explanatory theory of policymaking or governmental activity. Policy students looking for a counterpoint to their instrumental studies most likely will not find it here.

It is our view that the deficiencies of "mainstream" policy research and policy studies curricula are identical, and that both require a better grounding in contextual analysis. The goal of anchoring policy research within the context of fundamental values and institutions is relatively uncontroversial, even if the appropriate means are less certain. But asserting the need for contextual analysis within "applied" policy studies programs runs afoul of the entrenched interests and perspectives noted above. Defenders of such programs might object that our criticisms of narrow, noncontextual training are irrelevant when directed at an "applied" science because students here will really only be concerned in their careers with analyzing policy options that are conceived within a given and narrow range of values and institutions. Aside from noting the thorny questions of power and responsibility that are raised in this view, we would respond by emphasizing that the "applied" science of policy analysis flows from and depends on the "basic" sciences of political science, sociology, and so on, much as the applied science of medicine depends on the basic sciences of biology and chemistry. We no more want physicians who ignore the developing theoretical and research work of the natural sciences than we want policy analysts prescribing for the good of the body politic on the basis of unexamined assumptions or incomplete research.

But what exactly does context amount to and how would it be integrated into a policy studies curriculum? Our reading of modern political theory and of contemporary analyses of the state has revealed three aspects of context that seem particularly important for assessing the sources and impacts of policy—the economic context, the institutional context, and the cultural or ideological context. We shall describe each of these in turn and then indicate how we at Chicago Circle have integrated them into our doctoral program in public policy analysis.

The Economic Context. While it has long been recognized that the content of much public policy is distinctively economic, only recently has it been accepted that the very structure of economic activity may help condition the form and impact of state activities. In the case of the United States, a contextual view focuses on the American political-economic system as an historically specific, capitalist system which embodies predictable patterns of work, production, allocation, and investment. Historical analyses of the transformation in the economy and in state-economic relations can show how changing economic organization and values have provided a context for the elaboration of the great bulk of state activity today. Understanding the development of twentieth-century monopoly capitalism out of earlier, competitive market forms is essential to understanding the complementary transformation in the role of the state from the early stage of modest government involvement in economic infrastructure to the contemporary stage of state capitalism with its massive subsidization and regulation of productive enterprises.

Such historical analyses must, of course, be augmented by cross-national comparison. Contemporary policymakers, public and private, operate in a wide variety of economic contexts: state capitalism, state socialism, market socialism, state agrarianism, neocolonialism, and other hybrids. Each of these contexts embodies different ways of organizing production, distributing goods and services, and making investment decisions. A comprehensive understanding of policy activity, particularly given the increasing cross-national similarity in industrial technology, must take into account these varying economic contexts.

The Institutional Context. The structural or organizational form in which policymaking and implementation are conducted has a significant impact on both the definition of policy options and the substance of government actions. Indeed, much of the literature that we rightly regard as classic in political science is concerned primarily with this reciprocal relation between institutional form and political substance. In the United States, for example, the transformation of policy arenas from the relatively decentralized, market-based structures of the eighteenth and nineteenth centuries to the hierarchical, bureaucratic command and control structures which dominate public and private policymaking today has made possible the extension of government responsibility into daily life which is so characteristic of our time. This changing institutional context is particularly important for explaining and assessing the organization of state-economy interrelations in such varying forms as regulatory agencies, decentralized self-management, nationalized industries, or central banking and planning agencies.

A variety of traditional literatures fall under the rubric of institutional context, some of which, as we have noted, already find their way into most policy analysis programs. These literatures include organization and administration theory, history and theory of the modern nation state, legislative and bureaucratic behavior, federalism, legal and constitutional studies, and theory and behavior of the firm and corporation. Our intent in grouping these literatures together is both to support current curricula efforts and to suggest how these efforts may be extended. That is, this grouping shows how varied modes of organizing work, administration, and decision-making provide a context of institutional structure and values within which policy problems will be defined, and solutions will be implemented and evaluated. The use of comparative materials, illustrating both similar and alternative decision-making and administrative structures, would be especially valuable for demonstrating the range of matters falling within the contextual parameters.

The Cultural-Ideological Context. The existence of policymaking and implementing structures, and of policies themselves, presupposes that values and ways of understanding the world are sufficiently shared to make possible a mutually understandable realm of discourse about policy matters. In other words, policy activities—from recognition of problems and needs, through definition of acceptable solutions, to establishment of criteria for assessment—are conducted within the context of a particular culture, and often within the context of an ideological world view or public philosophy. In America, this context is a decidedly liberal one. Accordingly, a comprehensive understanding of contemporary policy substance and structure requires an understanding of the development of liberalism from early natural law and contract theory (which so influenced the Founders), through nineteenth-century utilitarianism, to twentieth-century pluralism. It also requires a parallel understanding of the competing traditions of political thought that have arisen or survived in opposition to liberalism. At the most basic level, even the latter ideological contexts have their own context in Western scientific rationality. A full understanding of the roots of both policy discourse and policy analysis thus requires a critical examination of philosophical and scientific epistemology through twentieth-century positivism and its contemporary successors and critics.

The cultural context most exemplifies the intellectual reorientation called for by a contextual approach. By considering our own values and ways of knowing as human products that are historically and culturally relative, the contingent and essentially political nature of both policymaking and policy analysis are revealed. When this insight is joined to knowledge of real structural contexts, the fundamental sources and systematic limits of particular policy options can be most fully understood by the "applied" policy analyst. Additionally, the bases of a comprehensive explanatory theory of state activity will be more readily available.

There are undoubtedly a variety of ways in which a contextual orientation might be integrated into a masters- or doctoral-level policy analysis program without sacrificing the benefits of traditional instrumental curricula. Our efforts to encompass both approaches within the political science division of the policy analysis program at Chicago Circle has convinced us of the difficulty of striking an appropriate balance between these foci. We offer our solution not as a panacea but as a touchstone for those similarly concerned with the design and quality of graduate education.

The Circle program consists of a qualifying phase, built around a series of interdisciplinary "core" courses, and four advanced specializations—economic policy, human services and physical resources policy, education policy, and the politics of policymaking.[4] The core courses, typical of those commonly offered in policy programs, provide an overview of the policy process, some basic economic training, quantitative methods, and research design. Among the advanced specializations, the "politics of policymaking" is concerned with the nature and consequences of the formulation, implementation, and evaluation of public policies. Students who elect this specialization are required to demonstrate competence through coursework and a general examination in three areas: the context of public policy, the process of policymaking and implementation, and one of several substantive policy concerns. The specialization also contains a theory and methodology division, though successful completion of the core is assumed to have satisfied minimum competence requirements in this area. Still, courses are offered each academic quarter in this division for students who wish to enhance their facility with evaluation methodology and theory. Taken together, the four divisions reflect the balance which we feel should be struck between contextual and instrumental approaches.

While the last three divisions are more or less self-explanatory, the context area obviously requires some elaboration here. As reflected in the earlier discussion, the program description speaks to the need to locate policymaking within "broad historical, economic, institutional and cultural contexts." Two courses have been developed which explicitly address the nature of these contexts, one focusing on the state and the economy, the other on ideology and culture. A description of each may help illustrate their respective emphases:

State and Economy: An analysis of the transformation of the functions and structure of the State that has accompanied the transformation from competitive to monopoly capitalism, competing explanations of the origins, and evaluations of the consequences of an interventionist welfare-state characterized by increasing centralization of decision making within the executive. Theoretical problems to be explored include: the relative autonomy of the State from economic determinants, instrumental vs. structural theories of the State, and the relationship between State growth and centralization and the persistence of capitalism.

Ideology and Culture: Examination of the ways in which policy making and implementing are shaped by a culture's world view and ideology while contributing to the production and institutionalization of that world view and ideology. Special attention will be paid to the influence, in liberal capitalist societies, of liberal individualism, utilitarianism, scientific rationality, legalism and Christianity. Examination of policy activity in noncapitalist and/or nonwestern societies will be included for comparative analysis.

In addition to these, a number of comparative courses are being offered that will address the same issues, but within the framework of an examination of some more specialized topic. Illustrative topics include comparative legal culture, comparative urban politics, comparative administration, and comparative public policy. Finally, students will be provided with general reading lists covering the basic issues of concern in this area.

The preceding approach to reconciling contextual and instrumental concerns is, of course, only a first step. Its major deficiency lies in the compartmentalization of contextual and instrumental matters into separate divisions within the specialization. Eventually, we would hope that the two would become combined in such a way that the design of nearly every course would be sensitive to the contextual, as well as instrumental, issues involved. Such a solution is not likely to be reached, though, until we in social science come to recognize the cultural and social relativity of instrumental knowledge and technique,[5] and are prepared to reorient our educational methods accordingly. Certainly this reorientation is best begun not at the graduate level of advanced training, but rather in the undergraduate curriculum. Indeed, had our undergraduate programs fostered a broad, historical, and cross-cultural consideration of political and social phenomena, the need for graduate program designs like ours would be less compelling. A reinvigoration of a genuine liberal-arts perspective in both undergraduate and graduate education is, in our view, the best way to make policy studies a creative and intellectually respectable field.

Notes

1. The sample was selected from the programs listed in the *Policy Studies Directory* (Urbana, Illinois: Policy Studies Organization, 1976). Information about the programs is based on that available in the applicable university and college catalogs. While there is bound to be some error in these descriptions, we trust that, as a group, they accurately reflect the general orientation of these programs and courses.

2. Duncan MacRae, Jr., "Policy Analysis as an Applied Science Discipline," *Administration and Society* 6(February, 1975):368.

3. These criticisms of policy studies have been spelled out particularly well in two recent articles. Stephen Elkin has characterized the work on policy outputs as theoretically thin, overly ruled by the availability of data, lacking sensitivity to the impact of non-local factors on local outputs, and based on trivially conceived conceptualizations of outputs as expenditures. See, Stephen L. Elkin, "Political Science and the Analysis of Public Policy," *Public Policy* 22(Summer, 1974):399–422. Kenneth Dolbeare has criticized the dependence on policy makers' goals and values, the usual focus on a single policy without reference either to other policies or to the broader socioeconomic context of government, the ignoring of the consumer's perspective in assessing impact, and the focus on incremental policy outputs to the exclusion of more fundamental levels of policy and impact. See Kenneth M. Dolbeare, "The Impacts of Public Policy," in Neil Cotter, ed., *The Political Science Annual, 1974* (Indianapolis: Bobbs-Merrill, 1974).

4. Additional specializations are in the planning stage (e.g., social welfare policy, social justice policy).

5. For a discussion of subjective aspects of ostensibly objective quantitative methods, see Philip L. Beardsley, "An Analysis of Some Relationships Between Moral Views and Statistical Findings, As Illustrated by the Hypothesis that Exploitation Causes Revolution," Paper presented at the Annual Meeting of the Foundations of Political Theory Group, Chicago, September 2-3, 1976.

6

The Politics of Policy Analysis

John L. Foster

Introduction

A major problem of any new and expanding field is developing appropriate curriculum boundaries. The problems of teaching policy sciences are certainly no exception. This paper will briefly survey the emphasis of present policy studies courses in American graduate level programs and suggest greater emphasis on an apparently neglected topic—the politics of policy studies.

Table 6-1 provides a rough estimate of the direction of current graduate level offerings in the policy studies area. It is based upon catalogue descriptions of 158 graduate and cross-listed graduate/undergraduate courses offered by 72 universities during the academic years 1974–1976. This is not an exhaustive list of policy studies courses, inasmuch as some catalogues were unavailable, and courses offered by departments *other* than political science, public affairs and administration, and urban studies were not included. However, it seems to be at least a useful preliminary indicator of the direction of the field.[1]

The 158 courses surveyed seem to fall into the following seven categories:[2]

1. *The Policymaking Process.* The emphasis in this category is on the general impact of the process on policy results. Most courses are oriented toward

Table 6-1
Distribution of Policy Studies Courses

Topic	Number with Primary Emphasis	Percent	Number with Secondary Emphasis[a]	Percent
Policy Making Process	50	32.5	3	25.0
Politics of . . .	12	7.9	0	0.0
Substantive Policy Areas	41	25.2	3	25.0
Program Evaluation	19	11.3	3	25.0
Policy Analysis Techniques	17	10.6	2	16.6
Politics of Policy Studies	5	3.3	1	8.4
Other	14	9.3	0	0.0
Totals	158	100.1%	12	100.0%

[a]Courses with clear emphasis on two categories are listed twice, once in the primary column and once in the secondary.

the federal level, but a few focus on American state or local process, or the cross-national level. The category also includes more specialized topics such as Congress and policymaking and the role of the bureaucracy in the policy process.

2. *The Politics of. . . .* These entries cover the policymaking process within a substantive policy area (for example, air pollution, welfare, transportation, education). Some common subtopics in these courses are the historical involvement of government in the area, political structures and process pertinent to policy development in the area, some technical background of the field, and possible future developments.

3. *Substantive Policy Areas.* These courses are either broad, general surveys of major American public policy topics, or more in-depth treatments of specific policy areas. Normally they trace the historical development of policies within an area (once again pollution, welfare, education, and defense are examples), discuss the impact (or lack of impact) of past governmental activity in the area, outline key theories or concepts within the field, and conclude with future options and prospects. These courses generally skim over politics and policy process issues, unlike the "politics of . . ." courses described above.

4. *Program Evaluation.* Program evaluation entries are essentially applied social science research methods courses. They usually stress research design, measurement, data collection, statistical techniques, as well as interpretation and application of results.

5. *Policy Analysis Techniques.* Terms such as policy analysis and program evaluation are used almost interchangeably but the courses in this category primarily have a future orientation rather than the existing program orientation of the program evaluation topic above. Some common subtopics in the policy analysis category are systems analysis, simulation, social indicators, alternative futures, delphi, and scenario construction.

6. *The Politics of Policy Studies.* The substance of these courses is the major topic of this chapter and will be described in greater detail later. Briefly, they cover issues such as: What type of analysis alters policy decisions? What hurdles exist to the conduct of analysis? What is the appropriate role of analytical expertise in the political process?

7. *Other.* This final category contains fourteen courses which did not seem to fit any of the previous six categories. They include: three practitioner-taught colloquia, eight topical policy seminars, two normative issues in public policy classes, and one seminar in social choice models and public policy.

This summary obviously is only a crude indicator of the present direction of policy studies education at the graduate level. Catalogue descriptions often do not list all subtopics covered, can be quite misleading, and are not legally binding. Classification of courses is subjective and the sample here is not necessarily random. Within these limits, however, table 6-1 suggests two generalizations about the present state of policy studies education. First, much of policy studies (specifically the policy process materials and the politics of ... offerings) appears to be part of traditional political science. Second, teaching many of the remaining courses (the substantive policy courses and general surveys) seems to require a level of technical knowledge which is not developed in most political science and public administration doctoral programs, but is the bailiwick of faculty in some other discipline.[3]

Politics and Policy Studies

These observations are not meant to denigrate present policy studies education efforts,[4] but it does seem reasonable for political scientists and public administration specialists to devote a great deal more attention to the politics of policy studies topic than is suggested by table 6-1. The topic is quite close to our expertise. However, it is seldom covered in traditional legislative and executive process courses. It is also very unlikely that other policy-related disciplines will cover the topic at all. Finally, it does not require developing a knowledge of matters such as the chemistry of air polution, relationships between money supply and inflation, and the volumes of research on educational techniques, which may best be left to someone else.

Politics of Analysis

Politics of policy studies courses could cover at least three subtopics. The first may be labeled the politics of analysis. This essentially deals with the question of how we can conduct the most rigorous possible research within the constraints of the real policy world. One consideration is the utility of various research designs. The classical experimental design is the most rigorous methodological tool available, but its usefulness in policy research seems quite limited despite a great amount of current interest.[5] Factors such as the frequent inability to randomize subjects, withhold services to establish a control group, and engage in the duplicity necessary for placebos place great constraints on the experimentalism movement. A careful treatment of what quasi-experimental designs have been used in, or are most appropriate to, a variety of policy research topics would be very useful.

A second item under this subtopic is funding. Policy studies are expensive, and support normally comes from either governmental grants or private foundations. Several sessions covering funding sources and the politics of grantmanship would form another portion of the course.[6]

Finally there are the political pressures on the analyst to consider. A frequently cited anecdote from the New Jersey Negative Income Tax Experiment concerns the pressures to release results as political support for the Nixon Family Assistance Program when only the most preliminary findings were available.[7] There are other published reports of similar dilemmas, and suggestions about how to deal with them.[8] Also, most faculty with consulting experience are likely to have anecdotes, so it should not be difficult to prime several class discussions of this issue.

Analysis and Policymaking

A second politics of policy studies subtopic concerns the impact of analysis on policymaking. The incremental decision literature suggests that systematically collected information (which includes policy studies) does not dominate the normal decision processes. However, even strong incrementalists concede that some information can affect public policymaking under certain circumstances. Wildavsky's article "Rescuing Policy Analysis from PPBS" suggests that analysis will have the greatest impact when the policy questions: (1) involve expensive choices, (2) pertain to new or growing programs, and (3) ask which program techniques are most apt to achieve a previously agreed-upon goal.[9] A major section of a politics of policy studies course should cover what analysts can, and cannot, do to increase the likelihood that their efforts have some policy consequences in a variety of areas.[10]

Another similar topic pertains to what role or model is feasible for a policy studies profession. MacRae suggests an engineering analogy in which analysts are the applied arm of a pure science field.[11] Axelrod uses the medical metaphor.[12] Both imply that policy analysts would be hired to produce specific policy recommendations for clients which would be drawn from the basic theoretical research of the social sciences. Another possibility is the lawyer or advocate model. If a policy studies profession attains influence over policy it may come through a process of competing groups hiring different analysts to present their case in the most favorable possible light. No doubt this is an unpleasant notion to many advocates of policy studies inasmuch as it would likely require de-emphasizing key value assumptions and skimming over evidence unfavorable to one's client. The advocate model is also unlikely to produce major policy changes, since groups able to hire analysts are likely already to be well represented in the policy process. This approach also has a tendency to use the scientific method essentially as a legitimizing device. On the other hand, such a role for policy studies does appear to be politically and economically feasible since organized groups always seek political ammunition. It *might* also produce better policy than no policy studies at all. Wildavsky argues that the most we can expect from policy analysis is to uplift the level of policymaking debate, and the lawyer style might at least accomplish that.[13]

Normative Issues of Policy Studies

This leads to several normative politics of policy studies questions. First, what professional standards are appropriate for a policy studies profession? Should the emphasis be toward the advancement of basic knowledge, or the more pragmatic task of providing a client with the most useful work? Conscious fraud is not justifiable under either approach, but the amount of emphasis an analyst places on unpleasant findings depends upon which professional model one follows.

Another professional issue is, what action is appropriate when clients, or employers, disregard an analyst's advice? Sam Adams in a recent *Harper's* article describes the frustrations and moral dilemmas which developed as White House and CIA officials ignored his Viet Cong troop strength estimates, and based (or justified) Vietnam War decisions with Defense Department estimates Adams perceived to be fraudulent.[14] Perhaps this is a particularly dramatic example, but one can imagine a number of instances in which an analyst is either consciously ignored or muzzled due to political considerations. What actions are appropriate for the analyst in these circumstances?

A final normative question is, how desirable is the possible development of a powerful policy studies profession? An expanding role for policy studies essentially is an expansion of the power of expertise. Expertise in politics often has elite-rule overtones. Perhaps this is not inevitable (the consumer movement suggests an example of expertise producing a better informed and more powerful mass public) but an unpleasant question arises whenever one considers policy studies and policymaking. What happens if policy studies, particularly the futures research, produce strong evidence that short-term choices of the public are likely to create long-term disasters? Who should rule in such instances? Present world population growth and energy consumption trends illustrate the dilemma well.

Conclusions

This paper is a recommendation for greater emphasis on the politics of policy studies portion of the policy curriculum. This suggestion is not meant to imply the exclusion of courses in policymaking process, evaluative and futures techniques, and the substantive policy areas. In fact, two possible positions for a politics of policy studies course are either as a core course introduction to a series of offerings on the other policy topics, or as a final summary class. Both positions would permit an emphasis and careful examination of these critical policy studies issues which appear to be buried in other courses, or ignored, at present.

Notes

I would like to thank David Reedy for Research Assistance.

1. Stuart Nagel and Marian Neef (eds.), *Policy Studies Directory, Second Edition* (Urbana, Illinois: Policy Studies Organization, 1976), is the major attempt to determine the nature of American policy studies education. This guide was based upon a mailed questionnaire to political science departments and the major policy-directed interdisciplinary programs. The response rate was 52 percent. The sample in table 6-1 includes 41 of the 78 schools reporting policy courses to the Nagel and Neef survey, and an additional 31 schools which did not respond to the questionnaire.

2. Several courses clearly cover two of table 6-1 categories. They are counted once in the "primary" column and a second time in the "secondary" column according to apparent degrees of emphasis.

3. Martin Landau notes that "to be faithful to his objective [the solution of practical problems] a policy analyst would soon have to engulf all of social science and a hell of a lot of hard technology to boot," in "The Proper Domain of Policy Analysis," *American Journal of Political Science* 21 (May 1977), p. 424. Landau concludes by noting that policy analysis must develop a more tightly structured domain in order to survive.

4. Some others are much more critical of the present state of policy studies. Heinz Eulau notes that "there is a great deal of fakery about the new public policy; almost anything goes by prefixing the noun of 'policy,' " in "The Interventionist Synthesis," *American Journal of Political Science* 21 (May 1977), p. 420.

5. Most program evaluation texts provide an introduction to these problems. For example see: Harry Hatry et al., *Practical Program Evaluation for State and Local Government Officials* (Washington, D.C.: The Urban Institute, 1973), pp. 39–70, and Carol H. Weiss, *Evaluation Research* (Englewood Cliffs, N.J.: Prentice-Hall, 1972), pp. 60–91.

6. An excellent source is Stuart Nagel and Marian Neef (eds.), *Policy Grants Directory* (Urbana, Illinois: Policy Studies Organization, 1977).

7. See Joseph A. Pechman and P. Michael Timpane (eds.), *Work Incentives and Income Guarantees: The New Jersey Negative Income Tax Experiment* (Washington, D.C.: Brookings, 1975).

8. Two general sources are Guy Benveniste, *The Politics of Expertise* (Berkeley: Glendessary Press, 1972), and Thad Beyle and George Lathrop (eds.), *Planning and Politics* (New York: The Odyssey Press, 1970).

9. Aaron Wildavsky, "Rescuing Policy Analysis from PPBS," in Robert Haveman and Julius Margolis (eds.), *Public Expenditures and Policy Analysis* (Chicago: Markham Publishing Company, 1970), pp. 461-81.

10. Several short treatments of the topic (in addition to Wildavsky) are Dror's discussion of "metapolicy" in Yehezkel Dror, *Design for Policy Sciences* (New York: American Elsevier, 1971), and Arnold J. Meltsner, "Political Feasibility and Policy Analysis," *Public Administration Review* 32 (November/December 1972), pp. 859-67. Two recent symposiums on the subject are Norman Beckman (ed.), "Policy Analysis in Government: Alternatives to 'Muddling Through,' " *Public Administration Review* 37 (May/June 1977), pp. 221-63, and Carol H. Weiss (ed.), "The Research Utilization Quandary," *Policy Studies Journal* 4 (Spring 1976), pp. 221-88.

11. Duncan MacRae, Jr., "Policy Analysis as an Applied Discipline," *Administration & Society* 6 (February 1975), pp. 363-88.

12. Robert Axelrod, "The Medical Metaphor," *American Journal of Political Science* 21 (May 1977), pp. 430-32.

13. Wildavsky, especially pp. 463 and 473-76.

14. Sam Adams, "Vietnam Coverup: Playing War with Numbers," *Harpers* 250 (May 1975), pp. 41-44 and 62-63.

7

Communications Skills and Policy Analysis: Exercises for Teaching

Ralph S. Hambrick, Jr. and
William P. Snyder

As many of the articles contained in this issue suggest, public administration and policy analysis courses increasingly emphasize the acquisition of complex conceptual and analytical skills. In many programs, perhaps most, this orientation is strengthened by requirements that students attain some level of proficiency with computers and data processing systems. Few would disapprove of this trend in the nature of academic preparation for public service careers. Certainly the complexity of the problems confronting political insitutions at all levels of government would seem to justify such an emphasis in preparatory coursework. To the extent that this trend continues, however, it creates a new problem: how to translate the methods and conclusions of technical analytic approaches into a form that is usable for decision-makers and comprehensible to the public. In the absence of effective translation—or bridging—between policy analysts and the groups they serve, the analytic and conceptual skills become meaningless. Skill at translation, in other words, is every bit as critical as analytic skills. It is this judgment which prompts us to suggest that this issue be given explicit and careful attention in policy courses.

Communications between policy analysts and decision-makers takes place at all stages of the analysis process—during problem definition, in the period of research and analysis, and during the presentation of results. Complicating communications at these several stages are the differences between the two groups. First, age differences are common, and a generation or more often separate the two. Second, different educational backgrounds and work experiences are usually present and serve as further barriers to communication. Third, in many governmental units, analysts are grouped in one part of the organization; their relation with decision-makers frequently involves issues of institutional rivalry and conflict. Finally, the perspectives of the two groups differ in important ways. Elected officials, for example, are strongly influenced by constituency pressures and reelection prospects. Analysts, on the other hand, have been trained to emphasize organizational and economic rationality; their policy recommendations are also colored by bureaucratic or personal interests. The net result is to strain further the credibility and applicability of analytic approaches.

Communication between expert and layman has always presented some difficulties, and the translation issue might be regarded as simply a variant of that problem. There are, however, some important differences. Most expert-lay communications difficulties are private. They arise between individuals and their personal advisers—attorneys, accountants, and physicians. In contrast, the translation problems we are concerned with here occur within public institutions. The decisions at issue affect the welfare and livelihood of large numbers of citizens. Unlike the dealings between professional advisers and their clients, which are generally privileged, the relationships between policy analysts and decision-makers are normally subject ot public scrutiny. Finally, the problem of effective communication of concepts and data to decision-makers is closely related to the process of informing the public of policy deliberations and decisions. Effective and sensitive communications between analysts and decision-makers, in other words, sets the stage for effective communications with the public at large. As the federal experience with the swine flu immunization program and the ban on saccharin clearly indicate, effective communication between analyst and decision-maker does not (and should not) assure public acceptance of such policies. But it can contribute importantly to public understanding of the issues involved and simultaneously enhance the credibility of government and the public's acceptance of public policies.

Communication Trouble Spots. Communication between analysts and decision-makers takes place in a setting and is influenced by factors other than the manner and style of the analysis being done. Efforts to improve communications are likely to be successful only to the extent that these factors are given attention. The checklist below indicates some of the trouble spots that need to be taken into account.

The Setting. The context in which policy analysis is undertaken is often taken for granted—analysts are often a part of the organization involved and assume they understand the setting. However, explicit questions about the context in which a policy analysis is undertaken are often illuminating.

1. Constituency, bureaucratic, or other responsibilities. How will these responsibilities influence the decision-maker's view of the problem and any proposed solution?
2. Other demands on the decision-maker's time and attention. To what extent will these demands limit the time available to the decision-maker to study and understand the analysis?
3. The backgrounds and technical skills of the decision-maker. Do they differ importantly from those of the analyst and thereby complicate the communications problem?

(In many instances, decisions are made by groups—for example, a city council— and the members of the group will have different backgrounds, constituencies, and responsibilities. In these circumstances, the setting involves a wide range of variables all influenced by the interactions and dynamics of the group involved.)

The Problem and the Analysis. In many instances neither the analyst nor the decision-maker initially understands the precise nature of the problem. Indeed, much research on policy issues serves primarily, and usefully, to define the central issues involved. Similarly, the research methodology to be employed obviously hinges on the definition of the problem. Yet, some common under-standing of the problem by both analysts and policymakers is an essential ingredient in successful policy analysis. The questions below may help analysts and decision-makers arrive at such an understanding.

1. The decision-maker's definition of the problem. Does it differ from that of the analyst (for example, a department head wants data to bolster his budget, while the analyst thinks he wants an information system to improve resource allocation within his department)?
2. The research design. Has the analyst developed a research design acceptable to the decision-maker, or does it involve more time and money than the decision-maker thinks necessary, or does it raise questions the decision-maker would rather have left alone?
3. The alternatives. Do those under consideration include both intuitively obvious approaches as well as those tentatively favored by the decision-maker?
4. Costs and benefits. Is the treatment of costs and benefits clear?
5. Incommensurables and spillovers. Is their treatment by the analyst explicit and comprehensible by decision-makers?
6. Does the analyst have an "ideological chip" on his shoulder (that is, if the decision-maker does not accept the analyst's values he is considered ignorant and ill-informed)?

The items indicated above clearly influence the effectiveness of communi-cations, and need to be taken into account when designing the analysis and presentation. It is not always possible to consider all of these factors, but some attention to them may have important benefits in terms of communicating the results of analysis to decision-makers. Responsibility for doing so, in most organizational settings, falls upon the policy analyst.

The Presentation. The manner in which the results of the analysis are presented should also be of central concern to the analyst. Some of the barriers to effective communication are as follows:

1. Language. Is specialized language necessary in the presentation or is the language simply foggy?

2. Writing. Is the report written to please other analysts, rather than to communicate with the decision-maker?
3. Stereotypes. Do the participants hold stereotypes of each other which are likely to cloud the presentation of the results of the analysis?
4. Patronizing. Do analysts "talk down" to officials (or do officials "talk down" to analysts)?
5. Does the analyst (or the decision-maker) think that the job is done when the analysis is finished?

Teaching Exercises. Obviously, not all the problems listed above can be solved by better training of analysts. Sensitivity to and training about these problems can make a difference, however. One aspect of such training is to have students participate in exercises designed to develop communication skills and sensitivities. The following list is indicative of what can be done.

1. Distill a written report to a
   a. written summary of specified length
   b. short oral presentation of specified duration (with visuals).

It is now common for research reports to contain a summary of findings and for conference papers and journal articles to contain an abstract. Similarly, even formal research reports are often presented in oral briefings. Having students prepare such summaries and related oral presentations, of other's work and of their own, can be a helpful skill developer. Such practice with feedback from the instructor and other students can be a useful exercise.

2. Develop charts and transparencies for a graphic/visual presentation from a
   a. quantitative analysis
   b. qualitative analysis.

It is possible for relatively sophisticated quantitative analysis to be presented in an understandable form. A variety of charts and graphs can be employed to dramatize the data being presented. But to do so is work which even the professional analyst sometimes talks himself into avoiding. A good way to impress students with the value of such work is to have them observe the presentation of—or to have them make a presentation on—the same analysis with and without such visual materials. Even when this point is obvious about quantitative material, it is sometimes lost with respect to qualitative information. But here too the visual can be used for structuring the presentation, for maintaining attention, and for dramatizing points which deserve emphasis.

3. Prepare materials for and give a presentation employing multimedia techniques; for example, slides, film strips, cassette recordings, closed-circuit TV, or even a movie (Super 8).

Before students leave a program certified as policy analysts (and perhaps the requirement should apply to those certified as university-level teachers as well), they should be comfortably familiar with a variety of communications aids. Moreover, they should know that the use of such aids is not only commonplace but expected in many organizations. Although an exercise of this nature requires some equipment and financial support, these resources are increasingly available at many colleges and universities and often can be made available for class projects. The principal point is to develop skills in adapting textual materials for use with such devices and determing which technique is most appropriate when. The available literature on audiovisual techniques (as well as some specialized education courses) offers valuable ideas on the use of these aids and techniques.

4. "Dejargonize" a report
    a. somebody else's jargon
    b. own jargon

One of the more common complaints about efforts to communicate academic or technical or policy studies is that they contain an excess of technical terminology which is difficult for the intended audience to understand. Rewriting a report or other material to remove technical language can be a useful learning experience. Since the jargon in an analyst's own field, especially his own writing, is likely to appear "natural," the best way to sensitize students to the issue is to have them translate writing from an entirely different field before tackling their own. This can help alert one to one's own use of language. An instructor could select passages for dejargonizing first from another discipline, from the field being studied, and then, closest to home, from the student's own work.

5. Develop an explanation designed for a decision-maker about the desirability or necessity of a particular methodological approach; for example, a sampling technique or an effectiveness measure.

One issue which sometimes separates decision-makers and analysts is the analyst's insistence on using some methodological device which to the decision-maker is excessively costly, consumes too much time, or is unnecessarily obtrusive in some manner. Students could be asked to develop an explanation in some context which is intended to convince the decision-maker of the necessity for a particular approach. A simple example might be the insistence on some representative or random survey-sampling technique as opposed to some less representative means. Such an exercise also provides a good opportunity for role-playing, with students alternating between analysts' and decision-makers' roles. An added benefit of the exercise may be the discovery that some methodological rigors are not necessary.

6. Prepare a set of questions which could be used with a decision-maker in defining a problem (and use them in role-play).

It is not uncommon for an analyst and a decision-maker to have quite different perceptions of the problem under consideration. This exercise is intended to give students practice in determining the decision-maker's perception of the problem. The decision-maker's statement of the problem is not always very precise or final, but it is an important datum for the analyst. A dialogue on the problem will help both participants arrive at a better understanding of the issues involved. Ideally, such a dialogue would provide an agreed-upon definition.

7. Restructure a research design to involve decision-makers in the conduct of the research and analysis.

Perhaps the most effective way for decision-makers to understand an analysis is to involve them in the study. Equally important, such involvement helps keep the analysis relevant and enables the analyst to get feedback from decision-makers. This exercise—perhaps involving a research design prepared by students earlier in the course—asks students to structure the policy research in such a way that decision-makers are actively involved. Obviously this is not possible in all cases. Payoffs can be great when it is possible, however.

8. Prepare a "talking paper" (that is, notes for an official to use in making an oral presentation).

The communication process does not stop when the analyst has conveyed information to the decision-maker. The official, in turn, may need to present the analysis (and the decision if it has been made) to interested groups or the public. The analyst may be called on to assist in this further translation. A "talking paper" provides practice in one aspect of this additional role the analyst may be asked to play.

9. Draft a letter (for signature by an elected official) or a press release responding to expected mail or press inquiries regarding a decision.

This exercise too involves communication with the public. It is likely to involve even further shortening and simplification of an analysis.

10. In terms of a specific policy issue (for example, the B–1 bomber or welfare reform):

a. have a student assume the role of analyst and describe the personal, constituency, and other pressures he might expect to find in a decision-maker
b. have a student assume the role of decision-maker and describe the personal, constituency, and other considerations that might be expected to influence the analysis.

This exercise is somewhat of a change of pace from the others. It can be useful, however, in sensitizing students to the differing perspectives which can be encountered and how these can affect communication.

Relation to Other Teaching Concerns. Building all or some of the above exercises into a policy analysis course or curriculum will require some time and effort on the part of instructors and students alike. It need not, however, significantly detract from learning other content. These exercises, or variations on them, can be woven into a course in ways which help, rather than hinder, mastery of other material. For example, an instructor (in relation to exercise 3) could let the class know he intends to use a variety of communication aids in the course. Part of the student's job would be to evaluate the effectiveness of these as a part of designing his own research presentation. Similarly, many of the other exercises could be used with regular course material. Distilling a written report (1), developing visual materials (2), dejargonizing a report (4), and preparing a "talking paper" (8) could all be based on journal articles, books, and/or research reports assigned during the course. If the course requires students to do a "real world" analysis, other exercises could be accommodated with existing requirements. Preparing a set of questions to interview a decision-maker (6), adapting a research design to include decision-maker participation (7), or thinking through the demands on a decision-maker (10) might strengthen an existing assignment.

Concluding Comments. Perhaps in policy analysis more than other fields it is true to say that a great idea (or just competent work) which is not communicated is worthless. This essay has suggested several ways policy studies instructors can seek to develop communication skills in their students. Clearly the list of exercises which has been presented is not exhaustive. Hopefully it will encourage the design of others.

The emphasis on communications as an important skill to be developed in students of policy analysis may have another payoff. The emphasis on communication may lead to more interesting and effective communications in the classroom.

8 Information-Gathering Skills for Policy Studies Students

Tom O'Donnell

In this chapter I shall briefly list and describe the basic kinds of information-gathering skills students in policy studies ought to acquire. To express these skills as concretely as possible, I have described them as if they were to be obtained by undergraduates in a liberal-arts program and how an instructor might approach teaching these skills in the context of a four-year undergraduate curriculum. The skills can be provided at other educational levels and through other pedagogical approaches.

This chapter assumes that students already have the conceptual background which permits the effective application of the information-gathering skills discussed here. In short, the student should be able to identify a policy and the arguments surrounding it; to identify factual elements and assertions; and to identify assertions of causal linkages between and among factual elements.[1] With these abilities, the student can determine what information is necessary for the analysis of the policy in question.

It is also assumed that students ought to learn these skills through using them to analyze a specific policy. Either the student or the instructor may select the specific policy, but at the very least the instructor should ensure that the policy selected is appropriate to the information-gathering skill being learned. The instructor should be aware that this may preclude the use of the same policy topic in learning all the skills enumerated below.

The discussion of information-gathering skills is divided into two parts: (1) those that deal with the discovery of existing information, and (2) those that deal with the generation of new information. Each part is presented as a learning sequence, with a progression from the more simple to the more complex information-gathering skills. In figure 8–1, I have suggested how these two sequences might fit into a four-year undergraduate curriculum of a policy studies student.

Discovering What Is Already Known. Students are all too often unaware of the full range of resources available in the library. They tend to equate library research with the use of books and general encyclopedias, the information-gathering skills generally taught at the secondary level. Unfortunately, these information-gathering skills are often the least helpful in determining the information necessary for analyzing a policy, since policy studies often require information not readily available in these resources. The student needs to be

Level:

Freshman

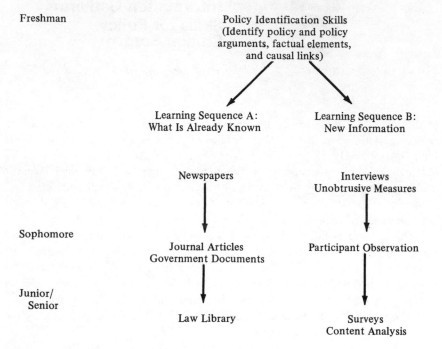

Figure 8–1. A Proposed Learning Sequence for Information-Gathering Skills in Policy Studies

introduced to other library resources and the skills necessary to use them in an applied context. The following learning sequence seems to be optimal for extending the student's skills in discovering what is already known.[2]

Newspapers. The first step is to have the student complete an assignment on a policy through the use of newspapers. The student should be introduced to the use of a particular newspaper index and taught how to use the microfilm on which most newspapers are stored. The *New York Times Index* and the *New York Times* are particularly appropriate materials, since virtually all academic libraries contain them and they are major sources in research. The student can begin to develop two important information-gathering skills in this way. First, he is introduced to the use of an index as a way of retrieving information. Second, he becomes acquainted with microfilm technology and how to use it. Both of these skills are required for other materials. Starting the learning sequence with newspaper research seems particularly appropriate, since the information to be found is generally less esoteric than in other sources, and thus easier for students to utilize effectively.

Journal Articles. At this point the student should be required to assemble findings from journal articles concerning the policy. To do this, the student needs to begin developing a series of skills. First, since he may be unfamiliar with the jargon of the subject in question, he will need to be introduced to the use of specialized dictionaries and thesauri. This will allow the student to construct a set of terms appropriate for the use of the specialized journal indexes. I would recommend the use of the *Political Science Thesaurus*, since it is perhaps the most complete terminological reference work appropriate to policy studies, and easily leads to the use of the *United States Political Science Documents*. Once the terms have been developed, the student should be introduced to the use of the subject specialty index and abstracts. General indexes (such as the *Reader's Guide*) perhaps should be avoided, since the subject headings may not be particularly appropriate for the topic (thus leading to needless frustration) and the general nature of the index leads the student toward popular magazines (and while they may be useful, students are probably quite aware of *Time* magazine already but unacquainted with academic journals). In addition, the student needs to learn the use of abstracts, since these can at least cut down research time and may often contain much of the information the student needs, thus saving a trip to the stacks or microform reader. In teaching the use of indexes and abstracts for policy studies, *USPSD* seems most appropriate, since it contains a variety of indexes (author, subject, geographic area, proper name, and journal), instructions on their use, and abstracts which identify other subject headings appropriate to the article.

Government Documents. For many students, government documents represent the most baffling problem in information retrieval. However, they are often excellent sources for information about a particular policy. At this stage, the student should be asked to complete an assignment involving the use of U.S. Government documents, which are more easily accessible in terms of indexing and retrieval than other government documents. Instructors particularly concerned with state or local policy, or policies of other governments, might consider introducing indexes and documents appropriate to these concerns. However, for a student's first experience, learning government document retrieval might be less frustrating and more rewarding if U.S. Government documents are used for the assignment. The student will need to be introduced to the use of the *United States Government Manual*, which will identify the agency related to the policy topic and determine the government author. This is important, since U.S. Government documents (as well as state and local government documents) are indexed by government author. This allows the student to use the *Monthly Catalog of U.S. Government Publications*, which contains an index to government publications.[3]

Law Library. At the advanced level, the policy studies student should be introduced to the law library, or at least to how to retrieve information about laws if the college library does not contain a specific law library. The ability to gather information about administrative law should probably take priority over statutory law, since the application of the law rather than the statute itself tends to be the focus of policy studies. Thus the policy studies student should be required to determine the governmental regulations appropriate to the policy. The *Code of Federal Regulations* and the *Federal Register*, its supplement, as well as its equivalent at the state level, would seem appropriate materials. Comparing two or more states' laws and regulations concerning a particular policy might be a particularly useful exercise for both developing information-gathering skills in this area as well as introducing the student to the comparative perspective.

Interlibrary Loans and Computerized Information Retrieval. Students on many campuses could make profitable use of interlibrary loan in retrieving materials not contained in their own library. Therefore, the student should be introduced to the use of interlibrary loans as early as possible in his undergraduate career. Computerized information retrieval systems are as yet not in widespread use, but will clearly emerge in the next ten to fifteen years as a major adjunct to library research. If such systems are available, policy studies students should be introduced to them as early as possible. In light of the above learning sequence, use of computerized retrieval might be introduced most profitably by using journal articles. If such a system is not available, introduction of the student to computer skills (especially in interactive mode) and a class session illustrating how computerized retrieval would work, using *USPSD*, would at least give the student a basis from which to learn.

Generating New Information. The information-gathering skills discussed in this section are often presented to the student in one course, entitled "Research Methods" or the like. This tends to result in an absence of application of the skills with a consequent lack of student mastery of these skills. It is probably better, where possible, to introduce these skills one at a time over the entire span of the policy studies student's undergraduate years. As with the previous section, the information-gathering skills are presented in a sequence from the simple to the complex, allowing for building the student's skills in a logical manner.

Interviews (Elite and Specialized). Interviewing skills are key to the generation of new information for policy analysis. As a first step, the student should focus on mastering these skills, and postpone until later the acquisition of other skills involved in surveys of sample populations. The subtitle "elite and specialized" refers to this distinction. Simply put, it means that interview subjects are chosen for their expertise or importance to the policy being analyzed, rather than as representatives of a population. For instance, a student interested in whether or not a local rape crisis center will be refunded might interview the head of the rape crisis center, the head of the agency in charge of city welfare services, the mayor, and perhaps one or two city councilpersons. Their views on the policy in question are important because they are actors in the situation and thus will themselves be part of the determination of the policy in question. While interviewing skills may well require years to perfect, the beginning student can easily use them effectively in this context, since only a few people need to be interviewed and the problems of survey design, questionnaire construction (elite interviewing is largely open-ended and unstructured), and statistical inference can be mostly avoided. Interviewing skills, per se, are also among the most useful skills, since they are transferable to almost any career context, from a doctor attempting to take a medical history to a potential employee interviewing for a job. A simple, but effective, training technique for interview skills involves having the student interview a "subject" (probably a student assistant) and attempting to elicit specific information through questioning. Preferably, the student should be videotaped during this session, and his technique, bearing, and success at eliciting the information critiqued by a trained individual viewing the videotape together with the student. If no videotape equipment is available, the student may be directly observed during the interview and critiqued from notes. Materials are available which discuss proper interviewing techniques,[4] and they should be used in conjunction with this exercise. Students can also, by viewing and analyzing the interview, begin acquiring participant observation skills (see below). Even if this individualized training is not possible, one general lecture/discussion/example session can prepare the student for actual field interviews. Simplicity of execution, relevance of method, and importance of technique make this an optimal "first skill" in this sequence.

Unobtrusive (Nonreactive) Measures. This skill depends upon "opportunistic observation" of evidence and is most useful in cross-validating interview-generated information. A past master of this art was Sherlock Holmes, who once observed that his partner, Dr. Watson, had made a wise choice of which of two medical practices to purchase. Holmes simply noted that the steps up to the door of Watson's office were more heavily worn than those to the other office next door, indicating a more prosperous practice. Such unobtrusive measures are "nonreactive" in that they are not subject to interviewer bias or interviewee manipulation. In and of itself, this technique is weak, but as a supplement to interviews it may provide useful information. For instance, Floyd Hunter, in his study of community power, was always careful to note pictures, awards, etc. displayed in the offices of those he was interviewing, which gave him insight into the activities and self-perceptions of the interview subjects.[5] A simple method for sharpening such skills would be to have the student observe someone's office for about fifteen minutes and then write a short essay on the interests, activities, and personality of the officeholder, indicating evidence from his observation which supports the assessment. As with interviewing, this skill may take long practice to perfect. However, for the beginning student, this skill has the advantages of ease of initial application and sharpening the ability to observe.[6]

Participant Observation. A widely used technique in sociology and anthropology, this information-gathering technique could have important use in policy studies. With its emphasis on precise observation skills, participant observation builds on the previous two skills which have observational components. The ability to observe critically the environment in which one participates may be a key skill for success in careers in policy formation and execution. Many undergraduates, however, receive little or no formal training in this skill, despite the fact that the curriculum may strongly advise internships and the like as important "experiential education." The result is that students participate in these activities without knowing how to observe properly, and thus learn less than they could. A simple technique for introducing observational skills is to have two or three student assistants play out a short scene (no more than ninety seconds) from a memorized script in front of the class.[7] It is perhaps best that the scene should appear spontaneous rather than rehearsed. Then ask the students to write down the following: a verbatim account of the dialogue; gestures accompanying each line; descriptions of the individuals in the scene—sex, age, race, hair color, clothes, and other distinguishing characteristics; length of time involved; and inferences about the individuals involved in the scene. This will sensitize the student to the distinction between observing and interpreting. A series of such scenes could be made available on videotape for students to observe and refine their skills. In addition, the student needs to become aware of the differences in observation which flow from being a participant rather than an observer. This could be accomplished by having half the students participate in a short simulation or in-class exercise, while the other half of the students observe, with both groups writing up a report of "what happened." Before comparing the reports, reverse the roles of participant and observer in another simulation. Debriefing can then focus on the distinction between "participant" and "observer" in terms of the type and quality of the information generated, and more sophisticated aspects of participant observation can then be introduced.[8] The possibilities for applying these skills in individual exercises are legion, since almost every student participates regularly in a variety of contexts (fraternities, sororities, clubs, committees, etc.) within the college which are amenable to participant observation. A possible exercise which every student can perform is to analyze, from a participant observation point of view, one or another of his classes. Information-gathering using this skill may well, as with charity, begin at home.

The three preceding information-gathering skills are recommended for the introductory level, inasmuch as they require little prior background for at least simple use. The next two skills, content analysis and surveys, probably can be most usefully taught after the student has acquired some facility with quantitative techniques and experimental design,[9] and so might be reserved for students at a more advanced level.

Surveys. As this has been one of the major tools for gathering information in the social sciences, its introduction to policy students is obviously necessary. This information-gathering technique draws on a variety of skills; I have discussed one of the most important, interviewing skills, above. Other skills which must be introduced at this point are how to design a sample survey (and alternative possible designs), sampling procedures and sample size, questionnaire construction (especially trade-offs between open-ended and closed questions), operationalizing conceptual definitions in the context of the survey questionnaire, and reporting and analyzing the results. Learning these skills will require a major block of the student's time, and thus ought to be taught in the context of a course in which original survey research is a major component. An alternative approach when this is not possible is to have the student complete the survey instrument but interview only a few people, rather than his entire sample. Otherwise, a mail survey is probably the least time-consuming and least limited by the student's resources, although telephone or personal interviewing are preferable. In the latter case, limiting the policy question in such a way as to localize the population being investigated to the college or university and/or its immediate environs may facilitate the applied use of survey skills.[10]

Content Analysis. This is a rather useful technique for generating new information out of old sources. By analyzing existing verbal records systematically, it is somewhat akin to using survey techniques to elucidate information from newspapers, historical accounts, or other records. It is an effective method for helping to determine decision-makers' *intent* in promoting a policy alternative. Its use to generate events data has received wide application in the study of foreign policy and international politics, although there is no particular reason why the approach should be limited by subject area. A rather simple way of introducing the technique is to pair two students in a team and have them analyze two different networks' evening news shows over a period of a week for "bias." Each news item should be timed, the subject of the item reported, and a judgment made as to whether the reporting seems positive, negative, or neutral toward the subject of the news item. At the end of the week, the two students should categorize the subjects and compare the two networks' news coverage in terms of time devoted to the subject, affective content, and the mix of subjects; other possible comparisons will occur to the students as well. If television news isn't feasible, the front pages of two different newspapers may be compared for the same time period, classifying each article by its length (and whether or not there is a jump), the size of the headlines, and affective content. Another approach is to look at the reporting of one particular policy over time in two different news sources. There are a variety of other ways to conduct content analysis, and the instructor might wish to introduce these in place of the above. In my opinion, this is a useful and much-neglected technique, and has the advantage of being relatively simple to execute, if time-consuming.[11]

Conclusion. This essay suggests important information-gathering skills with broad application to policy studies. Some pedagogical approaches, both in terms of sequences in which the skills should be learned and how the particular skills might be taught, have been outlined. Obviously, the essay is only an attempt at "beginning a dialogue on the educational objectives of policy studies . . . (which will) contribute to the process of developing consensus,"[12] which is an objective of this symposium. I would, of course, welcome suggestions and comments of others on this important area of teaching policy studies.

Notes

1. See William D. Coplin, *PS-6: Introduction to the Analysis of Public Policy from a Problem Solving Perspective* (New York: LRIS, 1975), and Ralph S. Hambrick, Jr., and William P. Snyder, *PS-13: The Analysis of Policy Arguments* (Croton-on-Hudson: Policy Studies Associates, 1976) for examples of teaching materials aimed at developing policy identification skills in an applied context.

2. See Merry Coplin, *PS-7: Library Research for Public Policy Issues* (New York: LRIS, 1975) for an example of teaching materials which aim at introducing students to library research for policy studies applications.

3. See J.E. Morton, "A Student's Guide to American Federal Government Statistics," *Journal of Economic Literature*, Vol. 10, No. 2 (1972) pp. 371-97, for an extensive review of federal economic statistics and their use and interpretation. In addition, there are sections on health and education statistics. The agencies which produce these statistics are identified and discussed, and an extensive bibliography is provided. This article is also available for classroom use as a Warner Modular Publication, Reprint 751, 1973, pp. 1-27.

4. See "Part VI: Guidelines for Conducting a Survey Interview," in Lawrence P. Clar, *PS-12: Introduction to Surveys and Interviews* (Croton-on-Hudson: Policy Studies Associates, 1976) for an excellent presentation on the "do's and don'ts" of conducting an interview. See also Lewis A. Dexter, *Elite and Specialized Interviewing* (Evanston: Northwestern University Press, 1970) especially chapter two, "Suggestions for Getting, Conducting, and Recording the

Interview." The entire book is an excellent, if somewhat academic, discussion of elite and specialized interviewing.

5. Floyd Hunter, private communication.

6. See Eugene J. Webb et al., *Unobtrusive Measures: Nonreactive Research in the Social Sciences* (Chicago: Rand McNally, 1966), for an extensive but somewhat technical discussion which extends this approach as an adjunct to other information-gathering techniques.

7. I am indebted to Dr. Dorothy Neff of Transylvania University for suggesting this classroom exercise.

8. See John Lofland, *Analyzing Social Settings* (Belmont, California: Wadsworth, 1971). An unexcelled presentation of field research methods from beginning to end.

9. See Lawrence P. Clark, *PS-11: Designs for Evaluating Social Programs* (Croton-on-Hudson: Policy Studies Associates, 1976), for an example of teaching materials using application of experimental design and experiments to policy studies problems.

10. Regardless of the approach taken to teaching survey skills, see Lawrence P. Clark, *PS-12: Introduction to Surveys and Interviews* (Croton-on-Hudson: Policy Studies Associates, 1976) for an excellent introduction and guide to acquiring the skills necessary for surveys in an applied context.

11. For an excellent handbook laying out the various options available for content analytic techniques, see Ole R. Holsti, *Content Analysis for the Social Sciences and Humanities* (Reading, Massachusetts: Addison-Wesley, 1969). For an exhaustive discussion of the technique and how to use it from the perspective of an historian, see T.F. Carney, *Content Analysis* (London: B.T. Batsford Ltd., 1972). For classroom materials introducing the content analysis approach in the areas of foreign policy and international politics, see Thomas J. Sloan, *CISE-12: International Interactions: Events-Data Analysis Applied to the Middle East* (New York: LRIS, 1975) and Stuart Bremer et al., *CISE-14: The Scientific Study of War* (New York: LRIS, 1975).

12. William D. Coplin, "On Teaching Policy Studies," *Policy Studies Journal*, Vol. 5, No. 1 (Autumn 1976) p. 127.

Part II
How Should It Be Taught?

Part II
How Should It Be Taught?

The question regarding teaching method also needs to be addressed if policy studies is to grow along the lines indicated. Again, the nature of policy studies leads one to conclude that there are no central pedagogical techniques. To some extent, this viewpoint is healthy since it is a basic tenet of modern education that multiple methods toward the same educational objectives are better than a single method.[1] The tenet is based on the assumption that different methods will capture the interest and build on the aptitudes of different students.

The danger is that instructors will be forced to use materials and strategies developed for disciplinary education. These materials and strategies are notorious for their emphasis on the theoretical and their denial of the applied. They almost always begin with the abstract and frequently introduce the applied as an afterthought.

We can illustrate the point easily. Most statistical textbooks and supplementary materials emphasize the use of statistics for hypothesis testing rather than as a basis for making reasoned decisions. There are some books which present statistical materials in the context of deciding about evaluating policy decisions.[2] However, the majority continue to present statistics in a theory-testing context.

Another example which might be cited is a recent book entitled *Introduction to Qualitative Research Methods*.[3] The book is a very competent presentation of the methods used in collecting information through various methods of direct observation. However, almost all of the discussion of how to use the methods are described in the context of generating and assessing hypotheses. Many of these methods could be easily used for monitoring social conditions to increase the capability of decision-makers to make or evaluate their policies, but a student would receive no new information on that use if he or she were to read the book. The striking thing about this particular case is that the authors themselves are heavily involved in policy research even though one would never know it from reading the book.[4] Similar points can be made about most existing educational material on surveys and interviews, content analysis, and social science methodology.[5]

For that reason, it is necessary to begin to identify materials and teaching strategies that will better serve the needs of policy studies educators. It is not simply a matter of choosing one method over another but rather of finding out how each method is designed to help students learn the mix of methods, concepts, and information which taken together represent the core of policy studies.

The selections in this section demonstrate the eclecticism and pluralism required by a field that purports to teach students how to apply social science

97

concepts and methods to the "causes and effects" of public policy. The chapters can be grouped into three categories: (1) modules, (2) introducing the real world, and (3) developing systematic thinking.

Modules

Chapters 9, 10, and 11 provide an introduction to a modular approach for teaching policy studies. Fairchild's chapter describes the characteristics of a modular approach and why it is particularly stuited for policy studies. Since the application of concepts and methods to an infinite variety of contexts is the policy studies field, a teaching approach which allows instructors to isolate specific educational objectives is particularly suited for delivering the educational goods. Newell and Glass's chapter places some detail on the framework presented by Fairchild by providing an example of how they have adapted a modular approach to the difficult task of teaching applied policy research skills in an introductory course. The final chapter in this group presents an excerpt from a learning package on benefit-cost analysis. Its prupose is to provide a concrete illustration of how the modular philosophy is translated into educational materials.

Introducing the Real World

A perennial problem for most social science educators, how to integrate policy studies theory and method into real-world information, confronts all of us most of the time. The chapters in this section deal with three ways in which the students can exercise themselves as they attempt to master the necessary concepts and methods. Duncan MacRae discusses how he uses case studies. Richard D. Bingham and Robert W. Biersack describe their use of field experience, and Margaret King Gibbs suggests ways in which community leaders can be used effectively.

None of these three approaches is revolutionary even in a field as "new" as policy studies. Nonetheless, they are difficult to execute because they require careful planning which all too frequently bores college faculty. Hopefully, the three chapters will provide instructors with the necessary motivation and some ideas on how to use teaching techniques that should be employed in every policy studies program.

Developing Systematic Thinking

All college faculty think that they are in the business of teaching systematic thinking. Those in the policy studies field are even more committed to such a goal. They face special problems, however, since the material of policy studies is diffuse with respect both to criteria of success and to the definition of the situation. Consequently, they face a special difficulty in getting students to think about applied problems in a systematic way. On the one hand, they can over-emphasize the "systems" by providing concepts and logical steps that are so abstract that only hypothetical examples can be generated. On the other hand, the need to introduce empirical materials can obscure basic principles of analysis.

The three chapters in this section demonstrate with concrete illustrations how systems of thinking can be presented in classroom situations. Mel Dubnick's chapter describes how the work of Elinor Ostrom and her colleagues at Indiana University has been adapted to the classroom. Students are provided with a framework through which they can dissect alternative policy proposals by expressing propositional linkages in a flowchart format. Donald G. Menzel's chapter discusses the application of a procedure first developed for the engineering curriculum. The procedure is called Guided Design. It involves a set of steps described as a "decision structure," a scenario and some group interactions. Finally, the chapter by Stahrl W. Edmunds presents a task and network approach to teaching about policy implementation. It shows how the concepts in the management literature applied to the study of public policy can be presented to students in a concrete way.

None of the chapters in this section argues for specific audiovisual or computer technologies. No bias against these approaches is intended, but it is clear both from these articles and from experience with educational innovation that the key to effective policy studies education is the development of structured activities forcing the student to interact directly with the material. The instructor is not so important as a source of information as he is to building a learning environment and to interacting with studetns as they seek to master that environment. Audiovisual and computer techniques can be used just as effectively as case studies and modules. In a field where many concepts and methods must be mastered so that they can be applied to the ever-changing information base, every pedagogical approach ought to be utilized.

Notes

1. For an excellent summary of the rationale behind the use of a variety of instructional technology see chapter 11 in *A Digest of Reports of the Carnegie Commission on Higher Education* (New York: McGraw-Hill, 1974). The chapter is a summary of one of the volumes of the Carnegie Commission Report. The full volume is also worth reading. It is entitled *The Fourth Revolution: Instructional Technology in Higher Education* (New York: McGraw-Hill, 1972.)

2. An excellent reader published under the auspices of the American Statistical Association is Judith M. Tanur (ed.), *Statistics: A Guide to the Unknown* (San Francisco: Holden Publishers, 1972). Also see Edward R. Tufte, *Data Analysis for Politics and Policy* (Englewood Cliffs, N.J.: Prentice-Hall, 1974), for an excellent presentation around cases and Gary Hammerstrom, *PS-10, Descriptive Statistics and Public Policy* (New York: LRIS, 1976), for examples of materials that approach statistics with a policy rather than a theoretical perspective. However, while one can find materials that present statistics in a way that helps the student make applications to public policy, the majority of materials are deficient in this respect.

3. Robert Bogdan and Steven J. Taylor, *Introduction to Qualitative Research Methods: A Phenomenological Approach to the Social Sciences* (New York: John Wiley, 1975).

4. One might speculate on whether or not the book would have been as well received as it has or, in fact, ever published, if the authors had made the presentation in terms of methods for collecting information for policy evaluation purposes.

5. To take a particularly ironic example, a book by Paul D. Leedy entitled *Practical Research* (New York: Macmillan, 1974) attempts to provide "cookbook" guidelines to researchers dealing with the whole range of topics starting with how to format a report, how to conduct library research, how to design and implement surveys and discuss statistics as well as quasi-experimental designs. However, the examples used in the book and even the exercises are classic theory-testing dissertation-style topics. A better title for the book would have been "A Practical Guide to Impractical Research." To find educational materials on social science data collection and analysis techniques that are applied one has to turn to texts on marketing research.

Modular Learning for Policy Studies

Erika S. Fairchild

Learning Modules

The words "module" and "modular" are used somewhat loosely in modern life and bid fair, in what has been called the "temporary society," to become increasingly standard terms in the vocabulary of most Americans. We have modular furniture, modular architecture, modular mathematics, electronic modules, learning modules, and now, policy studies modules. The common element in these varied uses of the term is that of self-contained units which can be shuffled in various ways in order to suit the needs of particular times or situations. The prime value of modules in general is flexibility and adaptability to change.

The concept of modules in the social science learning area is, if anything, even more loosely construed than in other areas, and the word seems to be used to describe learning units of almost any length and any description. A well-known management consultant firm, for example, runs short courses lasting from one to five days, and consisting of modules which last from a few minutes to several hours, each module designed to suggest one idea or involve the learner in one type of experience.[1] Several presses are distributing "modules" which are actually either original or reprint articles in various subject areas.[2] In general, however, learning modules are either packaged or instructor-devised units covering one small subject area, and which include: (a) particular learning or competency objectives, (b) readings, exercises, and experiences designed to achieve these objectives, and (c) some measure of feedback, testing, or evaluation to reinforce the learning experience.[3] Their length may vary from less than an hour to several weeks. Learning modules usually include some element of self-instruction.

The increased use of modular instruction in college courses can probably be seen as a response to several exigencies faced by modern educators. Often modules allow students to pace themselves according to their speed of learning and ability, thus obviating some of the difficulties involved in teaching students with different backgrounds and capacities.[4] In some situations, students may choose among modules within a course in order to tailor the course to their particular interests. In others, modules become minicourses providing one-credit options to students. Likewise, instructors using modular units may have greater flexibility in shifting, adding to, or subtracting from course material. Modular instruction lends itself to team teaching, with the greater use of specialists in subcourse areas. Perhaps also, given the attention-span problems of modern youth, who are conditioned by easy mobility and by the media to short, segmented, dramatic "happenings," it is more productive to tempt the student's appetite for learning with a smorgasbord of delicacies than with a heavy and less easily digested banquet.

Furthermore, the development of modular instructional units may be seen as part of a general concern with upgrading college teaching, and renewed awareness of the role of the university as a disseminator as well as a generator of knowledge. The activities of a vital and creative Division of Educational Affairs within the American Political Science Association, as well as the establishment of a journal devoted exclusively to teaching in political science,[5] are further evidence of the general trend to see good teaching as something beyond an inherent artistic talent which is possessed by some and beyond the reach of others. The recognition of the desirability of active involvement by the student, and the emphasis on learning as opposed to teaching, which are usually built into modular learning units, are also part of this trend.

Modular instruction does have some drawbacks. Where self-paced learning with varied options is built into learning modules, the possibility is strong that the student will not be motivated to proceed as rapidly as he is able, and various kinds of controls which obviate the advantages of self instruction must be built into the instructional system. The development of modular units by an instructor or a team of instructors involves a large investment of time and effort, and there may be understandable reluctance to make major changes in a course once a modular instruction system has been developed.[6] Thus a certain rigidity may be inherent in the system. Conversely, an instructor who is pressured to use an already-developed series of modules in an introductory course may well be resentful about, or unhappy with, a "canned" course. While these drawbacks can be minimized with various strategies, they do need to be considered.

Modules for Policy Studies

Policy studies per se are rarely the predominant element in introductory level political science courses. In contrast, modular course construction has achieved its highest development in introductory courses.[7] Policy studies, however, which are concerned essentially with the analysis of decision-making in relation to circumscribed governmental outputs, are peculiarly adapted to modular presentation. There are some difficulties, however. Yehezkel Dror summarized the dilemma in his 1971 work *Design for Policy Sciences*: "A main problem of policy analysis is how to put together its manifold concepts and dimensions and present a coherent and meaningful analytical study of discrete policy issues."[8] This is in effect the challenge for developers of modules in this area. The time-honored way to present particular policy problems has been through case studies describing the content and genesis of policy decisions. In fact, descriptive case studies of policymaking situations have been staples of public administration curricula in the past. Such case studies are certainly adaptable to modular presentation. In recent years there has been more emphasis on relating case studies to conceptual and theoretical frameworks.[9]

On a broader level, it is of particular interest to note the efforts of two organizations: the American Political Science Association and Policy Studies Associates. Armed with funds from the National Science Foundation, and concerned about both the lack of consensus about leading theoretical frameworks in political science and about the inadequate bridging of the gap between theory and practice in materials designed for student consumption, the American Political Science Association has commissioned the development of instructional materials known as Modules for Learning Analysis in Political and Social Science (LAPSS). These modules are designed to combine stimulating learning exercises with the development of awareness of the various conceptual perspectives which can be discerned in policymaking for such areas as health, criminal justice, and land-use planning. This effort at developing a "unity of theory and practice" (if we may be permitted a Maoist slogan) brings out quite clearly the tension between descriptive and prescriptive analysis which makes policy studies a peculiar mutant of the old "good government" school of political science.

The Policy Studies Associates series of modules is a more established one, which aims to present modular learning materials both in techniques of policy analysis (Policy Sciences Series) and in particular policy areas (Policy Issues Series). Here again the effort is to involve the student not only in the particularities of policy issues, but also in the possibilities for research and analysis related to these issues. Particular techniques for research and for analysis are covered by individual modules, and modules cover topics such as surveys and interviews, the analysis of policy arguments, descriptive statistics, and medical malpractice.[10]

In sum, the development of modular instructional materials which can be used as minicourses or as part of general courses in policy studies or even part of courses in particular policy areas remains a field where some important beginnings have been made, but where there is a need for further development. Developers and users of learning modules need to consider three important factors in relation to these materials. These factors are: (a) adaptability, (b) learning strategies, and (c) dimension.

Adaptability

Adaptability is of course not a problem if the instructor devises modules specifically for use in a particular course. In such cases questions about length, objectives, and scope can be tailored to the instructor's needs and the particular situation. Often the general framework of a course can be adapted to modular presentation. Thus an instructor who is teaching a course in criminal justice policy may wish to develop modules on intergovernmental relations in criminal justice, pressure group strategies, police practices, court administration, and correctional policy. In each case it is important to develop separate and discrete instructional materials, exercises, etc., for each module in the course (although it is certainly advisable to have some integrating concepts) so that the student is conscious of the modular structure and of the need to display competence in each of the separate units.

In the final analysis, if the instructor chooses to make extensive use of modular instruction, it is probably preferable to develop such individual instructional materials.[11] Nevertheless, packaged modules can be useful and provide important teaching aids for a minicourse or for part of a course in policy analysis. Here the developer of the module can be of assistance to the instructor if some flexibility is built into the module. This is especially so for modules which are essentially minicourses, lasting several weeks. It is natural for the developer to see the module as an integrated unit in which each part is important for an understanding of the whole; the instructor, however, may wish to spend only a limited amount of time on the subject matter under consideration and would appreciate a more accordionlike structure. This can be achieved by including optional readings and optional exercises which are not critical to the development of the module. In some of the LAPSS modules, for example, optional chapters and exercises are included and optional readings are suggested. Such flexibiltiy also allows the instructor to assign additional work to students who are able to handle it.

As mentioned previously, modules generally contain self-instruction elements and are, indeed, often entirely conceived as self-paced, audotutorial instructional units, with the instructor acting chiefly as facilitator, counselor, and evaluator. The developer, however, can provide for flexibility in relation to the matter of consuming the material. Team exercises as opposed to individual ones and provisions for class discussion, team reports, or individual sharing with the class can usually be built into the module by the developer. The important point for the developer to consider is how to make his module maximally useful without sacrificing its integrity as a learning experience. Conversely, the instructor who needs to consider the matter of linkages and course integrity often makes adaptations which will render the packaged module more appropriate in particular situations.

Learning Strategies

It is difficult not to wax enthusiastic about the possibilities for innovation and experimentation in teaching afforded by modular learning units. The small dimensions of the module allow both instructors and students to attempt experiments which may or may not prove successful. An instructor who spices a traditional course with a modular unit employing different learning strategies may find that this adventure proves to be the highlight of the course. The most obvious examples of techniques which can be adapted to modular form are simulations and computer-assisted instruction.

In the area of computer-assisted instruction, the American Political Science Association, again with the support of the National Science Foundation, has provided important leadership through the development of the series of modules known as Supplementary Empirical Teaching Units in Political Science (SETUPS). Using existing data sets, the modules take students through a series of exercises designed to familiarize them with the retrieval and analysis of computerized information on American and international politics. A minimum of technical knowledge is required to work through these modules, and instructors who have never before worked with computers use them in their courses.[12] The teaching units developed by Robert Boynton at the University of Iowa are also in this category.[13] Some of the various computer-assisted learning units, such as those on energy problems, environmental problems, and foreign policy, while not designed specifically with policy studies courses in mind, are particularly appropriate for policy studies courses. It is also not too difficult for an instructor, using personally acquired data, to develop a modular teaching unit for the computerization and analysis of this data, if he uses some of the extant materials as guide.

Simulations have been around for some time and vary from simple, home-made ones to elaborate, often computer-based policy games such as Inter-Nation Simulation (INS) and Community Land Use Game (CLUG).[14] Although not generally packaged as modules, these games can actually serve as modular units within a course consisting of modules, or separately in more conventional courses. Within the series of LAPSS modules, one has been devised specifically as a simulation.

Modular learning units also lend themselves to other kinds of teaching strategies. Voting games, prisoner's dilemma, and other games are usually of particular interest to students and can be included as all or part of a module. Audiovisual materials can also be easily structured into learning modules as individual or class assignments. Problem-solving by students working in teams is another important strategy and is often particularly valuable in fostering student participation and in illustrating processes of group dynamics as well as particular substantive issues. Student teams may also be used for unobtrusive field research and observation within the framework of a module. Some of the LAPSS modules employ the technique of conceptual mapping, in which students compare their own cognitive maps of distribution of services within a particular policy area with those of various policymakers and administrators.[15]

Perhaps the most important consideration concerning learning strategies which should inform the developers of modular instruction units is that of providing a variety of offerings and options to the student, ranging from class discussion to independent collection of data. This is not mere gimmickry; it is, rather, part of a philosophy of involving the student actively in learning, making decisions, and asserting himself in the educational process.

Dimension

Dimension refers to the length of a module (that is, the amount of time it would take a student or a class of students to complete it) as well as to the relative inclusiveness or specificity of the subject matter. As with adaptability, the matter of dimension is not as problematic when modules are developed by the instructor who plans to use them as when they are packaged for consumption by numerous instructors. The instructor who develops his own module does have some problems, however. He has to concern himself about the possibility of overkill in the use of any one teaching technique or in the use of modules themselves, and the problem of making modules so long or so complex that the student loses the sense of a self-contained and finite unit with specific and limited objectives.

The developer of a packaged module has these problems in intensified form, but he has to especially consider which facet of a policy issue is important enough to warrant the development of an instructional module. The obvious way to meet this difficulty is to develop a module which covers a particular policy area such as arms control policy or social welfare policy. Many areas of policy study, however, are too complex and diverse to allow for such an approach. All aspects of criminal justice policymaking, for example, could not expediently be covered in a single module. Even a module covering separate subjects such as police administrative policy or federal government involvement in criminal justice administration may be too cumbersome. In effect, if we can compare a course to a novel, a module can be compared to a short story. Like a short story, then, it should have a concentrated focus, and should not attempt to be a small novel. In this matter of dimension, or finitude, module developers may have something to learn from those who developed the case studies for public administration. These case studies, while often narrow in subject matter and lacking in theoretical focus, nevertheless were concerned with providing the student with an introduction to the reality behind an otherwise somewhat abstract subject.

Finally, in considering questions of dimension, the developer must contend with the lack of a leading disciplinary paradigm in approaches to the study of public policy. This is the problem which has concerned the originators of the LAPSS program and which has occasioned the peculiar structure of the LAPSS modules, in which the efficacy of particular paradigms such as decision-making theories and social structure thoeries are being scrutinized. While it is obviously not the obligation of developers of modules, which are teaching devices, to provide a forum for the exploration of philosophical questions, the theoretical and/or idelogical dimension is an important one and needs to be confronted at a conscious level rather than, as is often the case with policymakers themselves, at an unconscious level.

Conclusion

Modular instruction is not a final solution to the problems of teaching political science in general and policy studies in particular. Nevertheless, it is the author's impression that, especially in the policy studies area, it has great possibilities which have not been adequately explored. In fact, the need is for a kind of modular instruction for upper-level students which is different from that developed for introductory courses. Presumably the students in upper-level courses are at a more mature level, have had some background in social science, need less frequent feedback and evaluation, and are capable of handling more intense and less fragmented materials than are generally included in conventional learning modules. In an area of study which so closely intertwines descriptive and prescriptive analyses, the need is for modules directed not only at specific policy areas, but also at important methodological questions such as prediction of consequences of alternative policies, program evaluation, and research strategies.

Notes

1. Response and Associates, Dallas Texas. See, for example, The Emerging Woman in Management, a three-day course consisting of about twenty modules.

2. See, for example, University Programs, by General Learning Press (Morristown, New Jersey), and Warner Modular Publications, Inc. (Andover, Mass.).

3. See Michael Kozak, "Instructional Modules, a Summary," *Man/Society/Technology*, Vol. 35, #2, pp. 40–41, for a description of kinds of materials included in fifteen different learning modules surveyed by the author.

4. This is particularly so in modular personalized instruction systems such as those based on the Kellar Plan. See Ralph B. Earle, Jr. (ed.), *PSI and Political Science* (Washington, D.C.: American Political Science Association, 1975).

5. *Teaching Political Science*, a Sage publication.

6. The author, for example, participated in once-weekly meetings during an entire academic year for the purpose of developing the general outlines for a modular introductory Western civilization course. The actual construction of the course was accomplished by the instructors involved in it.

7. The reader might find it helpful to consult R. Diamond, P. Eickman, E. Kelly, R. Holloway, T. Vickery, and E. Pascarella, *Instructional Development in Higher Education* (Center for Instructional Development, Syracuse University, 1973), for a prescription for comprehensive restructuring of courses largely in a modular framework. This volume also contains a general bibliography on instructional innovations, including modular instruction.

8. (New York: American Elsevier Publishing Company, 1971), p. 60.

9. A well-known example is Thomas Dye, *Understanding Public Policy* (Englewood Cliffs, New Jersey: Prentice-Hall, 1972). Dye attempts to present nine case studies as examples of six different analytic models.

10. Policy Studies Associates is affiliated with the Council on International and Public Affairs and continues the *Learning Packages in the Policy Sciences* series of the Maxwell School at Syracuse University.

11. For a description of individualized modular development of an introductory course in international relations see W. Coplin, P. Eickman, M. O'Leary, "A Strategy of Educating Most of the Students Most of the Time in Political Science," *Teaching Political Science*, Vol. 1, #2 (April 1974), pp. 139–68; G. Brey, M. O'Leary, W. Coplin, R. Printup, "An Evaluation of a Strategy of Educating Most of the Students Most of the Time in Political Science," *Teaching Political Science*, Vol. 4, #2 (Jan. 1977), pp. 199–224. See also R. Diamond et al., *Instructional Development*.

12. For information evaluating SETUPS modules, see "Developing Research Skills," *Change*, Vol. 8, #6 (July 1976), p. 62; Maureen Fiedler, "Evaluation of SETUPS: Cross-national and World Politics," *DEA News*, #13 (Spring 1977), p. 2.

13. See, for example, G. Robert Boynton, *Public Reactions to Civil Disobedience* (University of Iowa: Regional Social Science Data Archive of Iowa, 1972).

14. For a guide to simulations in political science see C. Walcott and A. Walcott, *Simple Simulations* (Washington, D.C.: American Political Science Association, 1976).

15. For an example of this technique, see L. Weschler and M. Halloran, "Political Mapping: Policymakers, Citizens, and Service Delivery," *DEA News*, #12 (Winter 1977), p. 13.

A Modular Approach to Applied Policy Research

Charldean Newell and
James J. Glass

Introduction

Although policy studies and related programs have grown rapidly in recent years,[1] appropriate curricular materials have not been developed at the same pace. This article describes a modular administrative research methods course that will offer students, be they precareer or in-career, methods and techniques of research that may be used in the job situation. The course described stands in contrast to traditional methods courses in the social and behavioral sciences that emphasize theoretical research and hypothesis-testing.

In a traditional course, the student is exposed to a variety of methods, immersed in literature, and asked to devise a project using a research design and a method, with the project described seldom being carried out. The objective of such courses seems to be acquainting future academicians with the necessary tools of the trade to be employed in subsequent research. To an extent, an administrative research methods course is no different in that its purpose is the same. However, it does differ in its application of research design and methods by including techniques not normally covered by traditional courses and by emphasizing alternative ways of reporting research results. The special emphasis on report-writing is justified in that successful policy development and effective policy implementation and evaluation may well hinge in part or in whole on the skills of the practitioner in gathering accurate and adequate data, then presenting them clearly both to elected officials and to the public.

The concern here is that those individuals who on a day-to-day basis are responsible for determining policy alternatives, for making recommendations of optimum alternatives, for projecting the impact of those alternatives, and ultimately for evaluating the success of the policy package selected need a different approach to research methods than the discipline-oriented academic. They are not only engaged in continuous research but must assess the products of research brought to them by others in the organization.[2] Also, one must always consider that substantive policy changes so quickly that concentrating on what is known may be of only limited value. More important is a knowledge of tools, methods, and thought processes that equip the practitioner to deal with policy, whatever it may be.

Modular Approach

The particular perspective of the authors is that of a large Master of Public Administration program with both precareer and mid-career students. Thus, the discussion of research methods modules appropriate for practitioners stems from the orientation of a specific but interdisciplinary degree program that produces graduates who move into policy-related positions. The course in applied policy research is divided into modules for two reasons, exposure of the student not only to information but also to application of each method or technique and facilitating use of an individual module in an in-service or continuing education setting.

The teaching of applied policy research in a program where the student will soon be, or in many cases already is, in a position to utilize the information presents a particularly difficult problem. The traditional format in methods courses, where the student is exposed to many methods and techniques but uses none, is not appropriate. The modular or learning package approach would seem to be more valuable because the student is not only exposed to specific methods or techniques in each module but also has an opportunity to apply what is learned about gathering and analyzing information. Not only is it impossible to expose a student to a large number of methods and techniques in a one-semester course and expect the student to apply them, but it is also equally difficult to predict or select those techniques that would prove particularly valuable to the student. Nevertheless, those difficult choices have to be made. The modules described below reflect our value judgments as to those research strategies likely to be most useful to the greatest number of students.

Each module is divided into major ideas, learning objectives, and learning experiences. The fundamental learning strategy is "show, discuss, apply." Furthermore, there is an underlying learning objective that cuts across the nine modules, namely that the student's writing will show greater conciseness and clarity at the end of the course than at the beginning. The total package of modules is designed for presentation over a sixteen-week semester, some modules requiring only one week and some requiring as many as three weeks.[3] In addition, this course is the first of two that the student is expected to take, with the second semester providing options based on the student's needs. Choices for the second course include statistics and quantitative methods, policy analysis and evaluation, and legal research. Finally, it should be noted that there is no attempt made either in this explanation of the modules or in the course itself to distinguish between methods and techniques; in an applied course, the emphasis is on learning research strategies, not nomenclature.

The Nine Modules

Each of the nine modules is briefly summarized by outlining the main idea, the learning objective, and the applied experience. Four are then discussed in somewhat more detail as examples.

1. "Systematic Thinking": The central idea of Module 1 is the importance of thinking logically and of information-gathering as a basis for deciding or acting. The objectives for students are learning how to think through a problem and being able to distinguish systematically gathered information from randomly gathered information. The applied experience is an in-class hypothetical problem-solving exercise, requiring logic to find a solution.

2. "Ethical Considerations of Practical Research": The main idea in the second module is acquainting the student with the existence of ethical constraints in conducting research, with specific learning objectives of making the student aware of his own biases, of techniques that constitute invasion of privacy, of the importance of confidentiality, and the implications of sensitive research for elected officials. The applied experience is in-class role-playing with "ethically loaded" variables introduced in the simulation.

3. "Available Sources of Information": Module 3's main idea is acquainting the student with information that is already available. Objectives include familiarity with major data sources, the uses of such sources, and the limitations of available data. Included here are both primary sources, chiefly statistics readily available from public agencies, and secondary sources. Experiences include individual assignments for locating source materials and finding specific pieces of information. The related report also serves as an introduction to report-writing and documentation.

4. "Observation": This module is based on the idea that structured observation is a common information-gathering technique in public agencies. Objectives for the student include techniques of field research, reporting observations, and limitations of the method. The experience is a field project in which different teams of students are assigned a task of gathering information. Each team has a different project—such as substandard housing, traffic patterns, or leash-law violations—that requires data-gathering, data analysis, and reporting the results.

5. "Survey Research": The fifth module has proved to be one of the most needed as even small local governments have become more and more interested in survey data. The primary emphasis is on information-gathering. Learning objectives for students include the rudiments of sampling, questionnaire and interview schedule construction, maximization of return rates, interview techniques, applications, and preliminary analysis of data. The multiple objectives indicate that this is one of the longer units. The learning experience is the conducting of a simple survey project from the drawing of the sample to analysis of results.

6. "Evaluation": Module 6 is based on the need for practitioners to understand purposes and techniques of program evaluation. The learning objective is an acquaintance with the common techniques and purposes of such evaluations and an awareness of the political nature of the evaluation process. A simulated program evaluation is the experience, with an emphasis on relating information-gathering to purpose.

7. *"No Money, No Time, No Technique":* The authors designed Module 7 based on the main idea that the practitioner often has to make recommendations without much notice and with little time for thorough research. The learning objective for the student is developing the "best-possible" decision strategies in a highly constraining situation. Emphasis is placed on techniques that increase rationality in decision-making and problem-solving, as well as obstacles to be wary of. The students are given a description of a problem and the conditions for solving it, including limited time and resources, and must prepare a memorandum to the "boss" suggesting ways of getting the most relevant information for solving the problem.

8. *"Research Design":* The eighth module has as its topic one that in traditional courses usually comes at the beginning. However, our experience is that the learning objective of "putting it all together," that is, integrating problem identification, strategies for getting information, and techniques of analysis, is better accomplished toward the end of the course. In the research design module, the student experience consists of designing a research project suitable for the student's current or anticipated work setting. This module is directly tied to the final degree program requirement for our students, an administrative problem paper.

9. *"Writing Experiences":* Module 9 is the final module in the course. The main idea is that the students need to be exposed to a wide variety of situations encountered on the job, many of which involve directly utilizing research methods and techniques and all of which involve systematic thinking and writing that seldom are included in a methods course. Objectives for the students are virtually identical with the experiences called for: at the completion of the module, the student is expected to know how to prepare either a grant proposal or an environmental impact statement, to prepare an agenda, to handle routine correspondence and inter- and intraoffice memoranda, to prepare a résumé, and to do summary reports.

As an illustration of how these modules work, four of them are elaborated somewhat, with particular regard to the learning experience, that is, the actual application of a research strategy. "Systematic Thinking," "Survey Research," "No Money, No Time, No Technique," and "Research Design" have been selected to illustrate the diversity among the modules.

Systematic Thinking. This module introduces concepts and ideas the student will employ throughout the course. At this point, the student is provided initial exposure to the importance of logical thinking. Students are introduced to a "variation" of the scientific method (problem identification, identification of questions to be answered, gathering data, analysis, and reporting), which is compared to other, less logical methods, such as intuition and mysticism. The application of systematic, or logical, thinking involves two experiences. First, students select examples from newspapers and periodicals that both deal with public affairs and clearly illustrate either superior logic or an absence of systematic thinking. Consequences of the latter are examined. Second, they are given a problem and asked to describe the steps they would go through to be able to make a decision or recommendation. The second exercise is an introduction to research design; in the research design module the student becomes involved in a much more detailed application of this technique.

Survey Research. Because survey research is one of the more complicated modules with a number of objectives, it is one of the longest units. Two types of survey experiences may be utilized as part of this module, depending on circumstances. One survey would be a narrowly defined one in keeping with the students' beginning acquaintance with this strategy and with time limitations. Students might be assigned the task of surveying a neighborhood with clear boundaries as to citizen perception of city services; the number of services could be limited to, say, trash collection and drainage. The students would be responsible for drawing a random sample of which homes would be surveyed; drafting the survey instrument; making preliminary contact; interviewing an adult respondent in each selected home; organizing the data; and making a report. Because most of the students would lack statistical sophistication at this point, the analysis would be limited. Nevertheless, the students would have the opportunity to see the project through from beginning to end. A similar but more elaborate project would combine the efforts of more than one class, including one or more in statistics. The statistics classes would emphasize quantitative analysis of the data, but all classes would be involved in designing the survey and carrying out information-gathering. Such a project demands heavy faculty time commitments because of the coordination problems, but our experiences with such a survey—conducted in cooperation with a local government and designed to gain considerable information about attitudes toward city services and expenditures—indicate its practical value both to the students and to the local government.[4]

No Money, No Time, No Technique. Ideally, the best learning experience for this module would come from an actual on-the-job situation that arises for the student. In many instances, such situations are available because the students have begun preintern jobs with government or are in-career students. If no such problem is readily available, a hypothetical situation may be given to the student. As an example of the kind of problem we have in mind, we can cite a recent local example. One member of the city council announced to the press twenty-four hours in advance of a council meeting that he would press the issue of a 10 percent budget cut. The city manager's staff thus had little time to prepare a response, could obviously spend no money on defending against spending practices, and really could not use any traditional research strategy. Yet systematic thinking was called for. This kind of situation is useful for class purposes because the students must set forth specific information-gathering steps they would take, anticipate questions likely to arise, and prepare a report that could be used by the city manager. They are precluded from the nonsystematic approach of merely hoping the other council members can shut off debate on the matter.

Research Design. By this point in the course, we have discussed a variety of research methods and techniques. However, because the overall emphasis is developing the students' competencies so that they can actually conduct an applied research project and report on it, we are concerned lest the notion of research design get lost amid methods. This concern is heightened by the situation that occurs so often in practical research, namely that data are gathered by a number of individuals without any clear purpose or stated framework and with the end result that the purpose and techniques are not complementary. Thus, we view the research design module as the one in which the rest of the course comes together. Considerable emphasis is placed on the importance of improving rationality in decision-making and problem-solving while at the same time acknowledging both the barriers to and hazards of seeking rationality. The students are encouraged, however, to think in rational, systematic terms as an important step in improved public policy formation and implemenation.

This course is offered for students in an MPA degree program that requires a final administrative problem-solving paper. Accordingly, the applied experience for this module is the formulation of a research design that would be appropriate for the student's final report. The students must prepare a formal proposal that lays out a problem, indicates the research techniques that will be used to gather information about the problem and alternative solutions, and relates purpose to method. For example, one student might propose an evaluation of a program in which he has been involved as an intern or full-time professional. Another might identify a clientele need and seek means of meeting it. Another might suggest the unworkability of an existing policy and propose ways of modifying it. All would propose a scheme for gathering information and a system of analysis.

The particular project is a function of the student's interests. A student interested in administering programs for the aging might propose a longitudinal study with an experimental design to determine the effect of institutionalization on persons over sixty-five, with the purpose in mind of making recommendations about current institutional practices. Or a student interested in recreational administration might suggest a combination of observation and in-depth inter-viewing to assess problems associated with facility usage. Whatever the students' interests, whatever the degree program, the importance of design in a successful applied research effort can be emphasized.

Conclusions

Neither materials used in nor the format of traditional methods courses satisfies the needs of students whose interests lie in applied areas. While the admininstra-tive methods course briefly described in this article is geared to an MPA student, we think the approach could be used in a variety of other undergraduate and graduate programs that include some elements of policy studies. Each program would particularly need to modify the learning experiences to be specific to the students, and some of the modules might actually have to be replaced with others. For example, if a class were comprised mainly of students seeking careers in mental health and mental retardation, a module on control groups might need to be included. Other students may not need the module on writing. Nevertheless, we think the approach has validity and would recommend it either for a full course or for in-service training.

Notes

1. Even a cursory scanning of the annual editions of the *Directory of Graduate School Programs in Public Affairs and Administration*, published by the National Association of Schools of Public Affairs and Administration (NASPAA), reveals that the number of such programs has increased steadily.

2. An excellent set of reasons why the practitioner needs to understand the research process is given by Claire Selltiz, Lawrence S. Wrightsman, and Stuart W. Cook, *Research Methods in Social Relations*, 3rd ed. (New York: Holt, Rinehart and Winston, 1976), pp. 11-12.

3. For some modules, written reports are not due until later in the semes-ter. When one of the more complex modules—survey research, for example—is taught as a continuing education workshop, adjustments have to be made to accommodate written work.

4. Results of such a survey have been published by the Institute of Applied Sciences, North Texas State University, Denton, Texas, 1977. See James J. Glass et al., *Citizen Evaluations of City Services and Problems in Denton, Texas: Final Report*. This volume details survey methodology, citizen evaluation of city services, neighborhood problems, emergency services, and citizen participation. As an example of how the survey has been used by the city council, faculty

coordinators of the survey were asked by the mayor to appear before the council during budget hearings to provide information about citizen needs and citizen willingness to support a greater tax burden if better services could be obtained. The survey was conducted by five political science faculty members. Students from the respective classes were involved in all aspects of the survey process.

11

Modular Material: An Example from a Benefit/Cost Learning Package

William D. Coplin

The two preceding chapters present and argue for a modular approach to policy studies education. They emphasize the need for compact educational units in which educational objectives are clearly specified. They also underscore the need for a precise fit between these objectives and educational materials. Because a modular approach to education requires a highly precise structural relationship between learning activities and objectives, materials play a more central role than they do in most postsecondary social science instructional. For that reason, this chapter provides a concrete illustration of the kinds of educational materials that have been designed for modularized instruction.

The illustration is taken from a learning package distributed by Policy Studies Associates and edited by myself and Michael K. O'Leary. The learning package approach emphasizes small units and a close fit between learning activities and educational objectives. The activities may be a simulation exercise or some type of data collection or analysis activity. In some packages, conceptual skills such as application of the Thomas Dye framework to public policy analysis or benefit/cost concepts are provided. In other packages specific data collection (for example, surveys and interviews, library research) and data analysis (for example, descriptive statistics, program evaluation) skills are covered.

To illustrate, we have included the first section of a package that introduces benefit/cost analysis entitled *PS-14: An Introduction to Benefit/Cost Analysis for Evaluating Public Policy Programs*, written by T.R. Durham. Note the statement of objectives that appears at the beginning of the package and the attempt to get the student directly involved in the material at the outset of the package.

To the Instructor and Students on Objectives and Materials

The Primary Objective:

To introduce the basic concepts and techniques employed in benefit-cost studies so that you can begin to understand, criticize, and design such studies.

Upon Completion of This Package, You Will Be Able to:

Identify governmental program areas where benefit-cost studies can provide assistance in selecting among alternative program designs.

Recognize the need for and difficulties in assigning "benefits" and "costs" to features of governmental programs.

Distinguish between program *effects* and the associated benefits and costs.

Demonstrate familiarity with economic measures of benefits and costs.

Apply the technique of "discounting" to adequately compare future benefits with present costs.

Identify the relevant types of "externalities" in the comprehensive assessment of program net benefits and suggest techniques for evaluating these in economic terms.

Recognize various sources of possible error in actual benefit-cost studies (double counting, mislabeling of benefits or costs, violation of the "opportunity cost" criterion of true benefits and costs).

Additional Materials Required:

None.

Contents

120

Introduction

The purpose of this package is to introduce you to a style of analyzing governmental programs that is sometimes called benefit-cost analysis, or cost-benefit analysis. This approach represents a special case of "systems analysis" or "cost-effectiveness" analysis, which occurs when both benefits and costs can be quantified in comparable (dollar) terms. We will use the term "benefit-cost" throughout this package, but we are really referring to any study which attempts to evaluate the total costs and consequences of a program in a systematic manner, quantifying the associated benefits and costs using dollar amounts. Benefit-cost analysis is simply the mixing of a commonsense approach to decision-making with a little accounting (keeping track of what goes into a program and what comes out), and a trace of economics (to assist us in quantifying benefits and costs).

Over the years, certain practices and key concepts have emerged in benefit-cost analysis, and it is these practices and concepts that this package introduces. The package will provide you with: (1) some examples of benefit-cost studies, (2) the major difficulties and pitfalls involved in identifying and estimating the benefits and costs attached to a particular project, and (3) exercises to ensure familiarity with basic notions and encourage a critical attitude in reading or designing benefit-cost studies.

This package only starts you on the road to becoming a benefit-cost analyst who can provide professional services for a client, or have his work accepted by other practicing benefit-cost analysts. Substantial academic and practical experience would be necessary before you could consider that you had progressed any appreciable distance down that road. However, we believe that if you master the material in this package, you will be able to read and critically appraise benefit-cost studies which you are likely to see in your role as a citizen, and to appreciate the possible contribution that a well-conceived study may make regarding decisions on various matters of public policy.

In this package, we will be concerned with the application of benefit-cost techniques to public programs. Such programs are financed by transferring resources from private decision-makers, or spenders (consumers or businesses), to the government by taxing or borrowing. Public programs provide services for which the beneficiaries may or may not pay fees covering the costs of these services. Benefits (and costs) associated with these programs accrue to groups (often not the same groups) of persons. Benefits received (and costs incurred) may not be fully recognized or appreciated even by recipients or bearers. An additional and important distinguishing characteristic of public programs is that the benefits often are generated only over a lengthy time period, while the bulk of costs can occur early in the life of the program. It is this feature of public programs which identifies them as investments.

It should be kept in mind that government programs may take many forms, not all of which are as easily identifiable as investments as are such concrete examples as highway construction or dam-building. For example, government regulations to control pollution may require huge investments by business for compliance. Government-sponsored job-training programs, with an initial outlay of money and time, enhance skills to contribute to future increased productivity. Government research grants purport to have some of their "pay-off" in future benefits attributable to increased knowledge. Public health programs have their benefits realized in the form of reduced mortality of the general population.

Benefit-cost analysis may serve as a guide to decisions on whether to begin a new program, or which of several programs to initiate, and may also be used to evaluate programs which have been in operation for some time. In such cases, the decision would be whether to continue with a specific program, or which of several current programs should be continued. This latter type of application would appear to be more reliable, since a program which has been in operation for some time may provide better information on prices of outputs and inputs than one which is only in the planning stages. Both applications of benefit-cost analysis require elements of prediction or projection of future conditions: it is just as easy to abort a program prematurely on the basis of inadequate information as to launch one from a premature and overly optimistic outlook.

121

Finally, keep in mind that benefit-cost analysis provides a means for evaluating the effects of programs for comparison with costs—not a means for determining the effects to be evaluated. In a case such as a hydroelectric project, for example, the main effect of producing power is apparent. For others, such as air pollution control programs, the effects (such as reduced emission on air quality, effects of air quality on health), are less easily recognized.

We will begin by noting several similarities between government decisions to invest resources in a public program and business decisions to invest in new or improved products. There are, however, important differences between the scope of government decisions (the range of benefits and costs which must be taken into account) and that of business decisions. Although the logic of the analysis is basically the same for both types of decision-makers, these differences (and others, for example, the fact that public programs often do not generate income to pay for themselves) make the application to government programs somewhat tricky. This package will serve to familiarize you with these important differences, and with some of the complexities involved in adequately handling them.

Part I presents an example of a benefit-cost study, along with criticisms aimed at selected portions of it. Part II discusses briefly the underlying rationale for employing the benefit-cost approach to assessing government programs, and presents a comparison of business and government decisionmaking. Part II concludes with a section which makes the case for using market prices (actual or "simulated") to quantify the benefits and costs of a program. Part III is based on critiques of a benefit-cost study and discusses each critique as an illustration of the difficulty in the application of benefit-cost techniques. Each section of Part III includes an exercise to facilitate gaining competence in recognizing and handling each trouble spot. Part IV presents examples of benefit-cost studies, in which you can identify possible sources of error and suggest possible corrections.

Part I
An Overview of
Benefit-Cost Analysis

Why should government-endorsed and government-funded programs be subjected to benefit-cost analysis? Are not the celebrated checks and balances of the political process sufficient safeguards against ill-founded, ill-considered government undertakings? If anyone should require persuasion beyond that often provided on the average front page of the *New York Times*, the following example of what can happen may help convince the more sanguine. (This example in fact incorporates features of several specific and by no means isolated real-world cases.)

A. The Study

The Bureau of Reclamation (which, along with the Army Corps of Engineers, is in the business of building dams) has conducted a study to determine whether a dam should be constructed at a particular site on the Colorado River. Construction of dams along the river represents one part of the implementation of federal and state policies designed to develop the water resources of the American Southwest, and is the special responsibility of the bureau.

Since the language of the legislation directing the development of water resources requires providing the maximum possible benefits to the area, the bureau called in a team of analysts to figure out whether the benefits the region would receive from the particular dam project would be worthy of the cost of constructing it.

The report was finally submitted, and it showed that the dam would provide an estimated $2 billion in benefits during its lifespan, for an initial investment of $500 million. This looked like a good deal since the ratio of benefits to costs is 4:1, and it was decided to proceed with construction of the dam.

Exercise 1: Some Questions You Might Ask at This Point

If you were an individual or a government official concerned with the building of the dam, what kinds of questions might you wish to have answered before you accepted the estimated benefits and costs as true indicators of the worth of the dam?

List at least five such questions in the space below:

B. Citizen Response

Construction of the dam was delayed, however, because a local group of concerned citizens obtained a court injunction against beginning the project until a more thorough review of the supporting study could be made. Included in the evidence submitted by the citizens' group were the following observations:

1. Fully one-half of the $2 billion in benefits attributed to the dam will not be realized until ten to twenty years after the dam is completed; yet these future returns are compared directly with the immediate investment cost of $500 million.

2. The dam represents a multipurpose project, providing benefits in the form of increased agricultural output by irrigation, recreational benefits from the reservoir, hydroelectric power output, and flood control. However, nowhere in the report is there any mention of the facts that, in some sections, increased salinity of the soil due to irrigation will prevent the growing of certain valuable crops, or that a section of the river used extensively for canoe and raft trips will no longer be usable for these purposes.

3. The dam's benefits include future sales of sugar beets. The report shows that the value of this sugar beet output is calculated at current prices, even though beet prices have been declining steadily at 5 percent per year. Further, increased sugar beet production attributed to the dam is expected to be about 50 percent of the amount currently on the market.

4. One of the benefit elements, increased corn production due to the dam's irrigation system, is used entirely to feed beef cattle fattened in the area. Yet, both increased corn output and increased beef output are included among the benefits.

5. The benefits provided by the dam include hydroelectric power, valued at .09 dollars per kwhr. The total benefits from this source are calculated to be the estimated number of kilowatt hours produced each year, multiplied by the selling price. The citizens' group notes that residents and businesses of the region are currently obtaining this amount of power from fossil fuels, at a cost of .12 dollars per kwhr. Further, the power plant will be able to sell its output at .09 only because the funds used to finance the dam will be obtained at a rate of interest below that which must be paid by private companies through the use of tax-free bonds.

6. The bureau has estimated that 5,000 new jobs will be created during the construction period, and adds in benefits amounting to this number of jobs multiplied by the annual wage. The citizens' group points out that:
   a. the jobs are in fact a cost of the dam, not a benefit (adding them in effectively double-counts benefits already measured as the value of outputs produced by the labor) as embodied in the dam.
   b. not all of the jobs are new jobs anyway.
   c. if the jobs are to be figured in as costs, these calculations should recognize that some of the workers would have been unemployed if the dam were not built (and possibly collecting unemployment benefits), and consequently the true costs of employing them are much less than the going wage. (This adjustment would lower the cost of constructing the dam.)

7. The citizens observed that the analysts' study attributed to the dam savings in property loss from floods equal to the entire amount lost on the average per year (using the total losses for the last ten years for the estimate); however, fully one-half of the usual losses already are prevented by an improved dike system recently put in place.

8. Finally, according to the citizens' complaint, the dam requires that an entire tribe of Indians must be removed from their ancestral lands; this is, in fact, included as a cost in the analysts' report, but only insofar as the amount required to physically transport the Indians to a new government reservation and comparable housing.

9. As a parting shot, the citizens' group notes that the bureau's estimates have assumed that the dam will operate at full capacity over the next fifty years, with no allowance for various contingencies, including the possibility that it might fail completely and wreak havoc in excess of all anticipated future benefits.

Exercise 2: Comparing Criticisms

Compare the citizens' criticism with the questions you wrote for Exercise 1. Revise or extend those questions so that they cover the objections raised by the group. Indicate which of the points raised by the group relate to each of your questions, and explain why. If some of the citizens' points are not covered in your original questions, formulate questions which pertain to these points.

What is the purpose of all this? First, of course, is to observe that benefit-cost studies are used in certain areas of government activity to assess the value of specific programs, whether or not they are as concrete as the dam. However, as the above example suggests, not all these studies are done well, and taking their results at face value can lead to ill-advised endeavors. At the very least, the citizens' complaints show that there is some room for disagreement on the merits of the original study.

How should such studies be conducted so that the results provide a good basis for making decisions concerning government projects? One of our aims, in discussing systematically the different types of error in the case study above, is to indicate what types of mistakes are common (some obvious, some more subtle), and what can be done to correct them. In addition to noting examples of serious errors, we will try to identify the points at which various assumptions or forecasts are employed in doing benefit-cost analysis, and the factors upon which the validity of these assumptions may depend.

While some government benefit-cost studies are done poorly, many are not done at all. This can be of some concern, since government is faced with decisions as to which, of a vast number of possible programs, it should undertake, as well as to how much total resources should go into all government programs in a given period of time. This latter decision, which influences the extent of government participation in the economy and elsewhere, involves the justification for transferring resources (by taxing or borrowing) from the uses to which individuals or business firms would have put them, to purposes sought by the government. Even though the government may be acting in the perceived best interest of the people (just as we will see business firms acting in the best way to maximize their profits), it is possible to make mistakes. Benefit-cost analysis contends that such mistakes can be partially avoided or their magnitude reduced through a technique which seeks systematically to account in the best available way for all the benefits and costs associated with a specific government program. Government programs then can be compared in terms of their relative ability to provide benefits in exchange for the costs of undertaking the program.

C. Summary

Before we begin Part II, it may be useful to summarize specific points raised by the citizens' group, and relate them to some of the aspects of benefit-cost analysis which will be more fully developed in sections of Part III.

Citizens' Points	*Aspects of Benefit-Cost Analysis*
1. Future benefits are not compared with present costs.	1. Discounting and selection of a discount rate.
2. Not all consequences of the dam are included; omitted in particular are effects which adversely affect production in other areas even though these effects are not recognized in customary ways.	2. Externalities.
3. Valuation of future outputs does not take into account future demand and supply for the output conditions (particularly the increased supply due to the dam).	3. Shadow pricing.
4. Values are assigned both to an intermediate product and a final product.	4. Double-counting.
5. The full amount of expenditures on hydroelectric power are included.	5. Benefits valued as net savings.
6. Costs (jobs) are included as benefits, using the going wage.	6. Shadow wages.

| 7. Benefits are attributed to the dam incorrectly. | 7. Incremental benefits only or net savings caused by the dam should be attributed to it. |
| 8. The dislocation of the Indians and their loss is inadequately accounted for. | 8. Multiple objectives, distribution, and other nonquantifiable considerations. |

Finally, the citizens objected to treating future benefits, which are contingent upon a number of things, as equally certain to be received as are immediate costs certain to be incurred. The methodology for taking into account risks such as, for example, dam failure due to earthquake, is not well developed. But with some types of government programs (for example, expanding installation of nuclear power generating stations), such considerations may be very important.

The following learning packages are available from Policy Studies Associates (P.O. Box 337, Croton-on-Hudson, New York 10520) at this time:

PS#1   *A Programmed Introduction to SPSS (A Statistical Package for the Social Sciences): Revised Edition Incorporating Version 6 of SPSS*, Bruce B. Downing, Michael Burns, Barbara Haas, and Francis Hunt, Syracuse University.

PS#4   *The Good Society Exercise: Problems of Authority, Justice, and Order in Policy-Making*, Steven Apter, Hon Bramnick, and William D. Coplin, Syracuse University.

PS#6   *Introduction to the Analysis of Public Policy from a Problem-Solving Perspective*, William D. Coplin, Syracuse University.

PS#7   *Library Research in Public Policy Issues*, Merry Coplin with the assistance of Francis Hunt, Syracuse University.

PS#8   *Forecasting with Dynamic Systems*, Michael K. O'Leary, Syracuse University.

PS#9   *The Good Federalism Game: Participant's Manual for a Simulation of Intergovernmental Relations*, Rodger M. Gova and George G. Wolohojian, Syracuse University.

PS#10   *Descriptive Statistics for Public Policy Analysis*, Gary Hammerstrom, Syracuse University.

PS#11   *Designs for Evaluating Social Programs*, Lawrence P. Clark, Syracuse University.

PS#12   *An Introduction to Surveys and Interviews*, Lawrence P. Clark, Syracuse University.

PS#13   *The Analysis of Policy Arguments*, Ralph S. Hambrick and William P. Snyder, Texas A & M University.

PI#1   *An Introduction to Medical Malpractice.*

PI#2   *The Cost and Quality of Nursing Home Care.*

PI#3   *Patterns of Energy Consumption.*

PI#4   *Nuclear Energy.*

Introducing Undergraduates to Public Policy Analysis by the Case Method

Duncan MacRae, Jr.

Public policy analysis is the choice between better and worse policies with the aid of reason and evidence.[1] It is choice, rather than the cultivation of knowledge for its own sake. It is concerned with better and worse policies in an ethical sense—not merely selfish choice or that of economic man. It must thus proceed from a reasoned notion of the general welfare, the public interest, the good life, or that which is morally right. Both in the calculation of means to ends and in the systematization of ends themselves it involves reason. We may thus summarize it as rational, ethical, policy choice.

The Undergraduate as Prospective Citizen-Analyst

Undergraduate education has a vital place in this sort of choice. Graduate training has typically guided students to particular sorts of careers and jobs. The Ph.D. in a discipline has been an apprenticeship in research on the frontiers of knowledge; even if this knowledge has been used for policy choice, preparation for such choices has not normally been part of the training for the academic Ph.D. Only in political science has a candidate for the Ph.D. been allowed to deal with choice among political regimes or institutions; but this choice has been closely related to the literature of political philosophy (as contrasted, for example, with that of economics). The professions prepare students for particular roles in society where they do make valuative choices, justified by notions of the general good; but these choices are circumscribed by the particular professional roles into which the students are channeled, and by the values associated with them. The choice as to which professional roles should exist in the first place, or as to which of several professions should furnish the means to a given end, is not easily handled within the ethics of any single profession; for example, medical schools are often much more concerned with "health services" than with health policies that do not operate through physicians' services (for example, policies affecting nutrition and the environment). Similarly, graduate training in engineering or business often prepares the student to take his values from an employer or from the market, rather than to examine them in fundamental ethical terms.[2]

Fundamental ethical evaluation is thus the province of the citizen, who must formulate for himself criteria for policy choice that express his notion of rightness or of the general welfare,[3] without taking them from any external source. In the contemporary United States, college graduates constitute a significant portion of the citizenry. These graduates—especially those who may later be interested in public life—should thus be educated in rational and ethical choice.[4]

An introductory undergraduate course can define the field of policy analysis for students who may wish to study it further, or provide an interdisciplinary elective for students majoring in a conventional field of study centering about knowledge rather than action and choice. Since 1972 I have offered a course at Chapel Hill, "Introduction to Public Policy Analysis," which is intended as a foundation for an interdisciplinary degree program in this field.[5] The course is listed in three departments—political science, economics, and sociology—and I have usually taught it together with a colleague from economics. Our experience with this course, which centers about a series of case studies, is the basis for this paper.

Policy analysis focuses on effective choices rather than on knowledge per se. This notion can best be conveyed to the student by requiring him to make choices and communicate his reasons and recommendations. He must thus assume the role of an actor and participant rather than a passive spectator of the policy process. Our basis for teaching this role is a set of case studies, presented in written form or with the aid of other media; cases both exemplify the notion of choice and provide the analogue of a laboratory in which specific operational examples of general principles are learned. Specific examples are all the more important in policy analysis because the end product of instruction should be conceptual, interpersonal, and communication skills that are applicable to specific choices. These skills may also be developed later in internships, which are a frequent feature of instructional programs in policy analysis.

The basic unit of the course is a case which each student must read and analyze. Two weeks of class meetings are allotted to lectures and class discussion of each case. At the end of this period each student must submit a typewritten report of four to five pages, presenting his analysis and choice of policy. We require that the analysis be organized in relation to five questions:

1. Specify a given role that you will hypothetically assume as an actor in this case (mayor, governor, president, legislator, staff advisor, member of interested group, etc.). How is the problem (or opportunity) perceived by various persons and groups who are likely to be involved in the decision, or influenced by it? Distinguish the problem as they see it (the "problem situation") from your reformulation of it ("the analyst's problem").
2. State the criteria that you will use in evaluating alternative policies.
3. What are the principal alternative policies that should be considered?
4. What information is needed, and what is available to you, to estimate and compare the expected consequences of the various alternative policies in view of the valuative criteria you have chosen? Use the information available to choose a preferred alternative.

5. What political and organizational factors must be considered in your efforts to obtain the enactment and implementation of your proposed policy?

The detail of these questions may vary from one case to another; for example, when economic regulation is involved, we may ask the student to identify types of market failure that may be present.

The cases we have used are chosen to illustrate that the general approach of policy analysis applies broadly to policies that concern various aspects of the economy, education, health, and foreign policy. Most recently we have used the following cases for student reports:

1. "Martial Law in East Texas," by Warner E. Mills, Jr. (Inter-University Case Program, #53, 1960). The discovery of a large oil pool in East Texas led to a problem of regulation in 1931. Governor Sterling, after efforts to work through the legislature, declared martial law. The student is asked to choose an optimum level of regulated production (if he favors regulation) and to tell how he would bring it about. This case illustrates the externalities due to the "rule of capture" in oil drilling and the effects of policy on unrepresented consumers outside Texas.

2. "Income by Right," a series of three articles by Daniel P. Moynihan in the *New Yorker*, 1973 (by permission). The evolution of Nixon's Family Assistance Plan is considered as regards both its merits and its political difficulties in the Senate. Students are asked to choose a policy in this situation. This case illustrates problems of policies for income redistribution.

3. "Fluoridation in a New England Town," a case prepared by Dr. Thomas S. Plaut for the University of Michigan School of Public Health. An account is given of the organization of support for a fluoridation referendum in Newton, Mass., in 1960–61. Students are asked to judge the merits of both fluoridation (some information is supplied) and the means used by proponents to organize support. This case illustrates economies of scale and a possible merit good.

4. "The Charlotte-Mecklenburg School Busing Controversy (1965–71)," by Donald A. Hicks, H. Brent McKnight, and Michael Dailey, a case specially prepared for this course, based in part on papers previously prepared for other courses. A developmental account of the judicial decision, community politics, and issues leading up to the Supreme Court's affirmation of Judge McMillan's decision. Some data are presented, though not enough to permit prediction or evaluation of the long-run effects of the decision. This case is used to illustrate not only problems of equity, but also the mixture of private and collective goods in educational policy.

5. *Essence of Decision*, by Graham T. Allison (Little, Brown, 1971). A theoretically oriented account of the Cuban missile crisis of 1962. Allison's aim is to explain the crisis, while ours is to choose a right course of action, assuming the role of one of the participants. This book is especially rich in its

accounts of organizational processes and governmental politics; but statistical decision methods or those of benefit-cost analysis are less relevant here than in other cases. The film *The Missiles of October* has been of special value in teaching this case. The case illustrates the collective-good aspect of defense policy as well as effects on unrepresented persons outside the United States.

The purpose of a case-based approach is to give the student a realistic sense of the reasoning he must use as a citizen or as a public official. Reports are required in order to cultivate the skills in communication that are an integral part of policy analysis. Common principles are stressed throughout the discussion of these diverse topics.

The ideal case—to which the above cases are only approximations—should combine all the ingredients of policy analysis with realism and detail. It should provide information about how the problem or opportunity arose, and about the various ways in which it was viewed. It should suggest the values that participants used in argument or analysis, and which may be chosen by the student. It should outline two or more major alternative policies, including the policy of doing nothing, while leaving the student a chance to devise new alternatives of his own. It should provide enough data to allow the student to estimate the consequences of alternative policies in terms of the valuative criteria he chooses. It should give a rich enough picture of the political landscape, including the personalities involved, for the student to devise a plan by which he will work toward enactment and implementation and to anticipate what other actors may try to do. Finally, it is probably desirable that a case be open-ended, providing several plausible options for students to choose.

Cases with all these features are hard to find.[6] Some cases, written by political scientists, are good in their treatment of political feasibility and implementation, but lacking in statement of criteria for evaluating one policy in comparison with another; Marmor's *The Politics of Medicare* (Aldine, 1973) and Allison's *Essence of Decision* are of this kind. Other reports give excellent accounts of the methodology and scientific interpretation of a policy-related research study, but say little about how the study came to be done or how it was used or resisted. To combine analytic choice of policies with a sense of political possibilities is the essence of a good case study; the synthesis between these two types of skills can also be an important contribution of class discussion.

Concepts and Principles

The questions that the student must answer in his reports, and the ingredients that an ideal case should contain, both illustrate common elements that are stressed throughout the course. These ingredients are concepts and principles, drawn for the most part from existing disciplines, but having a coherence of their own as they relate to the analysis of policies.[7]

The teaching of cases as well as their selection or construction requires a clear sense of the concepts and principles, common to all cases, that the student is to learn. Case studies, no matter how rich and detailed, do not teach themselves. We make different abstractions from their reality and complexity for different purposes. Thus an initial section of the course must be spent in introducing the principles of policy analysis. This section occupies about three weeks in the semester with ten for cases and one for a summary of the course. The final examination requires the student to compare and contrast the cases in the light of these principles.

The principles of policy analysis may be related to particular disciplines and even drawn from them; but they cannot be taught from readings that are segregated into disciplinary compartments. The case-study approach is one means to avoid this segregation, but the same goal must also be pursued in the teaching of principles. To this end, I have been developing a set of text materials, together with James A. Wilde of our Economics department.[8]

The concepts and principles discussed in this introductory section of the course constitute a framework within which the student is expected to approach each case. They may be grouped under the following headings:

1. An assessment of the genesis of problems, related to the sociological notion of a "social problem" as well as to political and historical interpretations of the development of issues.
2. Characterization of valuative principles that are commonly used in policy analysis, including teleological and nonteleological ethics, efficiency and equity or justice, Pareto optimality and net benefit, and human development. These valuative principles should be expressed precisely enough to be connected with predicted consequences of policies.
3. Statement of policy alternatives in precise enough form that they can be evaluated, and preliminary choice of alternatives for feasibility.
4. Statement of simple models connecting policies with their expected (valued or disvalued) consequences, the relation of decisions to statistical data, and elementary use of decision trees.[9] The economic model of the free market, together with notions of various types of market failure, is presented; a useful introductory reading is James M. Buchanan, "The Bases for Collective Action" (General Learning Press module, 1971). Among the short cases (drawn from newspapers) used to illustrate these concepts are one on laetrile (illustrating demerit goods) and one on deposit bottles (illustrating externalities). Both are used with permission from author or publisher.
5. Assessment of organizational and political conditions for the enactment and implementation of the student's chosen policy, including constituencies, careers, and typical organizational goals.

To some extent each of these topics must be treated superficially in an introductory course. In fact, each topic above corresponds approximately to a more specialized or advanced course that can be offered in an undergraduate program, together with courses in a field of specialization and a final workshop course in which each student carries through the analysis of a problem of his own choice.

Some Practical Problems

The course has had an enrollment of from thirty to sixty students (sophomores through seniors). It has required special arrangements for team teaching, and involves extra effort by both students and instructors becasue it requires writing and detailed grading of essays at two-week intervals. If it were to be enlarged, it would require carefully trained teaching assistants who could conduct discussion sections and provide accurate criticisms of students' use of concepts from several disciplines. Accurate and prompt feedback is essential for students to gauge their progress in understanding and applying the principles. Papers should be graded for logical coherence, clarity of presentation, and mastery of principles, but not on ideological grounds. The clarity with which the student presents and uses his valuative criteria may be criticized, but his substantive choice of criteria must not.

Students' participation in discussion has been encouraged so far by questions to individual students from the instructors, or by general questions to the class about lecture material. Other approaches that could also be used are the invitation of guest lecturers with experience on particular policy choices or the encouragement of debate among members of the class about their contrasting policy choices.

If such a course is to introduce the field of policy analysis for students who wish to pursue it further, the course should be available to freshmen and sopho-mores. Up to the present, we have encouraged students to take at least one social science course concurrently with, and preferably before, this one. But if the materials and lectures can be organized in a clear and self-contained fashion, it should be possible to offer this course to freshmen.

We recommend the course to others on the basis of its success so far; yet we should also note ways in which it could be improved. Some of the cases used do not provide sufficient data for the student to develop elementary skills in applied data analysis. All cases are presented as "micro-histories" bringing events to a conclusion at enactment, failure of enactment, or implementation. Such cases tend to bias the student toward a "right" policy in a way that open-ended case histories might not, and they may not stress implementation sufficiently. The introductory presentation of principles succeeds to some degree in com-municating technical concepts such as "teleological ethics," "economies of scale," "collective goods," and "players in positions," but these concepts and others are complex for some students and may require improved teaching methods and materials; additonal exercises are being introduced into the text for this purpose. The course is thus recommended as having stood some of the tests of practice, but susceptible to further improvement.

Notes

1. Revised version of paper presented to the North Carolina Political Science Association, Raleigh, N.C., April 15, 1977.

2. See D. MacRae, Jr., "Professions and Social Sciences as Sources of Public Values," *Soundings* 60 #1 (Spring 1977), 3-21. A growing concern in engineering and business schools for social responsibility may, however, bring them closer to the perspective I am advocating.

3. This implies that the citizen's role does not conform exclusively to an economic or interest-group model, in which he would vote or participate only for narrow or selfish interests. See D. MacRae, Jr., *The Social Function of Social Science* (Yale, 1976), ch. 6.

4. Similar educational programs are also appropriate before college; see Richard C. Remy, "Promoting Citizen Competence," *Mershon Center Quarterly Report* (Ohio State University) 2, #2 (Winter 1977), 1-7.

5. Students majoring in Public Policy Analysis at Chapel Hill have done so under the existing provision for a B.A. in Interdisciplinary Studies; but a possible independent degree-granting curriculum in Public Policy Analysis is also under consideration.

6. An increasing number of policy-related case studies are being written in the various graduate schools of public policy and circulated among them. Cases used in professional schools may also be relevant, and the converse is also true; our case #1 above has been reanalyzed in Walter Gellhorn, Clark Byse, and Paul R. Verkull, *Problems in Administrative Law* (Foundation Press, 1974).

7. Examples of such concepts and principles are given in David G. Smith, "Policy Analysis for Undergraduates," *Policy Studies Journal* 5, #2 (Winter 1976), 234-44.

8. *Policy Analysis for the Citizen* (Duxbury Press, forthcoming, 1979).

9. If such a course were offered to students with a prerequisite of one course in statistics, a useful recent text might be William B. Fairley and Frederick Mosteller (eds.), *Statistics and Public Policy* (Addison-Wesley, 1977).

Teaching Policy Studies through Field Experience

Richard D. Bingham and
Robert W. Biersack

Although policy studies is one of the fastest growing areas of political science, little attention has been devoted to teaching policy studies courses. An examination of the journal *Teaching Political Science* from its inception in 1973 to date produced only one reference to teaching policy studies—a four-page "Teaching Note."[1] The journal seems to emphasize teaching an introductory course in political science or American government,[2] individualized or small group instruction,[3] and the use of games and simulations.[4] Yet policy studies courses, at least in our view, require special handling. Perhaps more than any specific subject matter, policy studies must teach an awareness of the policy process. The issue is important because in teaching policy science we are essentially training or educating people who are going to meet situations and experiences we cannot foresee. We are attempting to prepare students to make reasonably prudent judgments in the future. Merely telling them the answers as we see them today is probably not going to help them. As Dexter points out in his fine essay on relevance, it is not so much the content of the material studied which communicates awareness, it is rather the way the subject matter is handled.[5]

The importance of creating awareness in policy studies courses is demonstrated by recent criticisms of policy research. Policy researchers are often not aware of the needs of the agencies or individuals for whom they are conducting research. Nielsen, for example, noted that information produced in evaluations of social action programs is not used by those responsible for directing and improving public programs largely because the evaluations do not provide the kinds of information that program managers need.[6] Evaluators tended to examine the impact of the total program, monitor variables beyond the control of program managers, and assess the long-range outputs of programs. Managers, on the other hand, were much more concerned with specific program elements, with program components over which they had some control, and with the short range effects of the programs rather than long range outputs.

Wise also examined several studies of evaluations of federal programs and reported major weaknesses in many of the studies. These included: (1) lack of methodological know-how, (2) difficulty in securing cooperation from program personnel, (3) problems in developing specifications and guidelines for evalua-

The authors wish to thank Mary LeBlanc for comments on an earlier version of this chapter.

tion research, (4) lack of funds dedicated to evaluation, (5) problems in the communication of results from researchers to program personnel, (6) no systematic evaluation policy, (7) failure to spell out objectives.[7] He also emphasized the uncertainty of public decisions—noting that decision making almost always occurs under conditions of imperfect knowledge.[8]

The weaknesses identified by Nielsen and Wise are clearly related to the awareness that Dexter finds so important. But how can awareness be communicated to students? The traditional lecture approach hardly seems appropriate since policy researchers and evaluators themselves often fail to demonstrate an awareness of the needs of the organizations they are researching or evaluating. We suggest that awareness can best be stimulated by an action orientation. We agree with Kent that an action orientation should be brought into policy studies by using current problems—providing the basis for task orientation and for the organization of the student's thinking.[9] Taking Kent's argument one step further, we suggest that actual field experience provides the type of action orientation necessary to create awareness.

Field Experience through Internships. In response to demands for relevance, academic institutions have been giving increasing attention to internships as an educational approach.[10] Murphy described the growing popularity of internship programs as a response to increasing demand for professional schools of public administration.[11] Ideally internships represent a bridge between the theoretical concepts traditionally stressed in the classroom and the practical decision-making environment of the administrator in the public sector. It is the interplay between these two frequently conflicting environments which holds the key to success as well as the potential for failure of the internship experience.

The educational goals of most internships are to give the student a perspective of admininstration and to provide an opportunity to apply university training to actual situations. A well-planned program familiarizes the student with applied administrative practices, provides practical experience in management in an organized manner, and provides the intangible benefit of contact between the intern and an experienced administrator.[12] The key to this learning process is interaction—interaction among the student, the faculty adviser, and the agency supervisor under whom the intern is placed. A "dramatic" internship clearly provides a valuable educational experience.[13] The experience does not become dramatic by itself, however, but requires careful planning and frequent communication between the intern, his agency supervisor, and the faculty adviser. Creating the bridge from the classroom to administration is not a simple task—nor is it easy to make the internship experience meaningful.

Many interns find themselves in a "look, but don't touch" situation. Often they are given little responsibility or authority and thus never fully comprehend the responsibilities of management.[14] Weak internship experiences of this type can often be blamed on the faculty adviser—described by some as "the weak link in the internship chain."[15] Faculty advisers must clearly establish the goals and objectives of the internship, maintain frequent contact with the student, and provide meaningful evaluation of the intern's performance. Advisers must insure that the following common problems of internships are avoided: Interns are often "oriented to death"; the agency spends all of the internship period "training the student." Interns will often "go native" and become so involved with the agency and agency personnel that they lose all objectivity. Interns may not be meeting the objectives of the internship.[16]

There is also a tendency on the part of agencies to place interns in what amount to dead-end positions that are of little educational value. It is thus necessary for faculty advisers to plan the program in cooperation with the supervisor to insure that the student has a significant role to play within the organization and, in particular, to insure that the student is exposed to and participates in the decision-making process. Continued interaction between the adviser and the supervisor can insure that the experience at least has potential value; its realization, of course, depends on the abilities and initiative of the student.

Advisers must also carefully consider each organization in which an intern is placed. In some cases problems are virtually unavoidable. If the agency is under great pressure, or undergoing structural change, there may be a tendency to push the intern into the background. The involvement of the intern in the agency may also be limited by the student's commitment to the university or to his position in the agency.[17]

There also may be problems associated with the evaluation of the program as well as the individual student. As Williams pointed out, "types of learning accruing from internships, which students especially recognize as important, may differ from criteria evaluated in most classrooms."[18] Williams recommended the adoption of a series of evaluative tools, the most important of which is the written report by the work supervisor. Thus the value of the experience, both in mastery of important concepts and satisfactory completion of work assignments, may be judged by those most involved in each particular phase of the program.

While internships have historically been associated with graduate programs, particularly those in public administration, there is an increasing trend toward the use of internships in undergraduate education. This trend is exemplified by the almost overnight success of a unique program called the Washington Center for Learning Alternatives, designed to provide an internship experience for undergraduate students. Within its first two years of operation more than 120 colleges and universities have cooperated with the center to offer public affairs internships in Washington for undergraduate credit. Through the program students have an opportunity to work in the executive, legislative, and judicial branches of the federal government and in various public interest offices and agencies in Washington. The center provides housing for the students and both work and instructional programs. The work phase consists of thirty-six hours per week of supervised work in an office or agency that relates to the broad interests of the student. The instructional phase consists of a formal course meeting one night per week and a seminar that includes a series of lectures. At the end of the semester the student's performance in both the internship and the academic coursework are evaluated and forwarded to the home university, which determines the student's grade and awards credit. Since the center does not grant academic credit it does not need accreditation. While the internship experience offered by the Washington Center has been uneven, as might be expected with any new program, the broad appeal of the experience, as demonstrated by its successful beginning, clearly indicates that it is filling an important need in undergraduate education.[19]

While internships, when properly administered, are able to integrate theoretical principles with the skills best developed in a working environment, we question their utility for policy studies. Internships, after all, are designed to provide admininstrative experience and are heavily oriented in this direction. This is not to say that internships have no value for students interested in policy science but only that there are probably better ways to provide a policy experience—especially for undergraduate students. We suggest that a field experience through class research projects will provide the type of experience most relevant to policy studies work.

Field Experience through Community-Based Research Projects. A number of universities have incorporated a field experience into undergraduate policy studies courses through community-based research projects. Projects of this nature are able to overcome the weaknesses of internships. They also give students the opportunity to learn through trial and error and guidance from the instructor not to make the mistakes Nielsen and Wise found so common. Activities at Syracuse University, Marquette University, and the University of Wisconsin–Milwaukee exemplify such approaches.

In the spring of 1976 the Public Affiars Program at Syracuse introduced a "Community Link" project to tie academic coursework for undergraduates to community-based research training.[20] In December 1975 approximately seventy organizations in the Syracuse area were solicited for applied social science research projects that could be completed in about fifty hours by undergraduate researchers. During the first two weeks of the spring semester, project staff members contacted each organization, submitting a proposal to clarify the project proposal and to inform the organization that students were being matched with the projects—students were then assigned a project based upon their interests and skills.

During the first six weeks of the semester students underwent training and were required to complete either an independent study minicourse or a three-week seminar on survey design and interviewing. Minicourses included "Benefit-

Cost Analysis," "Designs for Evaluating Social Programs," and "Descriptive Statistics and the Analysis of Public Policy."

Toward the end of the training period each student contacted his or her employer to discuss the details of the project. Students then entered a six-week period of project work. During the project period the students met with their advisers on a weekly or biweekly basis, turned in brief reports summarizing the status of their projects, and kept advisers aware of any developing problems.

In mid-April all projects were completed and the students turned in two copies of their final reports to the Community Link Coordinator. One copy was sent to the participating agency for evaluation while the other was kept for grading. Evaluation of the experience by both students and employers was an integral part of the semester's program. Students formally evaluated the mini-course or research seminar after completion of the training period. Once the project period was complete students returned to the classroom to discuss their experiences and to make recommendations for course improvement. Each student was asked to pinpoint a specific problem he or she faced in completing the project and to make recommendations for solving that problem so that future students might benefit from his or her experiences. A list of heuristics was developed from the recommendations, and each student completed a short paper on the three heuristics most important to his or her individual project.

Employers also played an important role in the evaluation process. The Community Link Coordinator mailed each employer an evaluation form along with the copy of the final project. Employer evaluations returned after the spring 1976 semester were quite favorable—eleven employers were highly satisfied with the projects, fourteen were satisfied, and three were dissatisfied. Thus almost 90 percent of the employers were pleased wtih the experience and with student performance. A number of employers also wrote personal letters expressing positive views of the program—most such letters praised the students for their interest and initiative.

Many of the final reports were quite sophisticated and clearly illustrated the importance students placed on the projects. For example, one student surveyed a number of police departments throughout the country to complete a manpower scheduling project, and another evaluated a home health aides program.[21]

A somewhat different approach to community-based policy analysis is exemplified by a project undertaken in the spring of 1976 by undergraduate students in "Public Policy Analysis" at Marquette University. The students spent the entire semester developing a detailed desegregation plan for the City of Milwaukee. The project was conceived in January 1976 when District Judge John W. Reynolds held that the Milwaukee public schools were unlawfully and unconstitutionally segregated and appointed a Special Master to oversee the desegregation efforts. The Special Master reacted enthusiastically to the students' proposal to develop a desegregation plan, met with the students to discuss the project, and agreed to furnish the students with all the data needed to complete the project. The Department of Political Science assigned the students a project room for the semester, and the university agreed to provide typing and reproduction support.

During the early weeks of the semester the students conducted extensive library research into methods of school desegregation (for example, magnet schools, clustering, pairing) and developed a series of detailed goals for their desegregation plan. They sought to preserve the concept of neighborhood schools, to insure that the burden of desegregation fell equally upon both white and black students, to prevent violence, and to minimize both "white flight" and the use of busing.

The students then developed and applied a questionnaire to the case histories of desegregation in thirty-one cities, using the case survey method. (The case survey method involves the use of closed-ended questions applied to a series of independently undertaken case studies.[22]) Since the questions were closed-ended, the information from each case study was quantified for use in statistical and comparative analysis. The questionnaire attempted to measure the comprehensiveness of the desegregation plan in the thirty-one cities, to identify the techniques used in desegregation, and to assess the desegregation effort in terms of meeting each of the specific desegregation goals set by the students.

The students then correlated the goal-related variables (compliance, lack of violent community response, racial balance, burden, etc.) with methods of desegregation including open enrollment, pairing, clustering, magnet schools, rezoning, educational parks, and busing. Based upon the findings, they decided that most of their goals could be met by concentrating their efforts upon a plan primarily utilizing three desegregation techniques—school closings, magnet schools, and a combination of clustering and pairing.

In working out the details of the plan the students devised and monitored their own work schedules, divided tasks among themsleves, and posted "work orders" in the project room so that the continuity of the project was insured. Regular class meetings were held once a week so that students could brief each other on the progress of various parts of the project and make additonal work assignments.

An integral part of the project was a press conference held near the end of the semester at which the students presented their plan to the Special Master and the public. The press conference assured the legitimacy of the project—students realized that their work was being taken seriously by the community. The press conference was covered by Milwaukee's three commercial television stations, both daily newspapers, and virtually all of the major radio stations. The conference was given heavy emphasis by radio and television news programs throughout the day and evening. Major write-ups appeared in both daily newspapers.[23] The community reaction was highly favorable, with more than 100 copies of the plan distributed, on request, to community groups. The Executive Assistant to the Special Master called the plan "one of the most practical and thoughtful plans yet received,"[24] and the attorney for the plaintiffs in the desegregation suit called it "sound and very impressive."[25]

The learning experience did not end with the press conference, however. During the weeks following the press conference the students were called upon to testify before a public hearing held by the Special Master, spoke at other universities in the area, and advised many citizen groups throughout the city concerning the preparation of desegregation plans.

Evaluation of the learning experience was difficult. Students were required to evaluate their own performance in the course and to evaluate the work of the other students in their working group. These evaluations were combined with the instructor's to determine final grades.

A similar undergraduate research project was undertaken at the University of Wisconsin–Milwaukee (UW–M) during academic year 1976-77. The project differed from the Marquette experience in that the research project supplemented traditional classroom work and involved a number of classes. Students in eight political science classes completed a technology assessment of refuse collection in Milwaukee—recommending that the city initiate an experimental program using a cart system of refuse collection. The two policy studies classes ("Science, Technology, and Public Policy," first semester; and "Topics in Technology and Public Policy: Technology Assessment," second semester) coordinated the year-long project, while other political science classes contributed to the project in areas where their input corresponded to their classroom experience.

Like the Marquette project, the UW–M research effort was based on a community event. In 1975 the Milwaukee suburb of Shorewood abandoned its traditional refuse collection method and adopted a one-man mechanized collection system. Each household in the community was issued an eighty-gallon high-density polyethylene container on wheels. Each household was informed of the day of the week its cart would be emptied and instructed to roll the fully loaded cart to the curbside for pickup on collection day. The collector, driving a side-loading collection truck, stops next to each cart, connects the cart to a hydraulic lift unit on the truck, and activates the lift mechanism which empties the cart and returns it to the street. The apparent success of the system in terms of increased citizen satisfaction and cost-savings generated substantial interest in refuse collection innovations in Milwaukee. Thus policy studies classes were presented with an opportunity to complete a research project with the potential for real community impact.

During the first semester the "Science, Technology, and Public Policy" students surveyed all cities in the United States identified as using the cart system and requested evaluations of each city's experiences. They contacted equipment manufacturers for descriptions and cost data for various collection systems and completed detailed studies of both the Shorewood and Milwaukee collection systems. A class in urban politics examined the use of citizen surveys in evaluating municipal services and suggested basic research questions to determine citizen satisfaction with their present collection service and amenability to a new collection system. A survey research class then designed survey instruments to be administered to Shorewood residents, Milwaukee residents, and Milwaukee aldermen.

A number of the students in the survey research class continued work on the project during the second semester, pretesting and refining the questionnaires, drawing random samples of Milwaukee and Shorewood residents, training student interviewers (drawn from several classes in urban politics), and analyzing survey responses. The "Technology Assessment" class then drew together the materials and reports produced by other classes, analyzed the reports and findings, examined technological alternatives, predicted the potential impacts of the technology, and produced the final report.

Again, a press conference played a central role in the project—providing the students with the opportunity to have their work seriously considered by city policymakers. The response by the media was again excellent, with extensive radio, television, and newspaper coverage of the conference and the report.[26]

While the three programs described above illustrate novel approaches to providing policy studies undergraduate students with an interesting experience, the descriptions do not answer two important questions. What did students learn from community-based research projects that they could not have learned in a more traditional classroom approach or through an internship experience? Do community-based projects create the awareness students will need in later life?

Advantages of Community-Based Research Projects. From the students' perspective, the field project at its initial stage is a vast, alien experience, and may be very disorienting to those who have had little or no exposure to nonacademic activity. To some extent, however, the students' apprehension is overcome by the enthusiasm for doing something different or "important." In the early stages of the project (perhaps as a result of inexperience) there tends to be a great deal of exuberance and willingness to take on any challenge. While this is unquestionably an asset, it is important for the instructor to make certain that the project is not too broad or ambitious. The instructor must make certain that the students understand the scope of the project and the commitment necessary to bring the project to successful completion.

If disorientation and lack of self-confidence are the first feelings students experience in a field project, the loss of these feelings may be the greatest advantage of such endeavors. The successful completion of community-based projects does much to instill self-confidence in the students. Students learn to "sell themselves" to employers or decision-makers by providing manpower or expertise that they could not ordinarily obtain. The talent for selling oneself is vital in any career and is frequently not fully developed in the traditional academic environment.

Field experiences also provide the student with an understanding of decision-making processes which cannot be fully transmitted in the classroom. Students trained by traditional formal courses to look for the "right" answer soon come to the rather frustrating conclusion that in public policy there may be no "right" answer, but rather sets of alternatives responding to various, sometimes conflicting, objectives.

Similarly, students soon realize that the type and quality of information they believe they need to make decisions with confidence may be nonexistent. Students thus tend to delay important decisions because they lack the evidence (and experience) that they believe they need. The time constraints imposed by the project, however, inevitably force the students to make decisions with limited information. This problem is, of course, intimately familiar to policy-makers in the public sector but is difficult or impossible to convey in traditional lecture format.

In group research projects, time limitations and deadlines also force students to organize their efforts precisely, delegate responsibility, and develop an appreciation for accountability. There are a wide variety of activities which must be accomplished, ranging in importance from making policy decisions to collating reports, but all vital to the success of the project. By being involved in the entire process, students develop organizational skills in a group environment which would not necessarily result from individual work.

Another advantage of field experience is the development of interpersonal communication skills necessary in any career. From the students' perspective, there are two levels of communication which are particularly important. The first of these involves communication within the group participating in the project. It is important, especially when dealing with controversial issues, to arrive at a consensus regarding policy decisions. Doing this develops techniques of negotiation and compromise important in public sector activity. It is also vital, especially in large groups with divided responsibilities, to maintain continuous interaction among the people concentrating on different aspects of the project. Solving organizational problems and insuring coordination of effort without domination by a single individual develops patience and a concern for various points of view which are not so directly encouraged in the classroom environment.

The other level of communication required in a field project is the discourse between members of the group and those involved in the project professionally or as concerned citizens. When issues are controversial and have a significant impact on the community, we have found that groups desiring information will frequently call upon the students, as they are likely to be more accessible than those most intimately involved in the program. This serves the dual purpose of providing information to people who might otherwise not be able to obtain it, and giving feedback to the students regarding community attitudes toward the project and how they might react to policy recommendations. Further, it forces the students to make goals and objectives as clear and concise as possible, and to present them in an effective manner. These skills are further refined when final recommendations are presented to the agency or individuals responsible for implementation. Students learn that the impact of their recommendations may depend in part on the effectiveness of their presentation. The ability to give a detailed report and answer questions makes the student aware of the necessity for thoroughness as well as the importance of justification of one's position.

The final important advantage of field experience for the student is the feeling of self-worth which one develops upon completion of a successful project. The recognition that one has contributed in a concrete way to the well-being of the community and gained the respect of individuals in positions of influence gives the students a sense of confidence in his abilities beyond the realm of textbooks and lectures. This recognition of what can be done as well as experience with the techniques of information-gathering and problem-solving are valuable for any career.

Disadvantages. While policy research projects present the student with the opportunity to develop a real awareness of the policy process, there are also some disadvantages which deserve mention. The first of these is the time requirement. Effective field projects inevitably take a great deal of the students' time; and while it is not so great as to make it impossible for undergraduates to participate, once they have committed themselves they must be willing to follow through if the project is to be successfully completed. It is conceivable that the desire to be active in the project will have an adverse effect on the students' other academic responsibilities. It is important, therefore, for the faculty adviser to make as explicit as possible the time requirements involved, and to discourage students from participating who are unsure of their ability to make the necessary commitment.

A related problem which is especially acute in large groups is the varying level of commitment to the project on the part of students. The programs with which we have been involved have had students working independently, reporting progress and findings to the relevant agency. In these situations it is possible for individual students to provide a minimum of effort without immediate repercussions. This is particularly true when other students are prepared to take a more active part and cover for these deficiencies. If these variations in effort become severe, the quality of the work produced may be reduced, and conflicts can arise within the group which also affect the outcome of the experience. It is probably undesirable—and impossible—to force absolutely equal involvement; but efforts should be made to distribute the workload equitably; and frequent progress reports should be required to prevent, as much as possible, great variations in involvement.

Another disadvantage stemming largely from class size is the difficulty in arriving at decisions acceptable to all the participants. When the workload is divided along substantive lines, different students examining different policy alternatives, there is a tendency to become an advocate of one's area of concentration. (For example, in the school desegregation project, students who examined voluntary approaches favored them, while others supported other alternatives.) Efforts at compromise can be difficult, and the interaction of personalities can detract from the overall objectives of the project. Many decisions may have to be made on a less than unanimous basis, presenting the possibility of alienation which is detrimental on many levels, the most important of which is future commitment to the project by those who "lose" on significant questions. This problem is not unique to student experience, however; and while efforts should be made to reduce the number of serious conflicts, some disagreement is inevitable, and the process by which it is settled is a valuable part of the learning process.

While the students' interest is likely to be high when the project puts them into a highly politicized environment, they also become susceptible to attack and manipulation by other groups who have an interest in policy decisions. Initially, the students may be challenged as "outsiders," and the use of somewhat sophisticated research methods may also be looked upon with suspicion in some quarters. The effect of these early reacitons in large part depends on the support the students receive from those responsible for final policy decisions. If these individuals provide public encouragement, acceptance throughout the community is more likely.

Another major source of problems in dealing with controversial issues is attempts at manipulation of the students by competing factions in the area. Those groups or agencies who do not support the project may try to suppress information needed for policy decisions. (In the desegregation case, some school administrators were reluctant to supply needed data because, we suspect, they thought the results of the project were not likely to be to their liking.) Further, advocates of various policy alternatives may try to enlist the support of the students in order to enhance their own position. While these efforts give the students exposure to political machinations they contribute little to the actual goal of the project, that being to develop sound public policy. It is easy for inexperienced students to be influenced by people on the outside who are seeking their support. The realization by the students that they have some "power" or that their opinions carry some weight could lead to decisions made purely on the basis of political impact. It is very important, when these overtures are made, to have the students step back and examine the various alternatives for their substantive value. In many cases the value of the students' work is related to their independence from the political environment; consequently, coalitions, either formal or informal, should generally be avoided.

Conclusions. Although we have suggested a number of disadvantages of community-based research projects, in general, students participating in such projects find the experience highly rewarding. They gain firsthand experience in developing public policy; and, while they often make mistakes, their experience makes them sensitive to the problems and weaknesses of policy research identified by Nielsen and Wise. We believe that a well-planned field experience makes an important contribution to policy studies education. It clearly creates an awareness of the policy process in the student. If we are trying to prepare students to make policy judgments in the future, carefully guided field experiences will aid in this preparation.

While internships have been a major source of field experience in the past, especially for students in public administration, we suggest that policy students might benefit more from a research experience. Faculty involvement in the research experience can be much closer, and instructors can point out the significance of events in the student experience. Students cannot be mere observers in a community-based research project; they are forced to come to decisions and to be able to support them as a group to the community.

Notes

1. George Kent, "Teaching Practical Policy Analysis," *Teaching Political Science* 2(October 1974):100–103.

2. For example Ronald C. Green, "Mentrex: An Experiment in Teaching American Government," *Teaching Political Science* 1(April 1974):225–36; Donald G. Tannenbaum, "Introducing Students to Political Science: Patterns and Issues in the Beginning Course," *Teaching Political Science* 3(October 1975): 63–82; Eugene F. Miller, "What Political Scientists Can Learn from Teaching American Government," *Teaching Political Science* 4(October 1976):3–30.

3. Ralph M. Goldman, Jeff Fishel, and Susan Hobart, "Small Groups and the Introductory Course in American Politics: An Experiment in the Organization of Instruction," *Teaching Political Science* 3(October 1975):37–62; Patricia Taylor, "Personalized Instruction: The Introductory Political Science Course," *Teaching Political Science* 3(April 1976):227–48; Steven M. DeLue, "Individually Paced Instruction and Political Science," *Teaching Political Science* 3(July 1976):391–400.

4. Steve Whitaker, "A Role-Playing Simulation of the United States Supreme Court," *Teaching Political Science* 1(October 1973):47–58; Walter C. Clemens, Jr., "Games Sovietologists Play," *Teaching Political Science* 3(January 1976):140–60; Fred S. Coombs and John G. Peters, "Computer Based Games as a Political Laboratory," *Teaching Political Science* 3(April 1976):249–62.

5. Lewis A. Dexter, "The Notion of Relevance and Issues in Communications," *Teaching Political Science* 1(April 1974):207–15.

6. Victor G. Nielsen, "Why Evaluation Does Not Improve Effectiveness," *Policy Studies Journal* 3(Summer 1975):385–90.

7. Charles R. Wise, "Productivity in Public Administration and Public Policy," *Policy Studies Journal* 5(Autumn 1976):99.

8. Ibid., p. 103.

9. Kent, "Teaching Practical Policy Analysis," p. 100.

10. Thomas P. Murphy (ed.), *Government Management Internships and Executive Development: Education for Change* (Lexington, Mass.: Lexington Books, D.C. Heath and Company, 1973):xiii.

11. Ibid., pp. 4-5.

12. Richard D. Heimovics, "An Intern's Perspective," in *Government Management Internships* (ed. Murphy), p. 25.

13. See Bernard C. Hennesy, "Old Interns Neither Die Nor Fade Away: After Ten Years, Another Sample," *DEA News*, Spring 1977, p. 12.

14. Heimovics, "An Intern's Perspective," p. 26.

15. Thomas J. Williams, "The Faculty Advisor's Role in Intern Supervision," *Teaching Political Science* 4(October 1976):102.

16. Ibid., p. 104.

17. Thomas P. Murphy, "Potential Pitfalls of Internships," in *Government Management Internships* (ed. Murphy), p. 39.

18. Williams, "The Faculty Advisor's Role," 105.

19. Jack Magarrell, "Washington Internships for Undergraduates," *Chronicle of Higher Education*, March 28, 1977.

20. Suzanne Grant and Julie Fitzpatrick, "Report to the Community Link Advisory Committee: Spring 1976," Syracuse University, 1976 (mimeographed); "Community Link: Course Guide for Spring 1977," Syracuse University, 1976 (mimeographed).

21. Eric Smith, "A Survey of Police Manpower Deployment Systems," Syracuse University, 1976 (mimeographed); Mary Delaney, "Evaluation of Home Health Aides Trends Over the Past Three Years (1973 thru 1975)," Syracuse University, 1976 (mimeographed).

22. Robert K. Yin and Karen A. Heald, "Using the Case Survey Method to Analyze Policy Studies," *Administrative Science Quarterly* 20(September 1975): 371-81.

23. "MU Class Offers Plan for Schools," *Milwaukee Journal*, April 28, 1976, part 2, p. 9; "Integration Plan Keeps Pupils With Classmates," *Milwaukee Sentinel*, April 29, 1976, p. 12.

24. "Integration Plan Keeps Pupils with Classmates."

25. Ibid.

26. For example, H. Carl Mueller, "Study Pushed Garbage Cart Plan," *Milwaukee Sentinel*, May 10, 1977, p. 5; "Carts for Trash May Be Tested," *Milwaukee Journal*, May 10, 1977, pp. 1-2.

Notes on Inviting Those Who Make Public Policy to Help Teach It

Margaret King Gibbs

From time to time every professor of public policy studies is confronted with the task of reconciling theory and practice so that the two do not seem to be contradictory. Textbooks and case studies deal (with varying degrees of effectiveness) with the recurrent problems of relevancy and pragmatism in the attempt to educate those who will soon be moving into policymaking positions at various levels of public and private administration.

To prepare graduate students seeking the Master of Public Administration degree at California State College, San Bernardino, the final class, entitled "Public Policy Analysis," has employed the procedure of using those who actually *make* policy, to teach how it is best formulated. Two years of successful experience have now been recorded, earning the unanimous enthusiasm and endorsement of the students completing the course. (Students' ages ranged from the early twenties to the fifties.) They agree that nothing in their reading has been as helpful and as stimulating as being able to hear and quiz public officials who are responsible for actively making policy decisions every day.

Several factors seem to have contributed to the effectiveness of the procedure. First, students themselves chose the area for discussion, basing their choice on the five most critical needs of the region. Second, they chose the top policymaker in that area to participate in the discussion. Third, they formed teams to prepare themselves with the appropriate background essential to fruitful discussion. Fourth, they greeted the guest speakers and presided at the two-hour seminars. Fifth, each seminar session was planned to give each student an opportunity to question the speaker. Sixth, all sessions were videotaped for replay and evaluation. Seventh, a low profile was maintained by the faculty member.

The usual academic preparation for the course included reading four textbooks (together with discussion of the ideas contained therein): *Bureaucracy, Politics, and Public Policy*, 2nd ed., by Francis E. Rourke; *Public Policy Decision-Making: Systems Analysis and Comparative Advantages Debate*, by Brock, Chesebro, Cragan, and Klumpp; *Public Policies and Their Politics*, by Randall B. Ripley; *Strategic Perspectives on Social Policy*, by Tropman, Dluhy, Lind, Vasey, and Croxton; and, more importantly, a series of six speakers who are decision-makers in the policy arena of public administration.

To illustrate the implementation and feasibility of the approach, a brief description of the activities follows.

Before selecting their speakers the students were asked to analyze and rate the five most critical problems facing Riverside and San Bernardino Counties (two of the largest in the United States, comprising a total of 27,437 square miles). After discussion and argument the students selected unemployment, air quality, rapid expansion of residential building, crime, and property taxes. The fifteen members comprising the class voluntarily divided themselves into five teams of three members each. Each team accepted responsibility for researching one of the agreed-upon subjects and for recommending speakers who determine policy in that area. Further class debate concerning the relative desirability of the suggested officials eventually resulted in invitations being issued to the chosen speakers. These were sent by the faculty person, Dr. Margaret Gibbs, in the name of the college. Each official was advised by letter of the nature of the class and told that he might discuss, for no more than fifteen minutes, the background information he found essential to the policymaking function of his office. He was also advised that after his initial statement he would be expected to field questions prepared in advance by the students. This "early warning" served to maintain the seminar format of the sessions, much to the delight of the students.

Each team chose its chairman, who researched the biography of the speaker, introduced him to the class, and presided over the seminar. This provided students, some of whom had not had this experience, an opportunity to preside and the responsibility for keeping the seminar moving. (The faculty member identified the tape series and number and made a very brief introduction of the student chairman, but otherwise assumed a "back seat" role.) To prevent any student from talking too much or too frequently, the chairman kept a running notation as to who had asked questions, so that all might have equal opportunity to converse with the guest speaker.

Prior to the arrival of the guest, the team involved briefed the rest of the class on major topics of concern in the field and subsequently received a list of possible questions which might be addressed to the speaker at the conclusion of his talk. This discussion of questions served to guide the chairman in his effort to avoid duplication and to cover as much of the subject as possible in the time available for the seminar.

During the seminar session students were extremely cooperative about the usual courtesies, However, as the session moved along questions became a great deal more incisive. At one time or another each guest speaker commented on the impressive knowledgeability of the questioners and seemed pleasantly surprised that the students knew so much.

In the seminar following a guest session, students and instructor reviewed and analyzed the most recent presentation, relating it to readings and theory.

Each session was tape-recorded by the able CSCSB audiovisual staff, directed by Dr. Robert Senour. The audiovisual records of these seminars are being collected in a library of tapes under the title "Policymaking in the Public Sector," which now has grown to ten tapes of one and one-half hours each. Last year's (1976) tapes were reviewed early in the quarter to educate this year's class. Furthermore, this year's students reviewed, on their own time, tapes of their own seminars before writing their evaluation of each speaker, as required by the instructor for a portion of their term grade. Because the comments so gathered from the students are a convincing indication of the value of the program they are included herewith.

A $50 honorarium was given to each guest speaker (with the exception of one speaker, Mr. Haltigan, an employee of the federal government). The honorariums were made possible by a minigrant of $450 for innovative teaching. In 1976 the speakers were: James Cox, City Manager of Victorville, California; Norton Younglove, Supervisor (elected) of Riverside County; Mayor Bob Holcomb (elected) of San Bernardino, California; State Senator Ruben Ayala; and James Cramer, District Attorney (elected) of San Bernardino County. In 1977 the speakers included: Robert Herbin, Assessor (elected) of San Bernardino County; Supervisor (elected) Dennis Hansberger of San Bernardino County; Sheriff Ben Clark (elected) of Riverside County; William Haltigan, Regional Director, Region IX, Employment and Training Administration, U.S. Department of Labor; Joseph "Jeb" Stuart, Director of the South Coast Air Quality Control District; and Robert Anderson, retired Chief Administrative Officer of Riverside County.

General Evaluations by the Students[a]

1. The technique of inviting guest speakers to the class of public policy has several advantages. First, it helps to narrow the gap between theory and practice by understanding what actually happens in comparison with theory. Second, it allows the students of public administration to gain valuable information about certain bureaucracies and their objectives and the problems they deal with. Third, it helps to eliminate some misconceptions about certain organizations and their roles. Fourth, it is a good exercise for the students in learning how to ask the right and relevant questions. These outweigh any limitations on the technique.

We have certainly benefited from the six guest speakers that were invited during this quarter, whether in terms of relation between theory and practice or in terms of general background information. Each guest covered several areas to the extent that when combined together we have a good, comprehensive understanding to many public policy issues. Emphasis should be placed on the differences in responses between elected and appointed officials.

---

[a]Numbers indicate different student writers, quoted verbatim.

2. The speakers invited to this class were definitely the high point of the ten weeks. All the speakers provided individual views of public policy within their realm. Having more than one speaker was important in terms of in-depth comparison of presentations and personality. I feel it is extremely beneficial to invite a policymaker to speak in the classroom because it removes the aspect of performance and one is able to seek definite statements regarding setting policy.

After evaluating the six speakers, I thought I would be able to choose the two that seemed most beneficial. However, I feel that it is the combination of the six with their individual roles and perspectives of policymaking today that proved so important to this class.

In all and individually, the speakers were excellent, and it is a good experience for students to go beyond books and theories to actually questioning and listening to these people expound on their areas of expertness. This student gained more from this than many books could provide. It's a look at reality, of real people with real problems, and it is satsifying to find such dedicated public servants who are willing to share their experiences with the class.

3. No public administration program can be considered complete without having an input from the users of its product. Students should have in their curriculum, the means to evaluate the difference between the theoretical versus the practical application of academic knowledge. Having prominent decision-makers as guest lecturers has considerable merit in performing this function.

Students are not prepared to apply academic solutions in the public environment, unless they can receive some direction from those responsible for decision-making policies. Having guest lecturers discuss their concepts of ethical behavior, their processes of decision-making, conflict resolution, their attitudes towards secrecy versus openness in decision-making, and the resolution of public pressure, provides students a model to establish their own standards. It is critically essential that guest lecturers remain part of the MPA program for all the above reasons.

4. A common thread that ranged through presentations by all speakers was the need for public involvement in the policy determination process to ensure proper implementation. Another aspect was the political/client relationship in almost all of the functions represented by the speakers. Each speaker left it up to us to determine the validity of his policymaking role. The roles of the various actors in the policy arena could be seen in each area of government and the need for evaluation of the effectiveness of policy was evident. The various management principles employed by each individual or functional area were geared toward achieving effective implementation of administrative policy and some form of public relations activity was prevalent in each area. The necessity for a political base was noted and the impact of federal or state control of policy and standards was one of the handicaps that appeared in each presentation.

155

Again, it was the firsthand opportunity to question individuals that are directly involved in the development and implementation of policy that was the most prominent asset of the guest lecturer series. This gives insight into the problem areas that cannot be gathered from reading, no matter how expert the author. The exposure to local matters has far more impact than a historical or theoretical approach.

5. The guest speakers program was a very motivating format in which the blending of theory was illuminated by those in responsible positions who actually influence the policy mechanism. The value of each speaker varied, but all contributed some key elements as bureaucrats or politicians and representatives of some facet of government.

In critiquing the speakers, I found it of great assistance to review the tapes available. The reviewing of these tapes aided in revealing areas I failed to comprehend during the actual session. Overall, the format was an affirmative experience. I anticipate using this information gained from this experience in a productive manner in future endeavors.

Specific Comments by the Students[b]

Robert Herbin, County of San Bernardino, Assessor

1. It is through the transmission of such information that speakers like Mr. Herbin offer a valuable addition to the study of public policy, that is, they allow the student to see what is actually occurring in a particular policy area.

2. The students were made aware of the high ethical and equitable standards which are necessary to function in the tax assessor's office. Policies were necessarily highly standardized and involved considerable participative management. This was an excellent model for studying the process of public decision-making.

3. This presentation was an excellent example of an elected official using "scientific" methods for policy formulation and implementation.

4. As public administrators, we will be exposed to many elected officials. In order to be successful, we must learn to read between the lines when necessary and not accept all information and comments as completely factual.

---

[b]Numbers indicate different student writers, quoted verbatim.

Supervisor Dennis Hansberger, San Bernardino County

1. Supervisor Hansberger was an excellent speaker to address the areas and concerns of public policy. He was able to field difficult questions and produce good answers that were valuable for students of public policy analysis. The supervisor depicted the pressure groups that influence policy with the largest pressure being the decision maker's personal judgment of the issue.

2. I feel that sessions of this type are necessary to develop well-rounded public administration scholars. Public administration students must learn to deal with the fine art of compromise, yet retain a high level of ethical behavior. In addition, he must attain the technical competence in obtaining rational, just and equitable policy decisions. Mr. Hansberger's lecture was an important ingredient in achieving this objective.

3. I feel that the presentation which was offered by Supervisor Hansberger was a significant learning experience. It was an opportunity to listen to an elected official's viewpoints regarding policy decision-making. What soon became evident was that elected officials may not always deal with a policy problem in a rational manner. As public administrators, we should be aware of such situations where constituents' interest will overpower pure rationality.

4. This presentation was a good example of an elected official who realizes the real-world limitations in policies.

Sheriff Ben Clark, Riverside County

1. This program has some informational value in regard to the Sheriff Department's policy formulation and implementation. The supplementary material that was provided alluded to innovative management schemes, but with his explanation of the department's operation, I wonder whether they are salient factors in policy development and delivery. The most revealing aspect of this session was the presentation of a personality of a politically conservative, powerful county sheriff.

William Haltigan, Regional Director, Region IX, Employment and Training Administration, U.S. Dep't. of Labor

1. Mr. Haltigan's openness and experience in the decision-making process provided us with the criteria and processes involved in his creation of policy. He provided some insight into the criteria of secrecy versus open meetings, public pressure and special interest groups, and other bureaucratic processes of government.

2. Mr. Haltigan is a prime example of a bureaucrat working within a system and recognizing the various aspects of policy.

Joseph "Jeb" Stuart, Director, South Coast Air Quality
Management District

1. Mr. Stuart's presentation was a great asset to the learning process. In his discussion over the two-hour period, I learned more on the workings of air quality management than I had previously gleaned from numerous texts. His philosophy that the solution to air quality problems must be a win/win compromise which will allow economic growth and cleaner air is more pragmatic than the oftentimes presented economic win at the expense of a clean environment. If one can read between the lines, it becomes clear that this basic philosophy permeates all of public administration. The most successful policies are those where all involved can perceive of themselves as winners. For this item of information alone, so often occluded in the textbooks we read, the presentation by Mr. Stuart was a most invaluable learning experience.

2. This presentation was a good example of a professional administrator who readily grasps the implications of policy information and implementation.

3. He provided some insight on how decisions are arrived at with a conservative board, laws established at higher levels which are inconsistent with local needs, and economic conditions which are already at critical levels. An ideal model, to study, of a highly political vulnerable organization.

4. In general, his whole presentation added much substance to the dynamics surrounding public policy formulation and implementation.

Robert Anderson, Retired Chief Administrative Officer,
Riverside County

1. Mr. Anderson was a gold mine of information. His discussion covered a wide spectrum of policy issues ranging from budgeting questions to the implications of federalism to local government. But the most significant aspects of Mr. Anderson's presentation centered on his repeated direct and indirect emphasis that public policymaking is affected by situational factors. That is, policy that may have strong support in one area may not be possible in a different environment.

2. I believe that Mr. Anderson presented the class with an informative and timely presentation. For me, it was a very important auxiliary in the educational process. Without his presentation, and the others that preceded him on the many facets of government, I don't feel that this course would have been as interesting, nor, more importantly, as highly educational as it was.

15 Comparing Policy Alternatives

Melvin Dubnick

The term "policy studies" is applicable to such a disparate variety of recent research efforts that teaching courses in that "area" has become a major challenge. Any choice of instructional approach necessitates the adoption of a particular perspective in policy analysis, usually to the exclusion of several others. Those of us who focus our courses on policymaking, for instance, tend to ignore the vast literature on policy impact, and vice versa, while others among us who consider policy "substance" primary, generally do so by giving short shrift to questions of policy cause and consequence. Attempts to develop a course syllabus which is both sufficient to "cover" these various perspectives while managing to "fit" all relevant information into a semester (or quarter) session are often nightmarish experiences which only the most masochistic among us can possibly enjoy.

If this dilemma seems familiar, then you are probably a political scientist. As a discipline, we have been plagued for years by what Ted Lowi has termed a "fission and confusion in theory and research."[1] In spite of this (or perhaps because of it), the teaching of political science has been characterized by an obsession with being "authoritative" and "comprehensive"—two qualities, Lowi notes, not conducive to searching inquiry in the classroom.[2] Thus, many of us end up by burdening ourselves and our students with dull, never-ending texts and even duller, seemingly never-ending lectures. This does little more than convince our detractors that we are quite capable of creating boredom out of excitement, irrelevant abstractions from the mornings's headlines, and inconsequential busywork out of potentially instructive assignments. Many of the articles in this symposium and much of the work accomplished through (or promoted by) professional organizations[3] indicate a growing disenchantment with traditional modes of political science education. They also reflect the substantial efforts currently underway to guarantee that policy studies education will not fall into the same mold.

One such effort is the focus of this article: the work of Elinor Ostrom and her colleagues at Indiana University. Ostrom has developed a teaching strategy which can prove useful for those bothered by the usual overreliance on texts, lectures, and some of the more empty "innovations" in instruction techniques. It concentrates on the analysis and comparison of policy alternatives, but not to the necessary exclusion of concerns for policymaking or policy impacts.[4] Nor is the approach severely limited in application, for it has demonstrated applicability in any number of substantive policy issues and on both graduate and undergraduate levels. Much of what follows is derived from her approach as described and reported on in several sources as well as my own experience in attempting more limited applications in a variety of courses and contexts.

Basic to the strategy is the obvious (yet little utilized) contention that policy decisions reflect choices among competing policy *premises* as well as alternate conclusions. Policy choices are (more often than not) made from among several explicitly stated programs of policy action, each competing with the others for endorsement and adoption. The debate generated by the presence of several policy possibilities is usually substantial, especially in matters where an issue's salience for society is relatively high. This debate tends to create a "literature" of its own, ranging in form and quality from simplistic editorial diatribes to sophisticated scholarly treatises. A characteristic common to these writings is the "advocacy" position assumed by authors who seek to convince, persuade, and otherwise "sell" their policy position to a given audience. Advocates of policy positions are thus, by necessity, "rationalizers"; that is, they intentionally undertake to posit a "reasonable" argument on behalf of their policy choice and counter to opposed or competing positions. In so doing they invariably express (sometimes overtly, but oftentimes covertly) the "theory" underlying their proposed "solution" to a given policy problem. This "theory," once made manifest in a clear and logical form, explicates the policy proponent's understanding of the issue environment, the problematic situation involved, and the specific factor or factors upon which a solution is contingent. Thus, a policymaker's choice not only involves adoption of a particular policy action (that is, conclusion), but also acceptance of the "theoretical" underpinnings of that specific alternative.

There is nothing new or unique in this view, for policy advocates have always been open to challenge on grounds that their premises and assumptions are questionable. As a foundation for policy research, however, this approach has come into its own only in recent years,[5] particularly in the work of "public choice" analysts. On a very general level, Vincent Ostrom's discussion on the paradigmatic roots of traditional public administration demonstrates how extensively the premises of a given "theory" can dominate an entire "field,"[6] let alone the policies advocated by practitioners who follow that tradition. On more specific policy grounds, Robert L. Bish and Vincent Ostrom apply the search for underlying assumptions to various schools of metropolitan government reform,[7] as has Elinor Ostrom and others who have based numerous research endeavors on the results.[8]

Since the teaching mode discussed below is based on this analytic approach, a very brief sketch of the latter will be helpful in understanding the tasks students are asked to accomplish. Philosophically this approach owes much to the work of John Dewey,[9] but methodologically it traces its roots back farther. Credit is given to geologist T.C. Chamberlin who, in an 1890 article in *Science*, posited the "method of multiple working hypotheses." In applying this method, the "effort is to bring up into view every rational explanation of new phenomena, and to develop every tenable hypothesis respecting their cause and history." Having accomplished this task, the investigator has "tentatively neutralized the partialities" which would otherwise accompany the adoption of a particular theoretical contention. Thus, neutrality established and alternative hypotheses arrayed against each other, the analyst

proceeds with a certain natural and enforced erectness of mental attitude to the investigation, knowing well that some of his intellectual children will die before maturity, yet feeling that several of them may survive the results of final investigation, since it is often the outcome of inquiry that several causes are found to be involved instead of a single one.[10]

The "investigation" consists of devising "crucial" or "critical" experiments which posit and test the competing hypotheses. The hoped-for result: a finding which offers more credence for one contention than for others.[11] Vincent Ostrom expresses the utility of this approach for analyzing the competing theoretical assumptions of public policies.

Where we have two theoretical explanations that reach contradictory conclusions, empirical research can be propitiously conducted to test the empirical warrantability of the two competing explanations. If evidence derived from empirical research *consistently* supports the conclusion derived from one explanation as against the contradictory conclusion derived from another explanation, then we would appear to have a basis for supporting the use of one language system as supplying the better set of intellectual tools.[12]

While there are many problems with the actual application of this methodology (especially in the "soft" social sciences), its value for instruction in policy analysis is potentially quite high. The principle ingredient in the approach is student access to the literature generated by a debate over a given public policy issue. As might be expected, Elinor Ostrom uses the issue of metropolitan government reform, with special emphasis on the institutional form of police services in urban areas. In a study guide developed by Professor Ostrom, students are presented with a variety of materials ranging from a short brochure advocating consolidation for Multnomah County (Portland), Oregon, to a lengthy report issued by an Advisory Commission on Intergovernmental Relations.[13] There are, of course, no restrictions on the issues to which this approach can be applied: health-care delivery;[14] environmental and consumer protection; government regulation of business; energy production and conservation policies; antiinflation and antiunemployment policies; poverty policies; and so on. In short, there is a wealth of "raw material" available for use with this approach.

Given a particular issue area, the instructor will find it advisable to select three or four articles representing contending positions for use in student assignments. Without such preselection, the search for appropriate articles becomes time-consuming and wasteful of efforts which are more appropriately expended on analyses of the competing positions themselves.

Having provided the essential raw material for student assignments, the following steps should be followed: [15]

(1) After carefully reading a pamphlet, brochure, editorial, or article advocating a certain policy position, the student is asked to reread the piece, but this time to find specific phrases, sentences, or paragraphs used by the author to justify the proposal being presented. The student should transcribe that justification on a separate sheet, making sure to note the statement's source to facilitate future reference.

(2) Next, the student converts those transcribed statements into propositional "if . . . then" form. This step presumes, of course, that the student understands the nature and format of propositions which assert relationships among independent, intervening, and dependent variables. Consider the following examples derived from a recent article highly critical of the U.S. health-care delivery system. [16] In a space of several paragraphs, the following statements were noted:

1. "The faults of American medicine do not lie primarily in inadequate medical technology but in the fact that health care is a commodity that must be purchased. . . ."
2. ". . . No capitalist society has ever started from the premise that medical care is a right. In some capitalist countries a strong labor movement has won the right of medical care. . . . The American ruling class, however, has been able to impede the development of a labor party. . . . The oft-cited paradox of the richest country in the world having such backward social welfare programs is no paradox at all. Such is the logic of capitalism. . . ."
3. "The American medical system remains relatively unmodified by concessions to the working class. . . . The overwhelming majority of medical services are for sale to the highest bidder. Most physicians operate on the 'fees-for-service' principle."

From those three statements a student can deduce the following propositions:

1. Treating health care as a commodity is positively related to problems of the American health care system.
2. a. The more capitalist the society, the greater the treatment of health care as a commodity.
   b. The stronger the labor movement within a capitalist society, the less likely health care will be treated as a commodity.

163

3. The more capitalist the society (where health care is a commodity), the more service is provided to the highest bidder, the more likely a "fees-for-service" system will be in force.

A major attraction of this instructional approach is its demand that students know and be able to undertake the critical task of uncovering and explicating hypotheses from statements where such propositions are frequently well hidden. This is not a talent often stressed in courses and texts on political science methods, despite its obvious value for generating research topics.

(3) Having thus completed a "propositional inventory" of a particular policy position statement, the student is next asked to "link" the various propositions, thereby making explicit the logical form or "theory" underlying an advocate's proposal. Often this linking process is a simple matter of finding variables which "overlap" in two or more statements. At other times linkages are implicit and must be "reasoned" from a careful reexamination and analysis of the inventory. In my use of this approach, this task has proven to be the most challenging and exciting for most students. In a sense, they are asked to bring together parts of a "puzzle" for which they have found and cut the various pieces. The thrill of "fitting" the parts together soon becomes part of the process.

The entire procedure is greatly facilitated if the student is able to express propositional linkages graphically, that is, in "flowchart" form. Using the health-care propositions explicated above, each can be shown graphically, as in Figure 15-1 (see page 164). This graphic representation provides a foundation for the linking which can result in the flowchart shown in Figure 15-2 (see page 164).[17]

In this way the student is able to develop a comprehension of the logical underpinnings of particular policy alternatives. Again, this is not an activity stressed in courses on research methods, thus leaving the task demonstrating flowchart construction to the instructor.[18]

(4) Repeating steps (1) through (3) for other assigned articles, students will eventually have propostional inventories and flowcharts representing the assumptions and premises underlying several alternative policy choices. This material provides the basis for comparisons which would highlight points of agreement and disagreement among the competing "theories." For an example, in the metropolitan reform literature analyzed by the Ostroms there are several schools of thought, the most prominent being the "consolidationists," who favor the merging of smaller, overlapping governmental units into a larger, single jurisdiction. Basic to the consolidation position are the assumptions (that is, hypotheses) that larger jurisdictions produced more efficient urban service delivery and that fewer jurisdictions within a given area will do the same. These fundamental tenets are challenged by other reform positions which adhere to the assumptions of "community control" and "public choice" perspectives. The opposition on

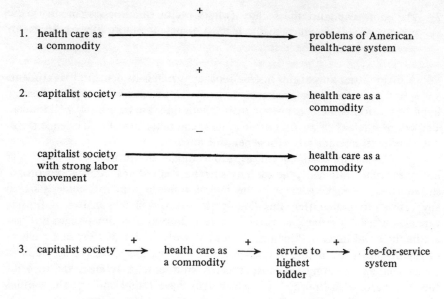

Figure 15-1. Examples of Individual Propositions

these and other specific points among those competing policy perspectives is evidenced in the comparisons students make by carefully analyzing their flow-charts. In a similar fashion, students also find points of agreement, for example, government efficiency is positively associated with lower per capita tax burdens by all three schools of thought. There are several ways for such comparisons to be expressed, and the instructor might consider assigning an essay topic that will have each student compare and contrast two specific policy proposals on the basis of propositions and logic derived to this point.

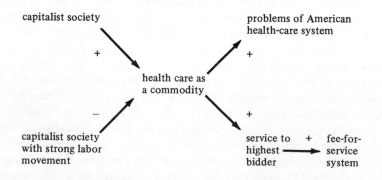

Figure 15-2. Completed Flowchart

(5) At this juncture there are several options open to instructors. While some may choose to stop, others may wish to extend the assignment by having students design and carry out formal research projects testing the empirical warrantability of competing hypotheses susceptible to critical experiments. If Elinor Ostrom's experience is any indication, the massive commitments of time and other resources needed to support such a project are well worth the effort.[19] While few of us have such resources, it is still possible for a class to develop a research design which might be useful if the opportunity arose. Going through the steps of breaking down propositions into their component parts, operationalizing the resulting variables, determining if the operationalized relationship will be empirically testable, developing a sampling frame and specific measures for each variable, considering rival hypotheses and planning methods for examining their impact or controlling for their effects, and selecting modes of analysis to be applied[20]—these are tasks which can be contemplated and discussed in the classroom as well as carried on in the field.

As both a research method and teaching strategy, the comparison of policy alternatives through propositional inventories and crucial experiments has much in its favor. Its use in the classroom demands considerable effort from both student and instructor, but the results are well worth the time and preparation involved. Besides the immediate payoff in terms of an in-depth familiarity with alternative policy proposals for a specific issue, the student learns through experience how to contend with a policy choice situation. In addition to facilitating "reasoned choice," there are other benefits to be derived: students find the techniques for developing propositional inventories and reconstructing the logic of an argument extremely valuable in other courses where critical analysis is called for; their ability to generate interesting research questions also increases, as does their capacity and willingness to undertake formal research in the social sciences; most important, however, is the payoff derived from the fact that the policy studies classroom becomes a place for "searching inquiry," not just a location for marking time and accumulating credit hours.

Notes

1. Theodore J. Lowi, "American Government, 1933-1963; Fission and Confusion in Theory and Research," *ASPR*, LVIII (September 1964):589-99.
2. Ibid., p. 592.
3. For instance, the APSA's Division of Education Affairs and International Studies Association's Consortium for International Studies Education have been active in developing and advertising innovative instructional material and strategies for several years.

4. Ostrom's work, for example, posits the institutional form of policy-making systems as an issue and regards the consequences of policy choice in that matter to be a rationale for (and evaluative measure of) that decision. In this manner she links the three focal points of policy studies: policy substance, policymaking, and policy impact.

5. The dominant form of policy analysis, of course, concentrates on comparisons of policy conclusions and their consequences. For instance, compare the "public choice" methodology with the more frequently applied benefit/cost analysis technique.

6. See his *The Intellectual Crisis in American Public Administration*, revised edition (University, Ala.: University of Alabama Press, 1974).

7. Robert L. Bish and Vincent Ostrom, *Understanding Urban Government: Metropolitan Reform Reconsidered* (Washington, D.C.: American Enterprise Institute for Public Policy Research, 1973).

8. Elinor Ostrom, "Metropolitan Reform: Propositions Derived from Two Traditions," *Social Science Quarterly*, 53(December 1972):474-93; also Elinor Ostrom et al., *Community Organization and the Provision of Police Services* (Beverly Hills, Ca.: Sage Publications, 1973).

9. See Dewey's *The Public and Its Problems* (New York: Henry Holt and Co., 1927) and *Liberalism and Social Action* (New York: Capricorn Books, 1935), especially chapter 3.

10. This 1890 article, "The Method of Multiple Working Hypotheses," was reprinted in *Science* (148, 7 May 1965, pp. 754-59) and is included in the appendix of Elinor Ostrom's *Urban Policy Analysis: An Instructional Approach* (Washington, D.C.: AAAS, forthcoming).

11. On critical experiments, see John R. Platt, "Strong Inference," *Science*, 146 (no. 3642), 16 October 1965, pp. 347-53 (also reprinted in Ostrom, *Urban Policy Analysis*); Arthur L. Stinchcombe, *Constructing Social Theories* (New York: Harcourt, Brace and World, Inc., 1968), pp. 24-28; Imre Lakatos, "Falsification and the Methodology of Scientific Research Programmes," in *Criticism and the Growth of Knowledge*, eds., Imre Lakatos and Alan Musgrave (London: Cambridge University Press, 1970/74), pp. 91-196; and James C. McDavid, " 'Crucial Testing' for the Study of Complex Institutions," in *Problems of Theory in Policy Analysis*, ed. Phillip M. Gregg (Lexington, Mass.: Lexington Books, D.C. Heath and Company, 1976), pp. 137-47.

12. Vincent Ostrom, "Language, Theory, and Empirical Research in Policy Analysis," in *Problems of Theory in Policy Analysis*, p. 16.

13. E. Ostrom, *Urban Policy Analysis*.

14. See Melvin Dubnick, "Three Approaches to Health Care," a L.A.P.S.S. module currently under development for APSA's Division of Educational Affairs. The initial proposal for that module can be found in *DEA News*, no. 13, (Spring 1977):13.

15. Much of what follows is drawn from E. Ostrom, *Urban Policy Analysis*; Elinor Ostrom, "Public Policy Analysis," *DEA News Supplement* (Spring 1975) pp. s/2-s/6 and s/9-s/11; and Dubnick, "Three Approaches to Health Care."

16. This example is from Stephanie Coontz, "You Can't Afford to Get Sick," in *Life in Capitalist America: Private Profit and Social Decay* (New York: Pathfinder Press, Inc., 1975), pp. 69-102.

17. For a complete analysis of this and two competing health care reform proposals, see Dubnick, "Three Approaches to Health Care."

18. See G. David Garson, *Political Science Methods* (Boston: Holbrook Press Inc., 1976), chapter 5; also Nan Lin, *Foundations of Social Research* (New York: McGraw-Hill Book Co., 1976), chapter 2.

19. See William R. Grant, "Applying Political Theory," *Change*, 8 no. 6 (July 1976):64-67, for an interesting look at Elinor Ostrom's courses at Indiana University.

20. See E. Ostrom, *Urban Policy Analysis*.

Guided Design

Donald C. Menzel

Guided Design is a new instructional method that may prove very useful for teaching policy studies. It was developed at West Virginia University in the early 1970s by Charles Wales and Robert Stager, who felt that lectures and labs were especially weak in teaching young engineers how to solve open-ended problems and manage many complex decision situations which would confront them upon graduation.[1] What was needed, they reasoned, was a method for guiding students through open-ended problem-solving experiences. The method had to be systematic yet flexible enough to insure a genuine experience. Too much guidance (overly systematic) could stifle experiential learning while too little guidance could make the learning experience somewhat haphazard.

Systematic Guidance. The Guided Design method assumes that effective problem-solving requires one to:[2]

1. identify the problem;
2. understand the basic objective;
3. comprehend various constraints, assumptions and facts;
4. generate possible solutions;
5. establish criteria and select a solution;
6. analyze the chosen solution;
7. synthesize;
8. evaluate;
9. report findings and make recommendations;
10. implement the decision;
11. evaluate the impact and, if necessary, revise the solution.

These eleven steps constitute a decision structure for guiding the student through a desired learning experience. The steps are sequential but not necessarily unidirectional. A student might begin with Step 1 and proceed through several steps and then find it advisable to return to Step 1. This occurs frequently in the policy process—problems are constantly being defined and redefined. Moreover, as Charles Jones notes, many problems are never clearly defined by policymakers.[3]

This decision structure is the conceptual underpinning of the Guided Design method. Further guidance is provided by carefully prepared programmed instructions, feedback, and supplementary information. The instructions present the student with a decision task, for example, collect information, identify the problem, state the objective, etc. Upon completing the task, the student receives written and/or verbal feedback. The basic premise is that learning results from trial and error. Thus rapid feedback is essential. The student must have a yardstick to determine how convincing or correct the decision is.[4]

Flexibility. The decision structure and programmed material cannot in and of themselves provide the learning experience. Other key components of Guided Design are a scenario, small group interaction, and the instructor.

The scenario sets up the problem situation and defines the student's role. Both are important. The problem situation can be relatively simple or complex. Indeed, an objective of a Guided Design course might be to guide the students through increasingly complex problems. For an introductory policy studies course it would make little sense to focus at the outset on something as complex as the nation's air pollution problem. However, the course might begin with a problem such as open dump burning and proceed through more complex problems such as auto and industrial pollution.

The role assumed by the student is also an important consideration. The Guided Design scenario does not place the student in an "unnatural" role, such as that of the President of the United States. Rather, the student is given a role that can be assumed with ease. A scenario, for example, might be developed in which the student assumes the role of an intern in a state or local agency. For more advanced students, the role of a policy analyst might be employed successfully. The important point is that Guided Design exercises require the student to be an active participant and observer *as a student and not as someone else.*

The participant/observer role occurs in a small group context. This affords the student many opportunities to try out ideas. It also exposes the student to the dynamics of small group decision-making and provides genuineness and flexibility in the exercise. Moreover, the small group arrangement discourages a mechanistic style which can be induced when using printed materials.

The instructor's roles in a Guided Design course are not any less important than in the traditional lecture-discussion course. The instructor is an administrator, evaluator, and guide—but it is this latter role that is different. Instructional guidance is tied closely to group discussion and decision-making. The instructor moves freely from group to group, observing, listening, and, when appropriate, entering into the discussion. In a sense, the instructor is at once guiding and being guided by the students. The classroom situation approximates, as Esther Millon Seeman observes, ". . . a transaction between instructor and students, and a transaction among students themselves."[5]

An Example. A fully satisfactory example of a Guided Design exercise cannot be presented in this article. However, the type of material used can be illustrated and some perspective can be provided on what happens in the classroom.

The problem-solving portion of my introductory policy course begins with a simple but effective problem called the "sidewalk" problem. The scenario is as follows:

This past semester Aaron Springer applied for a university-city sponsored internship. Several days ago he received a letter notifying him that he had been accepted and would be assigned to the city manager's office. The letter instructed him to report to Mr. Elmer Freeman, the city manager, at 8 A.M. tomorrow morning.

The next morning Aaron arrived at Mr. Freeman's office, which is located in the municipal building, a few minutes before eight o'clock and was surprised to find two former classmates—Bill Wallace and Kathy Knotts—waiting in the outer office. Bill and Kathy, he quickly learns, have also been selected as interns and will be working in the city manager's office.

Mr. Freeman, who is a young city manager, arrives a few minutes later, greets each intern, and invites them into his office. Upon entering the room, Aaron notices that Mr. Freeman's desk and adjoining table are laden with papers and reports, and on one wall there are five or six large graphs with multicolored lines running in several directions. For the next fifteen minutes, Mr. Freeman explains the responsibilities of the city manager's office—which, in a nutshell, concerns solving numerous city problems of various magnitude and complexity. "A 'good' city manager is a 'good' problem-solver," he commented. He also made it clear that he does not have a formal contract with the city and could be fired by the city council if he doesn't do a satisfactory job of coping with problems such as collecting garbage, cleaning streets and parks, and fixing potholes.

"What would be," he mused, "a good experience for you interns?" Bill suggested that the interns and Mr. Freeman might mutually benefit by letting the interns work as a team on a problem facing the city. "That's an excellent idea," replied Mr. Freeman, "and I have just the problem for you to work on. Every winter my office is flooded with complaints about the snow on city sidewalks. Something needs to be done about this problem."

Instruction 1

Suppose you were one of the student interns, what would you do?

Upon receiving Instruction 1, the students invariably begin generating solutions to a rather ill-defined problem. Some think that modern science should be drawn upon to modify the weather or that the sidewalks should be constructed with solar heat–absorbing material. Other students suggest more mundane solutions such as having the city melt the snow or making the property owners remove it. The discussion is usually imaginative and colorful. Even the most pensive student tends to get involved.

The groups vary in the amount of time required to exhaust the discussion, although it is seldom more than fifteen minutes. The instructor, a teaching assistant, or a group leader, under some circumstances, determines when each group is ready for the printed feedback and subsequent instruction. The groups do not move through the material in a lockstep fashion but are encouraged to move at their own individualized pace.

Each group, of course, may generate a longer and/or better response than that provided on the feedback sheet. This is to be encouraged. The students should use the feedback but should not be dominated by it. The feedback for Instruction 1 is presented in the following way:

Feedback 1

After considerable discussion, the group listed the following solutions:

1. Use modern science to modify the weather.
2. Erect protective coverings over the sidewalks.
3. Insulate or install electric heaters.
4. Construct the sidewalks with solar heat material.
5. Make the property owners or tenants remove the snow.
6. Have the city hire a private firm to do the work.
7. Have the city Department of Streets pick up and remove the snow or use salt to melt it.
8. Have the city purchase a flamethrower and melt the snow.

At this point the students realize that they have not really defined the problem well enough to sort through their solutions. Thus Instruction 2 asks them to "backup" and carefully define the underlying problem.

Instruction 2—Identify the Problem

"Before we focus on a particular solution," Aaron remarked, "perhaps we should make certain that we fully agree on the nature of the problem."

What is the problem?

Feedback 2

The following possibilities emerged during the discussion:

1. It snows too much.
2. Snow gets on the sidewalks.
3. The snow is not removed fast enough from city sidewalks.
4. People can be hurt if snow is not removed.
5. It's not clear who is responsible for removing the snow.

"The basic problem," Kathy concluded, "is that when it snows people slip and fall and injure themselves on city sidewalks. The fact that it snows too much or that snow is not removed fast enough from the walks contribute to the problem, but they are not *the* problem."

Instruction 2 and Feedback 2 demonstrate just how difficult it is sometimes really to pinpoint a problem, even a "simple" problem. And, as the students continue to work their way through the "sidewalk" problem, they find problem definition a recurring issue. Instructions 3 through 5 require the students to determine empirically whether or not sidewalk-related injuries are widespread. The data provided in the feedback show that snow on sidewalks is more of an inconvenience than a health hazard. That is, the snow makes it inconvenient to shop, walk pets, and jog. The basic problem-solving objective then is *to determine the "best" way to prevent snow on sidewalks from inconveniencing people.*

With this objective in mind, the students return to the solutions generated earlier, establish criteria for selecting several plausible solutions, and finally select one solution. The instructions—I.6 and I.7—do not make these tasks especially time-consuming. This is, of course, by design. I do not make a major issue of constraints in this introductory exercise. The scenario at this point guides the students toward the conclusion that the best solution is an ordinance requiring property owners to keep their walks clear of snow.

Further instructions require the students to investigate the components of a regulatory ordinance, draft a model ordinance, and then compare it with a scenario-supplied ordinance which happens to be a local community's ordinance. The final instruction asks each group to revise their ordinance and present it to the entire class for acceptance or rejection. This is usually a spirited event that provides a rough measure of each group's success.

Conclusion. Guided Design exercises can be used in a variety of ways by policy studies instructors. As noted earlier, it might be desirable to work through increasingly complex problems with correspondingly less guidance. Ideally, the students should have improved their problem-solving skills sufficiently enough toward the end of a course to be capable of managing a problem with little or no instructional guidance.

Guided Design might also be employed in a truncated fashion if the instructor wished to emphasize one or more facets of the policy process. The instructor, for example, might wish to use one exercise to investigate policy implementation and another exercise for policy evaluation. The Guided Design decision structure is not fixed or rigid. It is not necessary to begin, as was done in the "sidewalk" problem, with problem identification.

The Guided Design method emphasizes concrete problems and problem-solving. However, this does not preclude a more theoretical usage. It might be useful, for example, to work through Guided Design problems that fit into regulatory, distributive, and redistributive policy categories. Such a scheme might demonstrate the strengths and weaknesses of these conceptual efforts in a far more convincing way than could ever be done in a lecture by the most learned scholar.

Guided Design is now used in twelve programs at West Virginia University, including the freshman engineering and the chemical engineering programs and a multidisciplinary course entitled "The Nature of Evidence." Data collected on engineering students over a six-year period show that students who take the six-credit freshman engineering Guided Design courses graduate with higher grade-point averages than other engineering students without Guided Design instruction. In addition, dropout rates have decreased. In the chemical engineering program, which employs either Guided Design or some other decision-making experience each semester, students graduate with significantly higher GPAs than other engineering students. The program's effectiveness has also been noted by employers during recruitment visits.[6]

These findings are preliminary but potentially very significant. They suggest that teachers can be much more effective by approaching a subject matter or an entire curriculum with a decision-making orientation. Such an approach might incorporate the Guided Design method to offer a real alternative to the hierarchical learning structure of most classrooms.[7]

Notes

1. A series of eight articles on the Guided Design concept was published in *Engineering Education*, V. 62 (February to May, 1972).

2. Charles E. Wales and R.A. Stager, *Guided Design* (Morgantown, West Virginia: West Virginia University, 1976), p. 14.

3. Charles O. Jones, *An Introduction to the Study of Public Policy* (North Scituate, Mass.: Duxbury Press, 2nd ed., 1977), p. 8.

4. It should be stressed that this is not a form of instructional behaviorism. For an interesting critique of instructional behaviorism see George L. Newsom, "Instructional Behaviorism: A Critique," in *Proceedings of the Thirtieth Annual Meeting of the Philosophy of Education Society*, edited by Michael J. Parsons (Southern Illinois University–Edwardsville: Studies in Philosophy and Education, 1974), pp. 336–50.

5. Esther Millon Seeman, "The College Classroom as a Transaction," *Dea News* (Spring 1977):7.

6. Charles E. Wales, "Better Teaching—Better Graduates," March 15, 1977 (mimeograph).

7. The interested reader might wish to consult the following articles for more information on Guided Design: F. Goldberg and Gene D'Amour, "Integrating Physics and the Philosophy of Science through Guided Design," *American Journal of Physics*, V. 44 (September 1976), and Gene D'Amour and Charles E.

Wales, "Improving Problem-Solving Skills through a Course in Guided Design," *Engineering Education* V. 67 (February 1977):381–84.

It should also be noted that there is a film on Guided Design and that the Exxon Education Foundation offers a number of grants which can be used by faculty for released time to develop Guided Design material.

17 A Task and Network Approach to Teaching Policy Studies

Stahrl W. Edmunds

Recent literature has pointed to the need for policy studies to include implementation in order to improve their plausibility and use. The identification of work tasks and their sequencing into time networks to carry out policy into program implementation, provides an instructable way to improve the temporal, control, implementation, and evaluation aspects of policy studies. A teaching methodology for a task and network approach to instruction is presented along with an illustrative case and policy impact results.

One effective way to teach policy studies, at the undergraduate or graduate level, is through the implementation side of policy, that is, through a detailed identification and planning of the work inputs and outputs. These work inputs need to be arrayed into a sequence or process to yield the desired service delivery, or output, which is the goal of policy. The arraying of the work inputs or tasks may be viewed as a network of events, which becomes the policy process.

The advantages of this implementation approach to teaching policy studies are several: (1) the student learns from the specific to the general, which is a natural, experiential way of learning; (2) the student learns specific analytical skills in the process of constructing the task networks; (3) the results can test the feasibility of policy alternatives in time, cost, capability, and incremental benefits; (4) the specification of policy in terms of feasibility brings policy study closer to the needs of the policymaker and practitioner; and (5) the policy becomes accountable and capable of evaluation.

The disadvantages of this approach are two-fold: (1) the inductive nature of the implementation approach runs counter to the teaching proclivities of many academics whose thought runs from the conceptual or theoretical to the specific, rather than vice versa; and (2) the approach, which constitutes the format for a long exercise in a course, is more work for the student, who must master not only a methodology but learn enough about a substantive problem at the same time to apply the method.

These disadvantages are real enough to constitute barriers to the use of this teaching method, unless one can show means to overcome them, which is the purpose of this paper. Briefly, the means to overcome these barriers are to show: (1) that the inductive nature of the network approach leads immediately to concept and theory, which enables the instructor to deal iteratively with theory and practice, and the only issue is the starting point; and (2) that the student work-

177

load problem can be dealt with by simplifying and truncating the networks to reasonable scope, while still being instructive of the principle.

Even this much introduction may cause some to conclude that this approach to policy study is "not the political science that I know" and dismiss the teaching method as incongenial or arduous. However, I also intend to show that this implementation approach is in direct line with the current political science literature on policy studies, and therefore the method is not to be dismissed lightly. The next section relates the network approach to the context of current literature on policy studies.

Context of Current Policy Studies Literature

Sheffer (1977) traces two main lineages of policy studies, those attributable to Lowi (1964, 1970, 1977) and to Easton (1965). The Lowi typology characterizes policies by four dimensions (that is, distributive, regulatory, constituent, or redistributive) which link policy to political systems, forms of politics, clienteles, and power centers. As such, the Lowi typology has provided a pervasive tool for analyzing the political feasibility of policies. However, the impact of policy has been neglected in literature of this lineage, in Sheffer's assessment.

The Easton (1977) model transported the exchange paradigm of economics into political science by viewing the political process as an exchange of political "inputs" for "outputs." The exchange model opened new areas of analysis, particularly as to economic costs. If input costs and outputs are measurable, the political exchange can be maximized. However, governmental services are fraught with joint costs and free goods, which make the cost analysis ambiguous. Still more serious, in Sheffer's critique, is that outputs or outcomes are not necessarily identical with policy impacts.

Sheffer, then, sees a need to go beyond inputs and outputs to examine policy impacts in terms of spatial inclusiveness, temporal permanency, and disaggregation. Spatial inclusiveness refers to the extent to which policy reaches clienteles or decision centers at the periphery, versus the center, of the political system. The temporal aspect concerns the extent to which the time scale matches the delivery system to the needs of the clientele. Disaggregation refers to the extent to which policy cuts across multiple issue areas. Sheffer concludes that time and implementation are particularly important factors in complex political issues.

The task and network approach to policy studies, as we shall see shortly, measures the temporal dimension explicitly and provides partial measure for the spatial and disaggregation impacts.

Ashford (1977) sees the Easton model as contributing estimates to policy choices either for: (a) economic maximization, or (b) behavioral winning, of an issue. But this focus on estimates of policy variables is at the expense of formulation and implementation of policy, which determines its plausibility. Ashford proposes a plausibility paradigm which directs attention to how a variety of norms are achieved, which leads to a structural analysis of implementability. Only by restoring the plausibility of governance can we (the nation) revive the historic role of politics in legitimacy, aggregation of support, equality, and national priorities, according to Ashford.

Peters (1977) takes a very similar view, characterizing the inability to aggregate support as a "leakage of sovereignty." The State has grown in scope, range of services, and decision areas. While it may make decision (policy) on a wider range of subjects, it may not be able to provide what it says it will, or control what it must. This lack of control or effectiveness has a negative effect on citizens, leading to dissonance and alienation, or a leakage of sovereignty. The remedy, then, is to provide feasibility and control in policy implementation.

DeLeon (1977) concerns himself with a third lineage of policy studies derived from Lasswell (1951, 1971) and Brewer (1975), in which the functional roles of the decision-makers are characterized as: initiation, estimation, selection, implementation, evaluation, and termination. In this classification, the Lowi and Easton models deal primarily with initiation, estimation, and selection, which is perhaps why policy impacts inherent in implementation, evaluation, and termination are neglected. DeLeon views the implementation process as the critical transition between policy thought and action. Implementation translates policies into programs and determines how they affect the population.

The action/implementation aspects of policy studies have, in fact, gained more currency in usage among state governments, according to Lee and Staffeldt (1977), than have the political aspects. Their survey findings show that policy analysis has not taken hold as rapidly among state legislatures, auditors, or governors as it has among the executive branches, which have used policy studies extensively, particularly in the budgetary process. Lee and Staffeldt suggest that one possibility, why governors or legislators do not use policy studies more extensively, is that the analyses are too weak technically to have much effect or inspire confidence.

Ripley (1977) takes a similar view, in saying the policy research should establish a clinical relationship with the policymakers. That is, the policy researcher may start with different goals than the decision-makers. Problem definition, to be usable, requires that cognizance be taken of both sets of goals of client and researcher. Moreover, the results of policy studies need to be stated explicitly in terms of the productive impacts.

In summary, then, the context of current literature on policy studies is to direct attention toward probing such areas as: (1) spatial, temporal, and disaggregation impacts (Sheffer); (2) plausibility of implementation (Ashford); (3) control (Peters); (4) program implementation and evaluation (deLeon); (5) legislative significance (Lee and Staffeldt); and (6) clinical relationships with policymakers (Ripley).

These six critique areas represent deficiencies in current policy studies, at least to these authors; and the purpose of the balance of the paper is to show the extent to which the task and network approach to teaching policy studies satisfies these implementation-type requirements. First, however, we need to review the literature base from which network analysis comes in order to define what it is and how it may be applied as method to policy studies.

The Literature Base for the Task Network Approach

The literature base for the task network is largely found in the fields of operations management, systems theory, control theory, operations research, and system engineering. Some of this literature is highly mathematical in formulating models, but the emphasis here will be on concepts and word-models more familiar to social scientists. Obviously this operations management literature, dealing as it does with inputs and outputs, has some similarities to the Easton model. However, the Easton model concerns itself with maximizing outputs in an economic sense, and what I have selected from this literature concerns itself with controlling the process. In this sense, we are addressing primarily the control, plausibility, and evaluation concerns of Ashford, Peters, and deLeon. The operations management literature base is too broad to be cited extensively in this paper, which is ultimately directed at teaching, but the references cited will contain bibliography for those interested.

Buffa (1976) defines operations management as the design of a productive system by which resource inputs are transformed or converted into useful services; and among his illustrations are medical services, the U.S. postal service, hospital, fire department, and university operations. The operating program, as a productive process (that is, a policy implementation alternative), is the unit of study; but an operating program always exists and interacts within an environment. The environment is everything other than the operating program, which means the environmental interactions may be political, technical, competitive, ecological, behavioral, economic, intelletual, etc. In whatever way this broad environment may affect the operating program, these effects become part of the (policy) study, if they can be foreseen. That means the policy study and its program implementation must be as holistic as the mind can conceive; but also, because the operating process is a conversion of resource inputs to a service, the study must also be specific in relation to events. Therefore, Buffa identifies the hallmarks of an operating system as: (1) interrelatedness of events, (2) wholism, (3) goal-seeking, (4) inputs and ouputs, (5) transformation, (6) entropy, (7) regulation or control, (8) hierarchy, (9) differentiation, and (10) equifinality.

The hierarchy of inputs and outputs is a means of establishing the interrelatedness of events. The hierarchy is a nesting of programs (or subsystems) within systems, that is, how an input is converted to an output. This nesting of inputs is accomplished by specifying the network of tasks to be done, through intermediate stages of conversion, to the final service. Perhaps the clearest description of this task networking is found in Nadler (1970), who describes work design in terms of "function determination," which means the specification of the purposes for which work is to be performed.

The Teaching Methodology of a Network Approach to Policy Study

The task network approach to policy study essentially combines: (1) a holistic management information selection process, (2) the hierarchy of function determination approach to work design of Nadler, (3) the conversion and control concepts of Buffa, and (4) the goal-seeking process of political science, such as Lowi, Easton, Sheffer, Ashford, Peters, deLeon, Ripley, Lee and Staffedlt, etc. The procedure and topical coverage of the course are illustrated by the diagram in figure 17-1 and include the following steps:

1. The concepts of issue analysis, policy study, implementation, and operations management are covered by lecture and discussion in the first two sessions, to give the student perpsective of the applicable literature (which has just been covered above) to be used as reference in the problem-solving stage of implementation to follow.

2. The class is asked to take a simple problem, with which all are familiar, like cleaning a house or car, preparing a meal, putting up a Christmas tree, shopping for a birthday, for the purpose of making an implementation plan. The implementation program shall identify purpose, issues, performance requirements, functions, tasks, and sequence—all of which may be used to construct a network of events (like a PERT network) showing the time and cost for accomplishment. These exercise problems are intended to be simple in the sense of having one or two issues, two or three functions, and perhaps a dozen tasks. Hence the exercise can be done in class by discussion or between classes as an assignment. The purpose of the exercise is to prepare the student for a more complex policy analysis and implementation which will be the subject of a term project paper, either on a group or individual basis.

3. The students are next asked to select a problem or policy in which they are interested for a term project paper, which they may do singly or in groups. The project should represent something with which the student is already familiar by experience or previous reading, so that the substantive additonal learning about the problem will be manageable and will allow the student time to concentrate

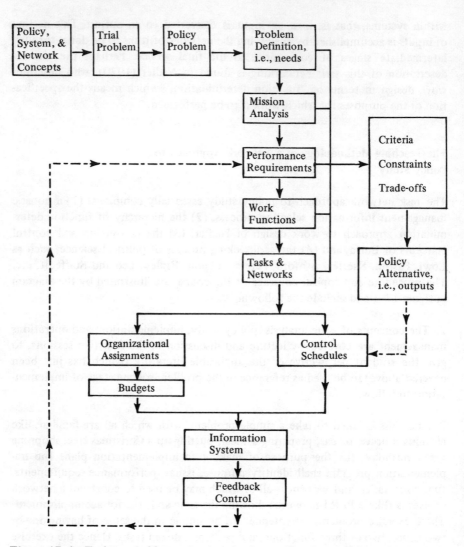

Figure 17-1. Task and Network Approach to Teaching Policy Studies—A Schematic Diagram

most of his/her effort on applying a task network methodology to a policy study. Many students with experience select a project from their work which represents a real problem to their institutions. Students without experience generally select some topic in which they have a special interest, and upon which they have done previous reading or papers. Examples of student policy study topics have been: selecting land-fill sites, consolidating city and county purchasing departments, developing a regional transit system, pyrolitic solid-waste disposal, expanding a local airport, providing animal rescue services, hydroponic food supply, emergency disaster medical treatment. Usually the students will interview and obtain information from government officials in the area about their project. The students for the most part have nontechnical backgrounds, and the technological data is obtained by reading or from local officials. Students are permitted to hypothesize techno-economic detail, particularly time and cost details, by reasonable estimates within a control total, if they are unable to obtain the data.

4. Having posed their policy problem, the students are then asked to conduct a wide-ranging inquiry on: Is there really a problem? If so, why? That is, the initial problem selection was made upon their own observation and immediate experience, and hence was deductive. The students are now to pursue inductively: What are all the other observations which may or may not confirm or further define the problem (Churchman, 1968)? These inquiries take the form of brief field policy studies, needs analysis, issue analysis, and identification of coalitions, leverage, public attitudes, voting strength (Bauer and Gergen, 1968). Out of this inquiry, which again is supplemented by interview, the student is expected to arrive at a hierarchy of issues and goals, with the ability to identify priorities and conflicts among them.

5. The students then do a mission analysis which is to specify one or a series of performance requirements which, if realizable, would provide delivery of a service which would satisfy a feasible set of policy issues determined in 4 above.

6. The mission performance requirements is broken down into a set of broad *work* functions which would have to be accomplished to realize the requirements (see Nadler 1970 regarding function determination).

7. The work functions are further subdivided into components, or subassemblies, of work, that is, the "nesting" of systems into a work hierarchy (Buffa, 1976).

8. The work components are again subdivided into tasks and activities which individuals perform. This yields three levels of work division (or three indentures) with perhaps one hundred tasks and activities which are essential to policy and program implementation. This level of work implementation is as far as the student is expected to go, although in real cases the task and activity identification (also known as the work breakdown structure) has been known to go to five or six indentures with literally thousands of tasks. The cost of planning and managing thousands of tasks in PERT (Program Evaluation Review Technique) networks under federal contracts has been known to cost about 7 percent of the total contract award. However, the smaller, three-level work breakdown structure, with several scores of tasks and activities, has proven feasible for instructional purposes.

9. As the students are preparing their work breakdown structures, they are instructed to ask themselves iteratively: What is the existing operating system or program? What is the ideal program? What is a feasible program? Thus the work breakdown structure successively reflects: (a) existing policy, (b) potential policy, (c) feasible policy. The existing policy is the work being done in the present state of the operating system. The potential policy represents what is technically or ideally possible. The feasible policy represents what is politically, economically, and temporally practical.

10. To arrive at an implemental program for a policy, the student must develop criteria to select a feasible program out of what may be ideal policy. The criteria normally contain a set of goals and a set of constraints. The goals are the performance specifications on a priority of issues determined in 4 above. The constraints are the political, economic, and temporal limitations hypothesized in paragraphs 4 and 9 above.

11. The constraints on feasible policy implementation are tested clinically (Ripley, 1977) upon important clienteles, coalitions, or policymakers to determine their range, latitude, or realism before they are incorporated into the criteria.

12. The entire work breakdown structure, with all its functions, components, and tasks, are examined critically to see: (1) the extent to which it delivers the performance specifications of the mission analysis, and (2) what trade-offs may be possible among the functions, components, and tasks by substituting different technologies, costs, or time sequences.

13. The trade-off analysis implies that alternative program concepts are being considered for the policy implementation; and indeed, the idea of alternative solutions should be brought into the discussion at steps 5 and 6 above. My teaching experience indicates that it is difficult for students to cope with a wide-ranging, inductive inquiry into policy and mission analysis (step 4) at the same time they are considering a wide range of technical or managerial solutions (steps 5 and 6). That is, the exercise becomes too open-ended for the inexperienced person (and sometimes for experienced persons). I therefore opt for leaving the issue and need analysis open-ended to arrive at policy options or missions, and leaving the alternative solutions somewhat closed until this stage (steps 9 and 13), where now the student is confronted with the question of whether time, cost, or performance can be improved by altering the work breakdown structure (that is, varying the tasks and technologies). This belated confrontation with the alternative solutions issue may cause the student grudgingly to revise his work breakdown structure with a new implementation means as he/she arrives at a better solution. However, the same kinds of revisions are typical in real policy implementation studies, and meantime the teaching method has confined the problem to a manageable instructional exercise for the student.

14. The student presumably now has arrived at a tentative, alternative program implementation plan for a policy, made up of a work breakdown structure of one hundred or so tasks which fulfill the performance specification (step 5), the multiple policy goals (step 4), and criteria (steps 10 and 11) by a feasible or cost-effective means (step 13). Some students feel at this point that they are finished, but we have not yet arrived at a program which is managerially accountable, evaluative, or controllable. The program is not yet governable or plausible (Ashford, Peters, 1977).

15. The plausibility or control of a program is established by constructing a network of events from the task and activity list. That is, the work breakdown structure is recast into concurrent or sequential events which define when, where, and what work will be performed. This networking can be done in the form of PERT (Program Evaluation Review Technique). To establish control, the student should identify time and cost estimates to each task or event on the network. These are simply marked in as number on the connecting lines of the network. It is at this point that students are allowed to hypothesize detailed estimates of time and cost if they cannot determine them from references. That is, for an instructional exercise, they should learn how to consolidate and use the estimates for control, rather than spending inordinate time on perfecting the estimates.

16. The tasks in the work breakdown structure are allocated to organizational units capable of performing them, among the operating agencies which will implement the policy. This allocation of tasks usually creates a matrix organization, in which existing governmental agencies may perform portions of the tasks in the network, but they are accountable to a program or project director managing the whole network of tasks and events.

17. Each operating agency, which has been allocated a set of tasks, is given a work order allocating a budget to perform those tasks and also given a time schedule by which the tasks must be done. These budgets and schedules are taken directly off the overall network and are merely the parceling out of assignments among performing agencies.

18. The student, now as program implementation manager, sets up a management information system, for each performing or operating agency, to show the monthly cash flow allowable to them under the budgets which have been allocated, plus daily, weekly, or monthly performance schedules within which tasks must be completed. The student then conceives of a reporting system to show: (a) actual versus budget expenditures, and (b) task performance against the schedule. Thus the student creates an exception reporting system to identify those agencies which are deficient in the time or cost in completing a task.

19. The student then specifies an evaluative or remedial mechanism by which he/she, as program manager, will review off-schedule performance for the purpose of determining its cause, its justification, replanning if the time and cost estimates were in error, or managerial remedy if the work performance was at fault.

20. The feedback control over policy implementation (step 19) now enables the student (program manager) to evaluate whether the policy has reached a stable state, or equifinality, or in policy study terms, whether the policy impacts are worth the program costs. In this evaluation, we are not entirely clear of Sheffer's critique of the Easton model, namely, that outputs do not necessarily equate with impacts. We have, however, done what Sheffer recommends, that is, disaggregated the outcome across multiple issue areas (steps 4 and 5). Hence, if the policy and mission analysis were done well in steps 4 and 5, as well as done clinically (Ripley) in conjunction with clienteles, then the outcomes should approximately equate with needs or impacts. At least we have specified performance requirements which can be checked by a postaudit survey with clienteles to see if, indeed, this service delivery meets their needs. Moreover, the management information system of exception reporting has yielded a governable, accountable, and efficient control over that work of events.

Extent to Which the Teaching Method Meets the Critique

Let us next examine the manner and extent to which the task network approach to teaching policy studies meets the critiques cited in current literature at the beginning of this paper. The critique is identified down the side of the table 17–1 below, with the appropriate reference to the teaching method identified by steps in the second column. The third column gives a crude appraisal (little, fair, or general) of the extent to which the critique is satisfied.

The network approach to teaching policy studies makes a contribution, if this appraisal is reasonable, to satisfying some of the existing needs in improving policy studies, particularly with respect to temporal, control, and implementation aspects of policy studies. The method does less well in the political

Table 17-1
Teaching Methodology as Satisfying Critique

Critique	Addressed in Teaching Method (by steps)	Appraisal of Satisfaction
Sheffer:		
1. Spatial inclusiveness	4, 5, and 11	Little
2. Temporal aspects	15, 16, 17, 18, 19	General
3. Disaggregation	4, 5, 11, and 20	Fair
Ashford—plausibility	15, 16, 17, 18, 19	General
Peters—control	18, 19, 20	General
deLeon—implementation and evaluation	6 through 19	General
Lee & Staffeldt—legislative significance and realism	13 through 19	Fair
Ripley—clinical relation	4, 5, 11, and 20	Fair

interaction of policy issues, that is, their spatial inclusiveness, disaggregation, legislative significance, or clinical relationships; but these political interactions are certainly not ignored; rather they are treated as amply as a heavily loaded one-term course allows. What this suggests is need for a companion course which treats the political ramifications in more depth. Indeed, the design of the network approach course presumes that such companion courses are generally available in schools of policy, political science, or public administration; and the need is to augment the policy implementation side of instruction.

Illustrations of the Teaching Method

The purpose of this section is to cite some additional references as to the use of the teaching method, together with a brief case illustration taking one functional analysis down to the third level of indenture in a work breakdown structure.

Cary (1977) has described an approach to teaching an introductory course in evaluation research which has many similarities to the methodology proposed here. The main differences appear to be that Cary takes an ex-post approach to evaluation, while the network approach, being implementation planning, is ex ante. As a result, Cary does not appear to get into similar detail as to tasks or networks.

Amplification of the major concepts behind the network teaching approach can be found in other writings of the author. The concept of treating the entire social process as a series of interactive decision networks is discussed in "Social Responsibility, Neglects and Reticulation." The construction of these interacting networks into an overall (first indenture) design for (1) society, (2) government, (3) business, and (4) voluntary institutions is found in *Basics of Private and Public Management* (Edmunds, 1978). An illustration of overall mission and policy analysis for society as a whole is given in *Alternative U.S. Futures* (Edmunds, 1978). Since the concept of top-level policy analysis, networks, and design is treated elsewhere, the illustration below is intended to focus on the work breakdown analysis.

In 1975–77, the National Science Foundation and the Energy Research and Development Administration funded a study for Imperial County, California, to determine a policy for geothermal energy development and land use within the county. The final product was to be a land-use zoning policy and plan. Imperial County contracted for an interdisciplinary policy study with the University of California, Riverside (UCR), and with the Environmental Quality Laboratory, California Institute of Technology. The research team consisted of: S. Edmunds, project director; Shawn Bieler and Tien Lee, geologists; Edgar Butler, sociologist; James Pick, demographer; Michael Pasqueletti, geographer; Adam Rose and Everard Lofting, economists; James Sullivan, public policy; Claude Johnson, remote sensing—all of UCR—plus Martin Goldsmith, engineer; Vincent Buck, political scientist; James Krier and Donald Hagman, lawyers— from Cal Tech. The research output consists of eight reports or monograms comprising nine hundred pages (available from the National Technical Information Service, Department of Commerce, identified as NSF/ERDA Grant No. 75-08793, "Geothermal Energy Development in Imperial County"). From this policy study, the County of Imperial then developed a generic environmental impact report and a geothermal element to its land-use plan, which reflected the policy implementation.

The mission of the policy study was to develop a land-use plan for the siting and encouragement of geothermal energy development consistent with (constrained by): existing agricultural production, environmental protection, water availability, improving employment, and promoting the general welfare. The general welfare was construed, upon consultation with clienteles, as conforming with the public attitudes of the citizenry, and as increasing the tax base.

The study was designed, in the proposal stage, with a work breakdown structure and task list to perform the mission stated above. The work breakdown structure was a three-level, or three-indenture, task list of about 150 tasks and activities. The section headings in the eight-volume report (NTIS) comprise the task list. An abbreviated form of the task list is shown below, where the first indenture represents the function to be performed, the second is the component work, and the third defines the task. The illustration below contains only the first two indentures or breakdowns, for the sake of brevity.

1. Assess the potential energy of the resource.
   1.1 Analyze the geophysical structure from well logs.
   1.2 Measure gravity anomalies.
   1.3 Measure heat gradients and flows.

1.4 Estimate heat in storage.

1.5 Analyze fluid composition.

1.6 Model hydrology of reservoir.

2. Assess the feasible engineering technologies for energy conversion.

2.1 Make technology assessment of well-drilling techniques and platforms.

2.2 Analyze alternative means and impacts of fluid transmission.

2.3 Estimate water requirements and impacts.

2.4 Make comparative analysis of flash-steam, binary cycle, and combined cycle energy conversion.

3. Analyze social impacts.

3.1 Analyze and project demographic structure.

3.2 Characterize social structure by education, occupation, income, ethnic origin, family status, etc.

3.3 Survey the public attitudes of the population regarding geothermal development.

3.4 Make leadership sutdy of decision-maker role and standing on geothermal issue.

4. Analyze geographic and environmental impacts.

4.1 Use remote sensing to analyze land use by parcel.

4.2 Map land parcels by use, ownership, and tax status.

4.3 Estimate acreage requirement of geothermal development and net displacement of agriculture.

4.4 Estimate the employment and crop effects on agriculture of geothermal conversion.

4.5 Identify environmental hazards or degradation from geothermal operations.

4.6 Measure or assess impact of environmental hazards together with abatement procedures.

5. Estimate the economic impacts, benefits, and costs.

5.1 Make a sector analysis of the economy.

5.2 Introduce a geothermal sector and estimate interactions.

5.3 Estimate employment, value added, and net economic product of the county with and without geothermal development.

5.4 Estimate the primary, secondary, and induced effects of geothermal energy on economic development.

5.5 Estimate fiscal impacts.

5.6 Identify net economic benefits.

6. Analyze the political decision structure.

6.1 Identify authority and jurisdiction of all agencies and governmental levels in geothermal regulation.

6.2 Characterize the existing regulatory structure.

6.3 Analyze the potential regulatory powers of the county regarding geothermal development under present or proposed legislation.

6.4 Identify the voting and political policy choices of the county in past relative to development or environmental issues.

6.5 Analyze existing land-use zoning practice.

6.6 Propose alternative land-use geothermal zoning, consistent with the above.

An example of a more detailed task list is shown in the next list below, and this level of detail would constitute the third indenture of the work breakdown structure. The example is given for component 5.3 of the economic impact study (from list above). Please understand, of course, that every two-digit work component above has a similar breakdown into a three-digit detail of tasks; and the whole of all the three-digit breakdowns is what constitutes the task and activity list of some 150 items for the project. Again, the whole list is omitted for the sake of brevity, and only the task detail for component 5.3 is shown for illustrative purposes.

5.3 Estimate employment, value added, and net economic product of the county with and without geothermal development.

    5.3.1 Balance the county input-output table developed in 5.1 and 5.2 above with state control totals re gross product, agricultural product, and employment.

    5.3.2 Adjust the 88-sector matrix in the input-output tables for county imports and exports.

    5.3.3 Add a geothermal energy sector to the exploratory drilling and utilities sectors of the table.

    5.3.4 Drive the geothermal sector with employment manning tables from Project Independence and a cost analysis of capital and operating costs.

    5.3.5 Project the input-output model, without geothermal, by the Dept. of Agriculture and Dept. of Commerce Office of Business Research data to the year 2020.

    5.3.6 Project the geothermal sector by the installed megawatts from the ERDA scenario.

    5.3.7 Use the linear programming coefficients to estimate, under both projections, the employment, value added, and county product by decades, 1970–2020.

The above illustrations, taken from an actual research program for a policy study, is clearly beyond the ability of students to calculate or resolve for themselves. But it is not beyond the ability of students to identify the kind of work which needs to be done at the three-digit indenture level shown above, given some reading and guidance from the instructor. That is, any intelligent student can identify the need for a sector analysis of an economy, if a new economic development is to be introduced, and put it into common-sense terms, even if the student does not know the jargon and technique of input-output models. A student version of the same task lists, which might be done in a course, might read:

5.3 Estimate the economic impacts on employment and output.
    5.3.1 Verify the sector analysis of the existing economy.
    5.3.2 Adjust the sectors for duplicate reporting.
    5.3.3 Create a geothermal sector.
    5.3.4 Estimate manpower and costs for geothermal sector.
    5.3.5 Project the economic sectors without geothermal energy.
    5.3.6 Project the economic sectors with geothermal energy.
    5.3.7 Derive employment and net output from the dollar projections in 5.3.5 and 6.

While a research director might prefer the first version of a three-level task list, to be assured that the researchers know how to do the work, the second student version is equally satisfactory from a management standpoint to establish control over the project, as long as time and cost estimates are attached to each task. On this basis, the task and networking concept becomes feasible as a realistic instructional tool for students to use, even though the technician (researchers in this case) might prefer greater nicety. The student is capable of learning the methodology and skills of implementation, work breakdown, and networks, even though he/she may not yet know all the technology needed to do the work. In this sense, perhaps, the network is a black box to the student, as it is to any general manager or policymaker. However, the student has learned how, at least, to plan work down to a sufficient level of detail so the policy can be implemented, costed, evaluated, and controlled. If students can learn that much, the next generation of policy study professionals will be able to carry policy implementation a large step toward wider utilization throughout government and among policymakers, including legislators.

Impacts of the Illustrative Study

The results of the illustrative study have been utilized by Imperial County to develop a geothermal element to their land-use plan, a generic environmental impact statement, and a revised zoning ordinance. The policy impacts, of the type which students would identify and measure regarding geothermal energy, include:

1. The amount and cost of potential geothermal energy.
2. The economic impact on agriculture.

3. Water availability.
4. Environmental impacts.
5. Land-use zoning options.
6. Income and employment benefits.
7. Fiscal benefits to local government.
8. Powers and jurisdictions of governmental levels.
9. Authorizations and procedures by government to implement geothermal development.

The benefit cost portion of the criteria would indicate that local government would derive very large fiscal benefits from geothermal development. Income and employment benefits to the population would be minor and environmental costs would be small.

The policy study would then show reasonable cause for proceeding with geothermal development, in this case, largely because the local government bureaucracy would have substantial motivation to gain the large fiscal benefits.

The implementation steps to encourage development would be a series of procedural steps including exploratory permits, zoning ordinances, conditional use permits, environmental impact studies by developers, environmental surveillance instruments, tax measures, assesment methods, budget effects, and infrastructure additions.

The task and network exercise, in this case, would provide the student knowledge of both the political benefits motivating the policy and of the managerial means needed to carry out the policy and realize the benefits.

Summary

The task network approach to policy study provides a practical way to teach program implementation in the political context of the issue preferences and constraints. As such, the task network approach, along with a companion course which probes into political interactions, can contribute to the development of the policy studies as a field by making them more plausible, controllable, clinical, evaluable, implementable, and identifiable (disaggregative) as to impacts.

References

Ashford, Douglas E. "Political Science and Policy Studies: Toward a Structural Solution," *Policy Studies Journal*, vol. 5, Special Issue, 1977, pp. 570–82.
Brewer, Garry D., and Brunner, Ronald D., eds. *A Policy Approach to the Study of Political Development and Change.* New York: The Free Press, 1975.

Buffa, Elwood. *Operations Management: The Management of Productive Systems.* New York: John Wiley, 1976, p. 71-154.

Cary, Charles. "An Introductory Course in Evaluative Research," *Policy Analysis*, vol. 3, no. 3, Summer 1977, pp. 429-44.

deLeon, Peter. "Public Policy and Political Development, *Policy Studies Journal*, vol. 5, Special Issue, 1977, pp. 596-615.

Easton, D. *Systems Analysis of Political Life.* New York: John Wiley & Sons, 1965.

Edmunds, Stahrl W. "Social Responsibility, Neglects and Reticulation," *Business and Society*, vol 16, no. 2, Spring 1976.

_____. *Basics of Private and Public Management.* Lexington, Mass.: Lexington Books, D.C. Heath and Company, 1978.

_____, ed. *Geothermal Energy Development in Imperial County.* ERDA/NSF Grant 75-08793, Washington, D.C., National Technical Information Center, Department of Commerce, 1977.

_____. *Alternative U.S. Futures.* Santa Monica: Goodyear Division, Prentice Hall, 1978.

Lasswell, Harold D. "The Policy Orientation," in Daniel Lerner and Harold D. Lasswell, eds. *The Policy Sciences.* Stanford, CA: Stanford University Press, 1951.

_____. *A Pre-View of Policy Sciences.* New York: American Elsevier, 1971.

Lee, Robert D., Jr., and Staffeldt, Raymond J. "Executive and Legislative Use of Policy Analysis in the State Budgetary Process: Survey Results," *Policy Analysis*, vol. 3, no. 3, 1977, pp. 395-406.

Nadler, G. *Work Design* (rev. ed.). Homewood, Ill.: Richard D. Irwin, 1970.

Peters, B. Guy. "Developments in Comparative Policy Studies," *Policy Studies Journal*, vol. 5, Special Issue, 1977, pp. 616-28.

Ripley, Randall B. *Policy Research and the Clinical Relationship.* Mershon Center Position Papers, No. 1. Columbus: Ohio State University, 1977.

Sheffer, Gabriel. "Reversibility of Policies and Patterns of Politics," *Policy Studies Journal*, vol. 5, Special Issue, 1977, pp. 535-53.

Epilogue
The Tribulations of
Innovation in Teaching
Policy Studies:
An Exchange of Memos

Ralph S. Hambrick, Jr.

Readers might be interested in the following exchange which occurred at a nearby state university between a professor and a university president about a proposed innovation in teaching policy studies.

To: President Smooth
From: Professor Unique

I have developed an innovative approach to teaching a policy issue which I wish to share with you. Since some of the more backward forces in state politics might raise objections to the approach, I would like your approval before proceeding (even though I have tenure). Knowing the high regard in which you hold quality education, I'm sure you will be sympathetic.

An important and controversial issue in American politics today is pornography. It is one of a number of issues we study in my course in public policy. A very significant part of the issue is definitional: just what is and what is not pornographic or obscene. This issue has taxed the most creative qualities of Supreme Court justices as well as judges at other levels. It is an issue which has demanded the attention of state legislators and city council persons; it has been faced by countless district attorneys and other public executives in the American political system. All of these officials have been forced to sit down and view films, magazines, and other materials to determine whether those materials are or are not pornographic. Students, too, should be forced to confront the tough decisions in American politics. How else can they truly learn the depth and significance of the policy issues facing the political system?

What I propose, then, is the following. I have developed a carefully arranged package of audiovisual materials which fit on a continuum from least obscene to most obscene. It begins with slides from last year's Miss America pageant, moves to the underwear section of the Sears, Roebuck catalogue and proceeds through a number of stages including some materials from *Hustler* and excerpts from recent French films.

The assignment to the student is the following: He or she is to study the landmark pornography cases, paying particular attention to the definitional problem, before coming to class. During the audiovisual showing, in which items are numbered for easy identification, the student is to decide where the line is to be drawn. As soon as the student decides where to draw the line, he/she is to leave the classroom and immediately prepare a written justification for his/her decision. The written assignment is due the following class period.

That is my proposal. It combines some of the best elements of education. First, it makes full use of audiovisual aids. Second, it actively involves the students rather than have them be merely passive listeners. Third, the content of the instruction is closely related to real-world issues. Thus, it meets most of the criteria for excellence in teaching policy studies.

I anxiously await your reply.

196

To: Professor Unique
From: President Smooth
   I reviewed your memo with interest; I am gratified to see faculty members take teaching seriously.
   But are you crazy, or what? Do you realize what would happen if you were to pull the
stupid stunt you described? Now it might be possible for you as a faculty member to hide
behind academic freedom. But what would happen to me? You see, it is us administrators
who have to take the heat for the dumb moves the faculty so frequently makes. I'm not
saying that's the way it ought to be, but that's the way it is.
   In sum, I absolutely, categorically forbid you to go through with the project you
described (whether you have tenure or not). I hope my meaning is clear.

P.S. [handwritten] Could you bring the materials over to my place Saturday night?

Index of Names

198

Index of Subjects

About the Contributors

Robert W. Biersack is a graduate student in political science at the University of Wisconsin–Milwaukee. As an undergraduate student at Marquette University he was a member of the "Public Policy Analysis" class developing the desegregation plan for the city of Milwaukee.

Richard D. Bingham is an associate professor of political science and chairman of the Department of Urban Affairs at the University of Wisconsin–Mailwaukee. He is author of *Public Housing and Urban Renewal: An Analysis of Federal-Local Relations* (1975) and *The Adoption of Innovation by Local Government* (1976) and has contributed articles to *Urban Affairs Quarterly* and *Social Service Review*.

Larry J. Cohen is an assistant professor of political science and acting director of the Office for Law-Related Research at the University of Illinois at Chicago Circle. His research is concerned with legal social control policy and dispute resolution in informal and decentralized settings.

Melvin Dubnick teaches public policy and public administration at Loyola University of Chicago. Besides his interest and activity in developing educational materials, he is currently involved in research on government regulation and administrative reform. He has recently published a simulation on public sector collective bargaining and is author of an **APSA LAPSS** Module on health care reform. An active member of **NASPAA**'s Undergraduate Program Section, he chairs its Task Force on Educational Materials Development.

Stahrl W. Edmunds is a professor and dean of the School of Administration at the University of Minnesota. He received the B.B.A. and M.A. from the University of Minnesota. His research and teaching interests are environmental administration, business economics, systems management, and policy and planning. His previous experience includes vice-chancellor of Administration, UCR, 1967–69; Industrial Development Advisor, U.S. State Department, Ecuador, South America, 1965–67; and twenty years' experience as a business executive for Hughes Aircraft Company, Ford Motor Company, Booz Allan Hamilton, National City Bank of New York, and Northwestern National Life Insurance Company.

Erika S. Fairchild is assistant professor of political science at North Carolina State University. She is the author of *Police Discretion*, one of a series of modules for learning analysis in political and social science which are sponsored by the American Political Science Association. She has also researched and published in the area of correctional policy.

John L. Foster is the acting director of the Master of Public Affairs Program and an assistant professor of political science. He has coauthored works on simulation models and written a number of articles on innovation in governmental structures.

Brian R. Fry is associate professor of government and international studies at the University of South Carolina, where he has just completed service as the director of the Master of Public Administration Program. He received the Ph.D. from Stanford University and has published articles in the *American Political Science Review*, the *American Journal of Political Science*, and the *Journal of Political Science*. He is currently working on research examining budgetary routines in state level resource allocation.

Margaret C. King Gibbs is associate professor at the School of Administration, California State College, San Bernardino, where she teaches courses in public policy analysis, local government administration, and organization theory. She has been a member of the Claremont City Council and the Board of Trustees of Citrus Community College and has published articles on property taxes.

James J. Glass is assistant professor of political science and director of the Applied Policy Research Program at North Texas State University. He is the author of several articles and papers on health planning and citizen participation. Currently he is involved in a study of citizen participation in planning for the aged. He is also a member of the editorial board of the *Southern Review of Public Administration*.

Ralph S. Hambrick, Jr., is visiting associate professor in the Department of Government and International Studies at the University of South Carolina on leave from the Department of Political Science at Texas A&M University. He has previously worked as research coordinator with the Center for Urban Programs at Texas A&M and as research fellow with the Syracuse University Research Corporation. Dr. Hambrick received the B.A. from Dartmouth College and the Ph.D. from Syracuse University. Recent publications have appeared in *Policy Sciences*, the *Bureaucrat*, *IEEE Transactions on Communications*, and the *Social Science Journal*. He is coauthor, with William P. Snyder, of *The Analysis of Policy Arguments*, a learning package published by Policy Studies Associates.

Ronald John Hy is associate professor of governmental research and political science at the University of Mississippi. He received the Ph.D. from Miami University. He is the author of *Using the Computer in the Social Sciences: A Nontechnical Approach* (1977). He has published in the *Policy Studies Journal*, the *Bureaucrat*, the *American Journal of Pharmaceutical Education*, and the

Educational Forum; and he has contributed to several state and local government books.

Edward T. Jennings, Jr., a Washington University Ph.D. (1977), is an assistant professor of political science at SUNY-Buffalo. He has contributed an article on state politics to the *American Journal of Political Science*, and he has co-authored *Distribution, Utilization, and Innovation in Health Care*, a monograph in the Learing Analysis for Political and Social Sciences Series of the American Political Science Association. His current research is in the areas of state and local politics and health and welfare policies.

Duncan Macrae, Jr., is a former president of the Policy Studies Organization. Originally trained in physics, he has taught political science and sociology at Princeton, the University of California at Berkeley, and the University of Chicago. He is now the William Rand Kenan, Jr., Professor of Political Science and Sociology at the University of North Carolina, Chapel Hill. He is the author of several books on legislative roll-call voting and of *The Social Function of Social Science*.

Donald C. Menzel is assistant professor of political science at West Virginia University. His teaching and research interests encompass innovation processes in the public sector, intergovernmental relations, energy and environmental policymaking, professionalization of public agencies, and the utilization of university-based expertise by state-local governments. Articles on these subjects have appeared in *Policy Sciences*, *Western Political Quarterly*, *Urban Affairs Quarterly*, and the *Water Resources Bulletin*.

Brian P. Nedwek received his doctorate from the University of Wisconsin-Milwaukee (1974) and is currently an associate professor, Center for Urban Programs, St. Louis University. He coordinates a seminar in the Public Policy Analysis and Administration doctoral program and monitors the field service internships at the Center for Urban Programs. He has just completed a study of human service classification systems and is completing work on a book entitled *An Introduction to the Study of Public Policy: A Reader in Public Policy Analysis and Administration*.

Charldean Newell is associate professor and chairperson of the Department of Political Science at North Texas State University. She is the author of several monographs, articles, and papers on state and local government, especially council-manager government. She is also editor of *The Municipal Matrix* and is currently involved in a study of differences in public and private decision-making.

Tom O'Donnell is an assistant professor of political science at Transylvania University in Lexington, Kentucky. He received the B.A. from Swarthmore College, and the M.A. and Ph.D. from Rutgers University.

Steven Puro received his doctorate from the State University of New York at Buffalo (1971) and is currently an associate professor of political science and a coordinating member of the Technological Studies Program at St. Louis University. He has directed the university's legislative and administrative internship programs. He recently completed a study of the selection patterns of U.S. District Judges for the Eastern District of Missouri and their civil liberties policies.

Robert M. Rakoff is an assistant professor of political science at the University of Illinois at Chicago Circle. His research has focused on the impact of the state on everyday life as ordinary people experience it ideologically and symbolically. A report on part of this research, concerned with home ownership, has appeared in *Politics & Society*.

David G. Smith is chairman of the Department of Political Science at Swarthmore College. Previous publications include *Political Science: An Introduction* (with J. Roland Pennock), *The Convention and the Constitution*, and contributions to the *American Political Science Review*, *Encyclopedia of the Social Sciences*, *NOMOS*, and *Modernizing American Government*. His current teaching and research interests are in the areas of public administration, public law, and health policy.

Michael P. Smith is an associate professor of political science at Tulane University. He is the author of *The City, Social Theory, and Urban Planning*. He and Edward T. Jennings have coauthored the recent teaching monograph *Distribution, Utilization, and Innovation in Health Care*, and he has coauthored or edited four other books, the most recent of which is *Organizational Democracy: Participation and Self-Management*, coedited with G. David Garson. His articles have appeared in the *Journal of Politics*, *Public Administration Review*, *Administration and Society*, Sage *Urban Affairs Annual Reviews*, and in various collections. During the 1978–79 academic year he will be a Visiting Scholar at the University of Essex, Colchester, England, conducting research on comparative urban policy.

William P. Snyder is associate professor in the Department of Political Science at Texas A&M University. He is a graduate of the United States Military Academy and received the Ph.D. from Princeton in 1963. Following duty as an instructor in the Department of Social Science at West Point from 1962 to 1966, he served in Vietnam, the Pentagon, and the Executive Office of the President. Prior to his retirement from the army, he was a member of the faculty at the United States Army War College. He is author of *The Politics of British Defense Policy, 1945– 1962, Case Studies in Military Systems Analysis*, and several monographs and articles. He collaborated with Ralph Hambrick on *The Analysis of Policy Arguments*, a learning package published by Policy Studies Associates.

Mark E. Tompkins, a Ph.D. candidate at the University of Minnesota, is serving on the faculty of the Department of Government and International Studies, University of South Carolina, and as director of Internship and Placement in the MPA Program there. He is currently working on research into the distributive implications of social costs and on resource allocation processes in state government.

About the Editor

William D. Coplin is director of the Public Affairs Program of the Maxwell School, Syracuse University. He has been chairperson of the Education Commission of the International Studies Association since 1973, and is the author or coauthor of such books as *Introduction to International Relations* (1971 and 1975); *Everyman's PRINCE: A Guide to Understanding Your Political Problems* (1972 and 1976); and *Quantitative Techniques in Foreign Policy Analysis and Forecasting* (1975). Professor Coplin has also coedited and coauthored, *Public Affairs Briefing Papers*, Volumes I and II for the *New York Times*. In 1976, he designed and implemented an undergraduate major in policy studies.